# Uncompromising Positions

# Religion and Politics Series

Mark J. Rozell, John C. Green, and Ted G. Jelen, series editors

*The Christian Right in American Politics: Marching to the Millennium*
John C. Green, Mark J. Rozell, and Clyde Wilcox, Editors

*Of Little Faith: The Politics of George W. Bush's Faith-Based Initiatives*
Amy E. Black, Douglas L. Koopman, and David K. Ryden

*School Board Battles: The Christian Right in Local Politics*
Melissa M. Deckman

*Uncompromising Positions: God, Sex, and the U.S. House of Representatives*
Elizabeth Anne Oldmixon

# Uncompromising Positions
## *God, Sex, and the*
## *U.S. House of Representatives*

ELIZABETH ANNE OLDMIXON

Georgetown University Press
*Washington, D.C.*

Georgetown University Press, Washington, D.C.
© 2005 by Georgetown University Press. All rights reserved.
Printed in the United States of America

10 9 8 7 6 5 4 3 2 1                    2005

This book is printed on acid-free paper meeting
the requirements of the American National Standard
for Permanence in Paper for Printed Library Materials.

As of January 1, 2007, 13-digit ISBN numbers will replace the current
10-digit system.
Paperback: ISBN 978-1-58901-071-0
Cloth: ISBN 978-1-58901-072-7

Library of Congress Cataloguing-in-Publication Data

Oldmixon, Elizabeth Anne.
    Uncompromising positions : God, sex, and the U.S. House of
Representatives / Elizabeth Anne Oldmixon.
        p. cm. — (Religion and politics series)
    Includes bibliographical references and index.
    ISBN 1-58901-071-X (pbk. : alk. paper) — ISBN 1-58901-072-8
(cloth : alk. paper)
    1. Church and state—United States.   2. Culture conflict—United States.
3. Legislation—United States.   4. Legislators—United States.   I. Title
II. Series: Religion and politics series (Georgetown University).

BR516.047 2005
322'1.'0973—dc 22                                      2005008370

*For my mother, Sue Oldmixon, and the memory of my father,*
*Bill Oldmixon—"compassionate conservatives"*
*in the truest sense.*

# Contents

# Figures and Tables

## FIGURES

## TABLES

# Preface

M y father used to regale me with stories of his days as an altar boy growing up on Staten Island, New York. He loved being an altar boy. For one thing, altar boys were excused from school to serve at funerals. For another, sometimes he and his friends had the opportunity to steal communion wine (unconsecrated, he was always quick to point out). He was raised and socialized in the pre–Vatican II Catholic Church. He yearned for a Latin Mass, he would not take Eucharist if he had not been to Reconciliation, and he did not care to see lay people on the altar. I am not trying to make my father seem overly pious. (The stealing of the Eucharistic wine should disabuse the reader of that notion.) My point is that I grew up knowing that religion was important. It was important to my parents, and they tried to pass that sense of importance along to my siblings and me. Professionally, I take from my upbringing the idea that religious values and participation in religious communities inform people's attitudes and structure their behaviors.

I grew up in Massachusetts, but my parents were not typical Irish-Catholic, Kennedy-loving Democrats. They were Republicans who had served in the military and voted for Nixon in 1960. When my father got out of the Navy in the late 1970s, he became a stockbroker. We were suburban Catholics. In that environment, my parent's partisanship (and mine) was defined largely by conservative economic policies, in the context of progressive New England politics, with a bit of hawkish foreign policy thrown in on the side. Social issues were of secondary importance to moderates residing in "Taxachusetts." In 2004 Republican Governor Mitt Romney testified before Congress in support of a constitutional amendment banning same-sex marriage. When I was growing up, however, Republican Governor William Weld supported gay rights and was prochoice.

Aside from self-indulgence, my reason for providing the reader with all this personal information is to drive home the point that this research emerged out of a profound dissonance experience. Moving south for graduate school, I was introduced to a different Republican Party. Certainly, conservative economic policies were important. The most salient issues, however, seemed to be the very social issues that were of marginal importance to Yankee Republicans. The Republican Party in which I had been raised in Massachusetts did not seem to be the same Republican Party that thrived in the South. I knew from my childhood that religious institutions served an important socializing function, but I did not appreciate the influence of conservative Christianity within the Republican Party. This personal puzzle became a political puzzle. Perceiving regional factions within the Republican Party, I analyzed floor speeches of the U.S. House of Representatives in hopes of measuring regional factions in the Republican Conference. This was my master's thesis.

I chose to explore this topic in the context of Congress because Congress is the national institution in which the regional factions of a party are brought together and govern. Specifically, I chose the House, as opposed to the Senate, because I believed that the smaller House districts might lead representatives to be more sensitive to localized concerns than senators are. Truth be told, moreover, I thought the House was simply more fun to study. My thesis research produced suggestive evidence that there are indeed regional factions in the House Republican Conference. Although representatives were articulating a similar agenda on the surface in the 103rd, 104th, and 105th Congresses, the South clearly was dominant. Moreover, once one scratches the surface, there appears to be a great deal of variation within the Conference. Supposed Republican homogeneity was wide, but not deep.

As this project evolved, my focus and theoretical framework changed. This volume more directly addresses contentious issues that seem to divide Yankee and southern Republicans. Taking a more holistic approach, the analysis also includes Democrats. Rather than focusing on regional dynamics, I draw heavily on cultural theory. My central argument is that political conflicts surrounding reproductive policy, gay rights, and school prayer represent a profound cultural cleavage at the mass level between religious traditionalism and progressive sexuality. Are cultural factions an ontological fact of American politics? Not necessarily (see Fiorina, Abrams, and Pope 2004). In reality, there may be consensus among many Americans on seemingly contentious issues. There are latent cultural factions that can be ginned up by elites, activists, and extremists, however. For example, in a May 2005 Gallup poll of 1,005 adults, 48 percent of respondents identified themselves as prochoice, and 44 percent identified as prolife. In the same poll, however, 76 percent indicated that abortion should be "always legal" or "sometimes legal" (margin of error ±3 percent; see http://www.pollingreport.com/abortion.htm). These data suggest that "prolife" and "prochoice" are *not* discrete categories—and that is the stuff of compromise politics and incrementalism. Cultural conflict, then, really is a style of argumentation that mobilizes latent cultural differences for strategic or ideological reasons (Leege et al. 2002, 26). For our purposes, we can be agnostic on that question.

What matters is that when cultural groups are mobilized, they apply countervailing pressures on political institutions to enact policies that are consistent with their vision of society. For the scope and purposes of this investigation, one group advocates for a society in which moral decisions, and thus policy choices, are informed by traditional Christian values; the other group advocates for a society in which moral decisions are made autonomously, and Christian values are relevant only to the extent that individuals choose to reference them. The question for this project is this: How do legislators legislate when policy conflicts are defined in explicitly cultural terms? After all, the House is an institution that is structured to engender compromise, and these issues do not seem to lend themselves to such compromise easily. What follows is my attempt to address that question.

In addressing that question, my goal in this project has always been to understand policy decisions made by legislators. Mayhew's (1974) elegant observation that legislators are "single-minded seekers of reelection" has become the guiding paradigm of congressional scholarship. We assume that legislators are goal-oriented, rational beings, and that goal orientation guides everything from voting behavior to staffing to the committee structure. Much of what we have done in the area of congressional studies for the past thirty years is derivative of *Electoral Connection*, and that is an appropriate homage. I hope this volume makes some small contribution by further expanding our conceptualization of legislator goals, providing an alternative to economic and class-based models. I also hope that viewing congressional politics through the lens of cultural theory moves us beyond the "realm of facts and reason," where we feel comfortable as social scientists, and into the realm of values and status, where political actors and the polity may be guided by feelings and loyalty to one's tribe as much as rational calculation (Mooney 2001, 5).

# Acknowledgments

Many people contributed to this project, and I am happy to have the opportunity to acknowledge them. Thank you to Larry Dodd, Ken Wald, Jim Button, Peggy Conway, Marty Swilley, and Debbie Wallen, all of whom are at the University of Florida. Larry and Ken, in particular, continue to be my professional sounding boards, and I am grateful for their mentoring. I also am grateful to my dear friends and colleagues Marian Currinder, Brian Geiger, Joshua Gordon, David Schecter, Peter VonDoepp, and Fiona Wright for their unfailing encouragement. Ted Jelen, Doug Koopman, and Ray Tatalovich all made helpful comments on this project, and I am most appreciative. Many thanks to John Green for generously providing me with invaluable data. Thanks also to my colleagues at the University of North Texas, especially Corey Ditslear and Michael Greig. I am indebted to the College of Liberal Arts and Sciences and the Dauer Chair (Larry Dodd) at Florida and the Research Office and the Political Science Department at the University of North Texas for funding parts of this research.

Richard Brown at Georgetown University Press has been terrifically helpful. Brian Calfano, Jen King, and Geoff Dancy provided me with very good research assistance. Thank you to Jeff Biggs and the Congressional Fellowship Program, for providing me with the opportunity to see Congress from the inside; Rep. Mike Capuano (D-MA) and former Rep. Joe Scarborough (R-FL), for allowing me to work in their offices; and Dan Muroff,

Rep. Capuano's former chief of staff, for answering my constant stream of questions. I also wish to thank the representatives and staff who allowed me to interview them for this project. They are busy people, and I appreciate their time. Thank you to my loved ones for their unconditional support: Carol, Katie, Mary, Bill, Kaoru, Joan, Emily, Erika, Allison, Maribeth, Anne, Erin, Christine, and Pam. They improve my quality of life every day.

Finally, I wish to recognize the 2004 Boston Red Sox, who won a world championship as I was finishing this manuscript (coincidence?). To be candid, the American League Championship Series and the World Series were distractions that constantly drew me away from my work. Even when I was at the office, precious hours were spent reliving the near-heartbreak turned triumph with my colleagues and fellow citizens of Red Sox Nation, David Mason and Phil Paolino. "Dirty Water" blared throughout the first floor of Wooten Hall on a daily basis. So, yes, the postseason was a distraction—but it was the sweetest distraction of all.

# Introduction:
# Guns, Race, and Culture

You are the light of the world. A city set on a mountain cannot
be hidden.

—Matthew 5:14

Inspired by the Sermon on the Mount, Puritan leader John
Winthrop preached to the early European settlers in North
America that they should model themselves as "a city upon
a hill."[1] In the years that followed, this image of America as a
Godly "city upon a hill" became a popular metaphor for the nation. Although the Founders ultimately designed a decidedly
secular government, Winthrop's sermon demonstrates that well
before the founding, the rhetoric of the nascent American community was infused with religious themes and a sense of provi-
dence. As President Reagan noted in his 1989 farewell address,
Winthrop coined this phrase as a way to "describe the America
he imagined."[2] In that America, religious values were considered
an unfailingly positive force. Winthrop regarded the relationship
between the new American community and their God as a "cov-
enant" that placed shared responsibilities and shared admonitions
on the group as a whole.

Although Winthrop imagined religion to be a positive, unify-
ing social force, the reality is that in the current era religion is a
source of conflict. Religion provides communities with a set of
correct beliefs and practices on which to model their lives. Yet the
effort to realize these shared values brings cultural groups into the

1

public arena, often in opposition to other groups. Indeed, in the twentieth century alone, religious values inspired different visions of the good life and animated both liberal and conservative political activism in support of those visions. The Catholic Church, for example, is a longstanding participant in political discourse, engaging in anti–death penalty activism while promoting economic social justice. Black churches are enduring centers of political activism in the African American community. In the mid-twentieth century they were joined by liberal Protestant churches and Jewish groups in their effort to end the status quo of American apartheid. The political conflicts over the regulation of pornography and alcohol have been infused with religious rhetoric. At the state and local levels, discussions of science curricula in education are unmistakably marked by a subtext of religious disagreement. Even in the areas of foreign policy and immigration policy, religious values strongly influence mass and elite-level preferences. Religion may not always be a source of political conflict, but it can be—and in a pluralistic society it likely will be. When this conflict occurs, cultures compete for legitimacy in the public space, and political institutions must provide resolution.

In the current era, American political institutions are called on to manage a highly salient conflict between two longstanding cultural groups of Americans: those who embrace religious traditionalism and those who embrace progressive sexual norms. In this book I investigate the politics of that conflict as it is manifested in the U.S. House of Representatives. I trace the development of these two cultures in contemporary American politics and then move to a discussion of legislative decision-making and leadership tactics. The underlying theoretical argument is that cultural conflict produces an absolutist politics that complicates traditional legislative norms. As legislators indicate, cultural issues draw on religious values and therefore are not amenable to compromise politics. To shepherd culturally significant bills through the legislative process, congressional leaders must develop strategies to overcome that difficulty. Adopting a weak form of partisanship that builds bipartisan coalitions provides one possible strategy, but the inclination of the Republican majority has been to embrace models of strong party government.

The conflict between religious traditionalism and progressive sexuality is only one of many twentieth-century cultural conflicts.

Others have raged over civil rights and gun control, to name just two examples, and Congress has resolved these issues with varying degrees of success. Thus, to fully understand congressional treatment of religious traditionalism and progressive sexuality, a review of how Congress has managed these other conflicts is useful.

## THE GUN CULTURE AND THE URBAN SOPHISTICATES

> You are of the same lineage as the farmers who stood at Concord Bridge.
>
> —Charlton Heston

When Charlton Heston accepted a fourth term as president of the National Rifle Association (NRA) in May 2001, he evoked an important national symbol: the freedom-loving patriot who is willing to die for his country. In using that image, Heston linked gun ownership to a larger culture that embraces the gun as a symbol of freedom. American settlers in the colonial and frontier periods depended on guns for their survival and livelihood. They owned and used guns for hunting, trapping, and protection. To protect the colonists from foreign armies and the indigenous population, able-bodied white men were expected to participate in citizen militias, bearing arms that they personally owned. As Spitzer (1998a, 8–10) notes, many historians credit these citizen militias with winning the Revolutionary War, defeating the best standing army of the day. Thus, learning to shoot became a necessary "rite of passage" for boys in the colonial and frontier periods.

After the citizen militias' "abysmal performance in the War of 1812," their importance for national defense dissipated. Moreover, as the country developed, the necessity of gun ownership for hunting and commerce also declined (Spitzer 1998a, 9–10). Nevertheless, the presence of guns in American society since before the founding, the importance of personal gun ownership in the Revolution, and the mythology surrounding guns on the frontier and in the present day have produced in many Americans a strong "sentimental attachment to . . . the gun" (Spitzer 1998a, 7). The tradition of personal gun ownership for hunting and as the last, best defense against tyranny still thrives.

The conflict over guns in contemporary America is a conflict of culture, and attitudes toward guns are structured by group-based loyalties and experiences.[3] As Spitzer (1998a) suggests, the gun control debate represents an enduring cleavage between the so-called gun culture—characterized by rural traditionalism and composed overwhelmingly of white, male, "old stock" Protestants who use guns for sport—and a culture of urban sophistication, composed of highly educated liberals, women, Northeasterners, descendents of recent immigrants, and persons who live in metropolitan areas and have little connection to traditional legal gun ownership (Spitzer 1998a, 12–13; see also Kleck 1996). The former group regards guns as a symbol of freedom; the latter group regards them as a symbol of barbarism and violence.

The politics of gun control in Congress has been characterized as a repeating pattern of outrage over a sensational gun-related incident, action by policymakers, and reaction by the gun lobby "that plays itself out with great fury but astonishingly little effect" (Spitzer 1998a, 13). Congress did not involve itself in gun politics until it enacted an excise tax on guns in 1919 (P.L. 65-254) as part of an effort to raise revenue. In 1927 Congress prohibited "the sale of handguns to private individuals through the mail." The 1927 legislation (P.L. 69-583) was not a robust gun control measure, however. It did not prohibit private couriers from transporting guns across state lines, and it did not prevent individuals from crossing state lines to purchase guns. More stringent controls that Congress considered at the time never made it out of committee (Spitzer 1998a, 103–4). The "first significant federal controls on firearms" came with passage of the National Firearms Act of 1934 (P.L. 73-474), which the Supreme Court upheld in *United States v. Miller*, 307 U.S. 174 (1939) (Jost 1997, 1114). Congress passed the 1934 statute in an effort to curb the organized crime violence that had thrived since Prohibition. Although the Eighteenth Amendment was repealed in 1933, gangland violence endured. The National Firearms Act restricted ownership of sawed-off shotguns and machine guns by requiring federal registration and levying a $200 excise tax on gun purchases. Broader registration requirements were dropped in the face of NRA lobbying efforts. Congress followed up with another gun control bill, the Federal Firearms Act of 1938 (P.L. 75-651), which required manufacturer and gun dealer licensing but made it difficult to prosecute individuals for providing guns to criminals. The 1938 statute marked another flaccid gun control effort (Jost 1997, 1116; Spitzer 1998a, 104–5).

After the Kennedy assassinations and the King assassination in the 1960s, Congress passed the Gun Control Act of 1968 (P.L. 90-618). Consideration of the bill was marked by intense lobbying efforts and fierce floor deliberation. The final version "banned the interstate shipment of firearms" (Spitzer 1998a, 108). Notably, Lee Harvey Oswald had purchased the gun he used in President Kennedy's assassination in this way. The law also prohibited gun sales to minors and felons, prohibited private ownership of bazookas and other destructive weapons, and required dealer licensing and recordkeeping. NRA president Harold Glassen characterized the bill as an effort to "foist upon an unsuspecting and aroused public a law that would, through its operation, sound the death knell for the shooting sport and eventually disarm the American public" (quoted in Spitzer 1998a, 107). Yet although this legislation had more robust controls than previous gun control efforts, it lacked the sweeping registration and licensing requirements that President Johnson wanted (Spitzer 1998a, 108; see also Jost 1997; Spitzer 1998b).

The Firearms Owners Protection Act of 1986 (P.L. 99-308) significantly weakened the 1968 statute. The 1986 bill relaxed some of the restrictions on interstate gun sales and eliminated some of the gun dealer licensing and recordkeeping requirements. Consideration of the 1986 statute produced an intense lobbying effort by the NRA, which supported the bill, and an array of policy organizations that opposed the bill. After the threat of a discharge petition, the bill was reported out of committee in the House and subjected to a barrage of amendments on the floor. Analysis of voting on the amendments indicates that opponents of gun control were concentrated in the southern and border states and, to a lesser extent, in the western and Rocky Mountain states. Members of Congress from rural parts of the country tended to support the 1986 anti–gun control measure more than their colleagues from urban areas (Spitzer 1998b, 179–83).

In the first two years of President Clinton's administration, Democrats held a majority in both houses of Congress and passed two significant gun control measures: the Brady Act of 1993 (P.L. 103-159) and the Assault Weapons Ban of 1994 (P.L. 103-322). The Brady Act instituted a five-day waiting period on gun purchases, during which time law enforcement could conduct background checks on gun buyers. The Assault Weapons Ban prohibited the sale and possession of nineteen different kinds of so-called assault weapons. The Brady Act remains in force, but the Assault Weapons Ban expired in September 2004.[4] Some legislators supported legislation that would have extended the ban for ten more years, and President George W. Bush indicated that he would sign such an extension. Bush did little to encourage legislators to act on the measure, however, and House Speaker Dennis Hastert (R-IL) indicated that he would consider scheduling a vote only if the Senate acted first. In March 2004, the Senate attached an assault weapons ban renewal to legislation that protected gun manufacturers from liability suits, but with the NRA's urging the bill was soundly defeated. Thus, Hastert did not schedule a vote in the House. Meanwhile, the NRA was so confident that the ban would not be renewed that, according to its executive vice president, Wayne LaPierre, the organization stopped running ads against it.[5]

Gun control is an "easy" issue (Carmines and Stimson 1980). Legislators and constituents understand and have well-formed opinions on gun control. As table I.1 indicates, about one-third of Americans support gun control at its current level, and about half support even stricter forms of gun control. Poll data indicate that 78 percent of Americans wanted the Assault Weapons Ban renewed. Yet sweeping reforms proposed during the New Deal, such as national gun registration, were never enacted. It comes as no surprise that gun control was strengthened during unified Democratic government in 1993 and 1994. Since then, however, the agenda of gun control advocates has regressed to the point that the five-day waiting period in the Brady Act is regarded as a major victory. By comparison to previous control efforts, it certainly is. Yet why have the reforms not been more sweeping? Many observers credit the strength of anti–gun control advocacy on the part of the NRA—through campaign donations and grassroots lobbying—with keeping gun control off the agenda and stemming a tide of reform (Spitzer 1998a, 135; Langbein and Lotwis 1990). Thus, even on highly salient issues where the expectation is of a robust electoral connection, interest groups affect the policy process. Of course, only 40 percent of Republican respondents in the aforementioned poll wish to see stricter forms of gun control, so the fact that the Republicans currently hold the presidency and majorities in both houses of Congress no doubt helps anti–gun control advocates.

**Table I.1.**    Support for Gun Control

*"In general, do you think gun control laws should be made
more strict, less strict, or kept as they are now?"*[a]

|  | More Strict | Less Strict | Same | Don't Know |
|---|---|---|---|---|
|  | % | | | |
| All | 51 | 10 | 35 | 4 |
| Republicans | 40 | 14 | 44 | 2 |
| Democrats | 65 | 4 | 27 | 4 |
| Independents | 48 | 12 | 36 | 4 |

*"About 10 years ago, Congress banned the sale and manufacture
of assault weapons. In your view, should Congress keep
or end this ban?"*[b]

| Keep Ban | End Ban | Not Sure |
|---|---|---|
| % | | |
| 78 | 16 | 5 |

[a]*CBS News* poll, November 10–13, 2003; *N* = 1,177 adults nationwide.
[b]*NBC News/Wall Street Journal* poll conducted by the polling organizations of
Peter Hart (D) and Robert Teeter (R), November 8–10, 2003; *N* = 1,003 adults
nationwide.
*Source:* http://www.thepollingreport.com.

A larger question is this: Why has congressional policymaking
moved back and forth on this issue for a century? Returning to
the beginning of this introduction, one explanation is that gun
control represents a cultural conflict in which policymakers are
forced to debate the ends, not the means, of policy. Gun advocates
concentrated in the rural parts of the country embrace a moral
order in which legitimate gun ownership is a part of everyday life
and a part of America's heritage. Gun control advocates—a population that tends to be more ethnic, more female, and more urban—feel no primordial tie to guns; they are not symbols of a
lifestyle and heritage these Americans hold dear. Accordingly,
members of the latter group regard guns as instruments of violence, and they prefer a moral order in which guns are absent

from everyday life. A profound divide exists between these two camps. Therefore, although many Americans support gun control, the issue remains nonconsensual and nonnegotiable. At least, that is how it is framed. Congress, then, is ill-equipped to provide policy resolution. As the political context changes, it is reasonable to expect the law to swing back and forth incrementally, with no statutory resolution.

## THE 1964 CIVIL RIGHTS ACT

> There is another reason why we dare not temporize with the issue which is before us. It is essentially moral in character. It must be resolved. It will not go away. Its time has come.
> —Senator Everett M. Dirksen, June 10, 1964

Perhaps no political issue exemplifies the politics of cultural conflict better than the struggle for civil rights for African Americans. The salience of this issue predates the Civil War. The U.S. Supreme Court's decision in *Dred Scott v. Sandford*, 60 U.S. 393 (1857) severely limited the ability of Congress to legislate on civil rights. Even after passage of the Civil War Amendments and the Civil Rights Act of 1866 (39 Cong. Ch. 31), Congress was impotent to advance a civil rights agenda. Real progress in this area would require a recasting of federalism by the Court (Kaczorowski 1987)—which would not come until the 1930s, when the Court reversed itself and began to uphold President Roosevelt's New Deal measures. With the Supreme Court's blessing of the New Deal, federalism was redefined so that the national government was able to exert influence over policy domains that traditionally belonged to the states. Yet obstacles to congressional action on civil rights remained. In particular, the relevant committee chairmanships were controlled by conservative southern Democrats. The South had been solidly Democratic since the Civil War, and the conservative chairs were not eager to allow strong civil rights measures out of committee (Lytle 1966).

Nevertheless, in 1964, with Democrats still firmly in control of both chambers, Congress passed the nation's most sweeping civil rights legislation to date. Why the change? One must consider the cultural dynamics. Fundamentally, culture provides members of a community with a guide for social interaction. It informs a community's understanding of how individuals should live with one another. Civil rights represented a cleavage between Americans who supported traditional social arrangements in which blacks and whites were segregated and blacks were denied economic and political rights and those who opposed such an arrangement, at least in principle. The former culture took root primarily in the rural, agrarian South and essentially captured the Democratic Party. The latter culture was more prominent in the industrial North—the cradle of the abolitionist movement. Moreover, if one could call any party the party of civil rights, it was the Republican Party, which had dominated the North since the Civil War. Efforts to advance civil rights for African Americans brought these two cultures into conflict.

The post–New Deal Democratic Party was a fragile coalition of rural southerners and northeastern labor interests. Both groups benefited from the economic relief of the New Deal, and they were able to maintain a majority coalition as long as civil rights was kept off the agenda (Benzel 1984). At the 1948 Democratic convention, the alliance was strained by Hubert Humphrey's efforts to attach a civil rights plank to the party platform. This effort alienated southern Democrats, causing a defection to the Dixiecrat Party that was substantial enough to give Alabama, Mississippi, Louisiana, and South Carolina to Dixiecrats in the general election. The migration of African Americans from South to North during the Depression and after World War II, however, provided urban Democrats in the North with a burgeoning constituency group. Democrats would lose southern voters by pursuing a civil rights agenda, but they would be able to mobilize African American voters into the tent of the Democratic Party (Leege et al. 2002, 109).

By the 1950s, elements of both parties could claim a civil rights mantel. Northeastern Democrats were reaching out to potential black voters, while Republican President Dwight Eisenhower was using federal troops to enforce the Supreme Court's decision in *Brown v. Board of Education of Topeka*, 347 U.S. 483 (1954), at the state level. Nevertheless, a coalition of conservative Republicans and southern Democrats blocked meaningful civil rights legislation in Congress for many years. Led by Hubert Humphrey, the social justice wing of the Democratic Party successfully advocated for a strong civil rights plank to be included in the 1960 platform, much to the agitation of Southern Democrats. John F. Kennedy was not an outspoken advocate of civil rights, however. Once elected, he adopted an accommodationist stance on race until 1963. Some observers attribute his belated activism in this area to a fear that he would alienate southern committee chairs who would quash other parts of his domestic agenda (Bryner 1998, 41; Leege et al. 2002, 109–11).

By the time Kennedy was elected, however, a civil rights social movement had developed and was engaged in peaceful protests and civil disobedience throughout the South. Unable to move Congress and the president, Martin Luther King and others organized the Southern Christian Leadership Conference (SCLC) and took their protests to the streets in hopes of garnering public attention and sympathy outside the South (Lytle 1966, 281). In response to King's efforts, mainstream and liberal Protestant leaders used their organizational strength to preach a "social gospel" advocating a new moral order on race. Jews and Catholics joined liberal Protestant groups such as the National Council of Churches in the religiously driven, broad-based social movement spearheaded by the SCLC (Findlay 1990). President Kennedy's accommodationist stance was untenable in the face of this growing civil rights activism. In the summer of 1963, Kennedy "called for an end to the old moral order of apartheid: 'We are confronted primarily with a moral issue. It is as old as the Scriptures and is as clear as the American Constitution. . . . Who among us would be content with counsels of patience and delay?'" (Leege et al 2002, 111).

With the development of a civil rights social movement and the president offering new leadership, the social bases of the parties were beginning to change at the mass level, and this change was producing change in Congress. Liberal Democrats were replacing progressive Republicans from the Northeast and Midwest, and a few conservative Republicans were starting to get elected in the South. In addition to generational replacement, some legislators changed their voting on civil rights, seeing the proverbial handwriting on the wall (Brady and Sinclair 1984; Leege et al. 2002, 109). As a result of national attention to sit-ins and protests at lunch counters and restaurants, Congress turned its attention to public accommodations.

In 1964, after President Kennedy's assassination, the House produced a compromise civil rights bill designed to win bipartisan support that would be strong enough to "overcome southern opposition" (Bryner 1998, 42). The 1964 Civil Rights Act (P.L. 88-352) prohibited discrimination in public places and in employment practices on the basis of race, color, national origin, gender, and religion, and it received a friendly reception in Emanuel Celler's (D-N.Y.) Judiciary Committee. Rules Committee chair Howard Smith (D-VA) indicated that his committee would not report out a rule for the bill, although he reversed his obstructionism under the growing threat of a discharge petition. Proponents of the bill successfully fought off almost 100 amendments, and the bill eventually passed with bipartisan support by a vote of 290–130 (Lytle 1966). The bill pitted northern Democrats against southern Democrats as much as it pitted Democrats against Republicans. The vote on final passage reflected a regional/ideological divide that was a sign of things to come. Northern Democrats supported final passage by a margin of 141–4, but "Southern Democrats voted 92 to 11 against" (Leege et al. 2002, 112).

The main obstacle to passage in the Senate was the filibuster. Sen. Richard Russell (D-GA) led the opposition. Russell coordinated eighteen southern senators into platoons, each of which took turns holding the Senate floor. Democrats did not have enough votes to invoke cloture, so they worked closely with Senate Minority Leader Everett Dirksen (R-IL) to win uncommitted Republican votes. While the solid South filibustered, the rest of the Democratic party worked on a compromise bill. On June 10, 1964, for the first time ever, the Senate invoked cloture on a civil rights bill, by a vote of 71–29. Forty-four Democrats and twenty-seven Republicans voted for cloture (Lytle 1966, 292–95).

Passage of the 1964 Civil Rights Act did not conclude congressional treatment of civil rights. Congress addressed voting rights and housing later in the 1960s, and it continues to revisit the issue of affirmative action. Nevertheless, the civil rights debate has been transformed since 1964. Racism remains pervasive in many segments of American life, and the major political parties still use racial symbols to mobilize and demobilize voters (Leege et al. 2002). By and large, however, the policy debate over civil rights is a debate over means, not ends. It is a debate over how to achieve a commonly agreed upon moral order. Politicians and parties argue over how best to achieve social justice, but they do not argue over what social justice is. The moral order in which blacks and whites are political equals is agreed upon in the mainstream of American politics. The way to ensure that equality, however, is a point of intense debate.

Why the transformation? Dirksen suggested that civil rights was simply an idea whose time had come (Lytle 1966, 295). Cultural conflicts exist over issues on which the public is deeply divided. The growth of the civil rights social movement and the publicity it brought to racial injustice in the South blurred the lines of the cultural conflict and won sympathy outside the South, making civil rights legislation difficult to obstruct.[6] Thus, when Kennedy discussed civil rights near the end of his presidency, he evoked symbols that were meaningful to Americans in both cultural camps: Scripture and the Constitution. Leege et al. (2002, 30) suggest that cultural cleavages endure until they are "resolved decisively by legislative action and social change." In this case, the relevant social change probably was the growth of a pro–civil rights majority at the mass level. This is not to suggest that racism disappeared. Rather, Americans rejected the old moral order of apartheid and were willing to embrace a new one. The new moral order envisions a society in which African Americans are afforded certain basic social, political, and economic rights. This social structural change allowed, enabled, and empowered Congress to legitimate the new moral order in law.

It is worth noting, however, that in 1964 Republican presidential nominee Barry Goldwater used the themes of racial difference and states rights in his campaign. He won Mississippi, Alabama, South Carolina, Louisiana, and Georgia by wide margins. By then, blacks were solidly in the Democratic tent. Nevertheless, it bears repeating that Republicans and Democrats in the current era are engaged in *instrumental* conflicts pertaining to race. As table I.2 suggests, Americans are divided over strategies for equality. Most notably, they are divided over affirmative action. Yet 80 percent of respondents in the same poll believe that diversity in education is "very important" or "somewhat important." There seems to be consensus on that goal. Thus, when President George W. Bush voiced his opposition to affirmative action practices at the University of Michigan, his argument was grounded in the idea that affirmative action treats people unequally on the basis of race, which he argues is unconstitutional.[7] He certainly did not argue that African Americans have no place in higher education or that diversity is unimportant.

**Table I.2.** Civil Rights and Affirmative Action

*"How important do you think it is for a college to have a racially diverse student body—that is, a mix of blacks, whites, Asians, Hispanics, and other minorities? Is it very important, somewhat important, not too important, or not at all important?"*

| | |
|---|---|
| Very important | 50% |
| Somewhat important | 30 |
| Not too important | 10 |
| Not at all important | 10 |

*"Do you think affirmative action programs that provide advantages or preferences for blacks, Hispanics, and other minorities in hiring, promoting, and college admissions should be continued, or do you think these affirmative action programs should be abolished?"*

| | |
|---|---|
| Should be continued | 53% |
| Should be abolished | 35 |
| Don't know | 12 |

*Note:* Associated Press poll, February 28–March 4, 2003; $N = 1,013$ adults nationwide.
*Source:* http://www.thepollingreport.com.

## GUNS AND RACE IN RETROSPECT

Congress has a long history of addressing cultural conflicts. In addition to gun control and the 1964 Civil Rights Act, one could speak of prohibition, slavery, pornography, abortion, gay rights,[8] and prayer in the public square. As a national legislature, Congress serves as the rhetorical stage on which disparate cultural groups come together to make policy and to legitimate a moral order. The 1964 Civil Rights Act and gun control legislation suggest that Congress is highly responsive to social structural changes. As group-based loyalties shift at the mass level, different cultural majorities are constructed within the institution. Congressional treatment of a cultural issue will move back and forth from an affirmation of traditional values to an affirmation of progressive values as those cultures grow and contract and compete with one another. Congress can provide resolution to an issue by legitimating a particular culture only as the polity approaches consensus.

The public is divided on the issue of gun control, and well-developed pro– and anti–gun control lobby groups have emerged to press their cases in Congress. Thus, the law develops in less than linear fashion as Congress responds to the ebbs and flows of cultural group strength. The story of the 1964 Civil Rights Act is different, but it also illustrates the dynamic of cultural politics. From 1866 until 1960, Congress passed a flaccid series of civil rights measures. In that era, the public was sharply divided into two cultural camps, and both camps found a home in the major political parties. Thus, division in Congress reflected division at the mass level. Change at the structural level produced a growing civil rights majority within the institution. The coalitional bases of the parties shifted, and by 1964 the civil rights majority in Congress was large enough to overcome minority obstructionism. Congress legitimated the new moral order and transformed the conflict over civil rights from an ends-based cultural conflict to an instrumental policy conflict. In legitimating the new moral order, Congress probably accelerated the atrophy of the old moral order.

## DEFINING CULTURAL CONFLICT

On the first day of college courses such as Introduction to American Government, undergraduates often are introduced to Lasswell's aphorism that politics is about "who gets what, when, and how." That description certainly rings true. In a democratic context, the people choose policymakers, and policymakers distribute resources. Ideally, the distribution of resources reflects the larger values and priorities of the polity. In distributing resources, policymakers implicitly determine, "Who among us is the most deserving? What behaviors should we encourage? What behaviors should we reward?" Students of politics often observe that the answers to such questions are informed by self-interest. Students of congressional politics often observe that the answers to such questions are informed by a specific kind of self-interest: electoral ambition. In this volume, however, I explore the possibility that policymakers sometimes ask a different set of questions: "Who is with us, and who is against us? Who is good, and who is evil?" Questions such as these are asked and answered in the context of social group identification and competition.

Social groups—whether they are racial, ethnic, class-based, or religious—develop shared cultures. *Culture* is a word that can mean everything and nothing. Because theoretical rigor demands something more precise, it is important to elaborate on what we mean by "culture." Scholars disagree about the meaning of this term. As the first part of this introduction suggests, this research proceeds on the assumption that culture provides people with a "moral order" (Wuthnow 1987). That is, culture provides "a shared sense of how people ought to live their lives and what social relationships are compatible with that vision" (Oldmixon 2002, 775). Within a political community, culture is significant in part because of the demands it makes on society at large. As people interact and adopt shared "moral orders," norms of behavior emerge (Wildavsky 1987). Individuals are expected to behave in certain ways, within certain boundaries. Cultural groups demand, with varying degrees of success, that society behave in accordance with that group's norms. In a pluralistic democratic society, competing cultural groups apply countervailing pressures in and on the institutions of government to legitimate their preferred ways of life—their preferred social relationships.

A few things are worth noting. First, the terms "culture" and "preference" are not interchangeable. Individuals have preferences; social groups have cultures. Culture is the fountain of preference. Assuming rationality, individuals *prefer* policies (in a political context) that are in their *interest*, as they understand it. Interests do not spring from the heavens, however; "they are conferred on objects and events through social interaction." Thus, "the origins of our preferences may be found in the deepest desires of all: how we wish to live with other people and how we wish others to live with us" (Wildavsky 1987, 4). Social interactions produce shared belief systems, or cultures. The preferences individuals acknowledge and embrace, then, are informed by culture and therefore should be consistent with a set of values and norms that promote a given culture.

"[C]ultural conflict," then, "is simply argument (and associated behavior) about how we should live. . . . Political conflicts* warrant the label of *cultural conflicts* when they involve disagreement about what society should or does prescribe as the *appropriate way of life*" (Leege et al. 2002, 26; emphasis in original). An obvious question is this: If one assumes that behavior is consistent with a widely diffuse set of cultural norms, why does political conflict emerge? If a polity shares the same culture, should not political discourse be marked by a "seamless web" of consensus? Not necessarily. In a pluralistic society, such as that in the United States, there is likely to be more than one culture. Social groups within a polity have an array of available cultures within which they can couch their behaviors. At the same time, individual cultures are likely to be rife with inconsistencies. They are more like "toolkits" containing "diverse, often conflicting sets of symbols, rituals, stories, and guides to action" (Swidler 1986, 277) than static, internally consistent guides.

Thus, the rational actor will pursue money, power, or self-esteem, but the rational actor also will pursue aggrandizement of group values that may or may not be connected to individual material well-being. This is the stuff of political conflict. Preferences can be easily ordered, and disagreement about preference ordering does not imply profound conflict. Cultures cannot be so easily ordered, and disagreement on the basis of culture is not easily resolved because cultural conflict "deals with what is perceived as right and wrong, us versus them" (Leege et al. 2002, 26). For example, if one argues among friends that *Slippery When Wet* is a superior album to *New Jersey*, and another person takes the opposite view, no harm is done. Their preferences differ, and the latter friend is wrong, but at least both enjoyed the music of Bon Jovi in the late 1980s. If one person argues that prayer should be permitted in public schools, however, and another takes the opposite view, that is a different story. These divergent views are informed by fundamentally different understandings of what society should look like and how individuals should interact. Cultures are more like Isaiah Berlin's "incommensurables" (Gray 1996) than like simple preferences.

Second, in this volume I pay close attention to congressional decision making on issues of reproductive policy, gay rights, and religion in schools because they are exemplars of a salient cultural conflict. No single set of issues is essentially cultural or moral, however. "Just as science finds its identity in its methodology instead of its subject matter, cultural politics defines itself by the style of argumentation over public policy instead of the type of public policy" (Leege et al. 2002, 13). Classification as such depends on the perception of relevant actors and the terms of debate. Therefore, a "policy dealing with sexual behavior need not necessarily be morality policy, just as a policy dealing with economic regulation might well be a morality policy" (Mooney 2001, 4). Abortion has taken on a moral frame, but it could easily be understood as a public health issue. Alcohol regulation provides another example: It can be framed as a public safety issue, as with drunk driving, or as an absolutist moral issue, as with Prohibition (Gusfield 1963; Meier and Johnson 1990).

A related point is that because cultural conflict refers to a rhetorical style that invokes *"social values, norms and symbolic community boundaries"* more than a precise catalog of issues, issues can take on and then lose a nonessential cultural framing (Leege et al. 2002, 27; emphasis in original). An issue may represent cultural conflict in one era but not in another. Either the institutions of government provide resolution, or the social structural environment changes so that the issue no longer represents profound conflict (Leege et al. 2002, 30). As I discuss in the first part of this introduction, the cultural conflict over gun control endures, but the cultural conflict over civil rights for African Americans does not. Instrumental discussions of civil rights continue to produce political conflict and continue to have moral implications, but the issue no longer represents a cultural conflict, per se. Prohibition is an example of cultural conflict that has been completely resolved at the federal level.

Though no issue is essentially cultural, scholars have identified certain characteristics that are common to cultural conflicts.[9] First, cultural issues are "easy" issues (Carmines and Stimson 1980; Leege et al. 2002, 28; Mooney 2001, 7). In their analysis of mass-level issue voting, Carmines and Stimson (1980) argue that when issues are "easy," the electorate (or, for these purposes, constituents) develop "gut"-level opinions and can act on them without much cognitive difficulty. Carmines and Stimson (1980) characterize easy issues on the basis of the following attributes: first, easy issues take on symbolic, rather than technical, significance; second, they are ends-based, rather than means-based, conflicts; and third, they remain on the public agenda for a long period of time. Because easy issues endure in the public consciousness, and because they are both simple and symbolic, they tend to be highly salient with the electorate. Therefore, vote-seeking political parties and candidates may politicize these issues to their own advantage. Indeed, elections have been won and lost because parties have been able to effectively portray their opponents as foils on the wrong side of an easy issue policy conflict (Leege et al. 2002).

In a legislative context, however, so-called easy issues may be difficult to resolve. Because these issues influence mass-level voting, legislators are expected to be highly responsive to their districts on these issues. Building majorities may be difficult, however, if district-level responsiveness becomes such an imperative that compromise is undermined. Development of a weapons system, reforming Social Security, the tax code, energy policy, Middle East peace: These are all complicated issues about which few members of the electorate have well-formed opinions. Thus, representatives may feel less pressure from their constituents to vote one way or another. In these areas, representatives are likely to have discretion to act as trustees. Americans do know what abortion and homosexuality are, however, and most people have strong feelings on these issues. Therefore, the expectation is that constituents are likely to exert pressure on and be influential with their elected representatives (Mooney and Lee 2000). A compromise policy may be obvious and apparent, yet it may be unavailable to legislators if they are constrained by their districts.

Second, because cultural conflicts are ends-based conflicts over how individuals should live as a society, cultural conflicts tend to be framed in an absolutist, nonnegotiable manner (Leege et al. 2002; McFarlane and Meier 2001; Mooney 2001; Meier 2001; Haider-Markel and Meier 1996; O'Connor 1996). This factor also complicates legislative resolution. When policy ends are agreed upon, compromise in pursuit of a common goal should be facilitated, even if the instrumentalities conflict. By virtue of the values-based nature of cultural conflict, however, the political lines of battle are drawn between good and evil, morality and sin, and the ultimate goals are in dispute. There is little room for principled disagreement, so the ability of opposing parties to compromise is severely limited. As Lowi (1998, xv) notes, "The observed political behavior [as it relates to moral issues] is more ideological, . . . less utilitarian, more polarized, and less prone to compromise." People feel most righteous with regard to these kinds of issues, and they are most inclined to support government intervention that advances their values (Mill 1863). Congress, however, is designed with rules and norms to facilitate compromise. Indeed, decision making in any organization is a matter of compromise (Simon 1957). Therefore, these issues are likely to engender a great deal of tension within each chamber. The increased levels of tension may encourage groups of legislators to regard each other as morally suspect, to regard politics as an arena of broad moral conflict, and thus to carry moral framing of issues into fields well beyond relevant policy issues.

Third, "[w]hile much law codifies rights and wrong," cultural conflicts engage values on which there is "no overwhelming consensus in a polity" (Mooney 2001, 4). As Mooney (2001) notes, there are many criminal activities that most people agree are wrong and deserving of state-sponsored punishment—kidnapping, theft, and rape, to name a few. Prohibitions against these activities are all based on the classically liberal value that society places on life, property, and individual integrity—integrity of one's person and one's possessions. No such consensus exists with regard to fertility control, gun control, prayer in school, physician-assisted suicide, or gay rights (Mooney 2001, 4). When the institutions of government are forced to consider these issues, when they are forced to legislate morality, many people will have a fundamental conflict with values embodied in and legitimized by the policies, regardless of what government does.

Fourth, all cultural groups experience some level of hypocrisy in their ranks. This observation is not to suggest that culturally animated advocacy is insincere. In general, however, there is some disjunction between public and private behavior, particularly when cultural conflicts emanate from regulation of perceived sinful behavior, as with homosexuality and abortion. Then, Meier (2001, 23) notes, "the correlation between public behavior and private behavior is less than 1.0." For example, public opinion data indicate that Americans overwhelmingly disapprove of pornography. Yet the demand for pornography is high (Smith 2001). Indeed, pornography is a multibillion-dollar industry in the United States. In another example from an earlier era, one might point to the suburban elites of Massachusetts who vociferously supported busing but were exempted from and unaffected by the policy.[10] In a legislative context, this disjunction between public and private behavior creates an informational problem for legislators because they do not get an accurate feel for the preferences of their constituents. Moreover, it places opponents of traditional values at a tactical disadvantage because rhetorically it puts them in the awkward position of "standing up for sin" by championing sex, drugs, and the destruction of the American family (McFarlane and Meier 2001; Meier 2001, 1999; Mooney 2001; Smith 2001).

## CONCLUSION

The politics of cultural conflict might not matter, except that cultural conflict is an enduring characteristic of American politics. Moreover, the prominent cultural conflicts of the post–New Deal era are likely to become more, not less, salient (Dodd 1993, 1981; Habermas 1973; Inglehart 1990; Lowi 1998; Tatalovich and Daynes 1998). One might be tempted to argue that because these issues are contentious, because they create difficulties for a legislature that is structured to seek compromise, and because they are largely symbolic, Congress should shirk, punt, or otherwise ignore cultural conflict. Practically speaking, this approach is difficult because constituents care about these issues deeply (Studlar 2001, 39), and cultural issues are used to mobilize voters (Leege et al. 2002). Moreover, failure to manage these issues directly may weaken the institution (Habermas 1973; Dodd 1993). To retain its legitimacy and the loyalty of the public, Congress must "demonstrate a reasonable capacity to recognize fundamental problems . . . , deliberate over the proper solutions to these problems, and enact legislation that addresses them in a credible manner" (Dodd 1993, 418–19). Any organization depends on external resources for survival, and legitimacy—the sense that an institution is entitled to govern—is the most vital resource (Zhou 1993). In the case of Congress, ignoring these moral issues, no matter how difficult they are, may compromise the legitimacy of the institution.

In the remainder of this volume I explore this political puzzle in the following manner. In chapter 1 I address the political foreground. I explore the extent to which goal-oriented legislators and staff perceive cultural moral conflicts and assess their strategies for coping with them. In chapters 2 and 3 I address the background: the social structural environment in which goal-oriented legislators act. In these chapters I chart the development of two distinct yet symbiotic cultural movements and their ability to pressure Congress to enact values specific policy. In chapter 4 I analyze specific decisions made by the House from 1993 to 2002, with a quantitative exploration of roll-call voting and cosponsorship decisions. In chapter 5 I discuss strategies employed by leaders to cope with these nonnegotiable cultural issues. Finally, in chapter 6 I explore future implications for cultural politics.

# 1

# Seeing and Believing in the Foreground

You're either fiercely opposed to it or fiercely in favor of a woman's right to choose, and . . . the middle of the road was the surest place to get run over.

—Republican staffer

Regardless of historical era and context, in the foreground of American politics members of Congress want things. They are purposive and goal oriented, and they act to achieve their goals. Scholars have elucidated an array of legislative goals that to varying degrees structure behavior, institutional organization, and institutional change. As I note in the Preface, Mayhew (1974) assumes that reelection is a legislator's singular goal. In his seminal work *Congressmen in Committees*, Fenno (1973) argues that legislators actively pursue policy, influence in the chamber, and reelection. Aldrich and Rohde (2001) suggest that legislators seek and balance policy and reelection goals. Dodd (1977, 1986a, 1986b) argues that legislators are primarily motivated by the quest for power and personal autonomy within the chamber, in the tradition of Machiavelli.[1] People are complex, so there is validity in all of these arguments. Indeed, it would seem absurd to argue that legislators are indifferent to any of these goals.

Unless one assumes that legislators have a pathological desire to hold public office—perhaps to make up for a lack of self-esteem (Barber 1992)—reelection probably is instrumental to policy and power goals. In and of itself, reelection is not a valuable commodity, yet without it none of the other goals is achievable. Generally speaking, then, when representatives consider legislation they must strike a balance so that power and policy are maximized and reelection is not compromised. If a representative determines that voting one way or another will earn the ire of his or her district and therefore compromise reelection, this calculation should inform the legislator's voting. If there is no effect, then the legislator is free to base his or her judgment on other, secondary criteria (Arnold 1990).

One way to distill the collective wisdom of congressional scholarship, then, is to suggest that competing legislator goals, and the need to find an equilibrium among them, structures many aspects of congressional politics. Yet congressional politics also appears to be influenced by background factors, or social structural factors. Whereas the pursuit of foreground goals is continuous, social structure is temporally specific. Simply, the argument is that societal—that is, exogenous—phenomena shape the internal politics of the institution and the pursuit of goals. This assumption was at the heart of Polsby's (1968) seminal explanation for House institutionalization, which was that as modernization and industrialization placed increasing demands on Congress, the institution became differentiated and professionalized. This structural assumption remains at the heart of Polsby's most recent volume (2003) on congressional change. It also has influenced Sinclair's (1990) discussion of Senate change and Young's (1986) portrayal of the nineteenth-century Congress, to cite just a handful of examples.

Which societal developments are salient to the politics of cultural conflict? Two trends seem to be particularly relevant. One is the emergence of the feminist movement and its embrace of progressive sexual and family norms, which I discuss in chapter 2. The other is the politicization of religious traditionalism, which I discuss in chapter 3. Both of these cultural movements were animated by changes in the opportunity structure. The endurance of these cultures is a result of the resonance of the values they espouse, an opportunity structure that remains favorable, and their ability to marshal resources such as money, leadership, grassroots support, and the like. Advocates of religious traditionalism and progressive sexuality are said to be engaged in a cultural conflict—at least as far as this volume is concerned—because they articulate incompatible visions of the good life, based on different sets of values. Congress, then, finds itself with the responsibility of managing this conflict because it is *the* national institution in which disparate constituencies are brought together to legislate—to make policy for the whole community. We expect Congress to be perceptive of and receptive to the advocacy efforts of these disparate cultures because legislators themselves may be cultural devotees or because of the presence of cultural devotees in the district, which produces an electoral connection that is relevant to cultural conflict. Either way, background social structure and foreground goal orientation interact to produce policy on moral, or cultural, issues.

## THE MECHANICS OF DECISION MAKING

Patterns of legislative decision making vary by policy domain (Clausen 1973), and the kinds of issues under examination in this volume constitute a policy domain that produces district patterns of politics (Lowi 1998; McFarlane and Meier 2001; Meier 1994). What can we say about congressional politics as it relates to cultural issues? Returning to the discussion of foreground dynamics, legislators have preferred policy goals and behave in ways that produce their preferred outcomes (Fenno 1973; Meier 1994). In the same way industrialization produced in some legislators an interest in policy goals related to child labor and monopolies, the emergence and politicization of progressive sexuality and religious traditionalism have produced an interest in policy goals related to those respective visions. Thus, a guiding assumption of this volume is that legislator goals will be policy oriented and that decision making will be influenced by the desire to legitimate legislators' preferred culture in law.

That said, it would be unwise to disregard the influence of the district on legislator behavior. Legislators may be guided by policy goals, but probably not at the expense of reelection. It bears repeating: Cultural, or moral, issues tend to be "easy." They produce gut-level reactions from the electorate that shape mass-level attitudes and behaviors. Because these issues are highly salient with constituents, legislator treatment of cultural issues is likely to affect reelection, and legislators are almost certainly cognizant of that fact. It

may be difficult, however, to disentangle the influence of legislators' true preferences from their desire to get reelected because with
salient issues, legislator preferences and modal district preferences
are likely to correspond. Moreover, many members—particularly
those with state legislative experience—have long track records
from which it may be politically difficult to deviate, even if they
wanted to. In an ideal sense, constituents know what they want,
and they know what they are getting in a legislator when they cast
their ballots. This should be particularly true with regard to abortion, which has been a component of the annual rhythm of the legislative process for decades. As the marginals in table 1.1 suggest,
public opinion on abortion has been very stable in recent years. In
the aggregate, Americans have longstanding attitudes on this issue,
and in theory this fact should facilitate correspondence between
legislator and district preferences.

This correspondence may be less clear with regard to school
prayer. Although the issue has been on the political radar for
many years, Congress considers it with less frequency, so it tends
not to be as high profile. Legislators have less of a track record,

**Table 1.1.** Abortion Attitudes

*"Do you think abortion should be legal in all cases, legal in most
cases, illegal in most cases, or illegal in all cases?"*

| Date | Legal in All Cases | Legal in Most Cases | Illegal in Most Cases | Illegal in All Cases | No Opinion |
|---|---|---|---|---|---|
| | | | % | | |
| 5/04 | 23 | 31 | 23 | 20 | 2 |
| 1/03 | 23 | 34 | 25 | 17 | 2 |
| 1/01 | 21 | 38 | 25 | 14 | 1 |
| 7/00 | 20 | 33 | 26 | 17 | 4 |
| 3/99 | 21 | 34 | 27 | 15 | 3 |
| 7/98 | 19 | 35 | 29 | 13 | 4 |
| 6/96 | 24 | 34 | 25 | 14 | 2 |

*Note: ABC News/Washington Post* polls, conducted most recently May 20–23, 2004;
$N$ = 1,005 adults nationwide.
*Source:* http://www.thepollingreport.com.

and constituent attitudes may be more difficult to intuit, as table 1.2 suggests. In a 2002 *Newsweek* poll, 87 percent of respondents supported inclusion of the phrase "under God" in the Pledge of Allegiance, and only 36 percent of the respondents in the same poll thought that government should avoid promoting religion. However, 45 percent consider the United States a secular nation. These findings suggest the possibility that legislators and constituents are operating with imperfect knowledge of each other on this

**Table 1.2.**   Religion in the Public Space

---

*"As you may know, a federal appeals court ruled this week that the Pledge of Allegiance is unconstitutional and cannot be recited in schools because the phrase 'under God' violates the separation of church and state. Do you think the phrase 'under God' should or should NOT be part of the Pledge of Allegiance?"*

| | |
|---|---|
| Should | 87% |
| Should not | 9 |
| Don't know | 4 |

*"Thinking about the issue of separation of church and state in this country today, in general, do you think the government should avoid promoting religion in any way, or not?"*

| | |
|---|---|
| Should avoid | 36% |
| Should not avoid | 54 |
| Don't know | 10 |

*"Which one of the following three statements comes closer to your view? The United States is a Christian nation. The United States is a biblical nation, defined by the Judeo-Christian tradition. The United States is a secular nation in which religious belief, or lack of it, isn't a defining characteristic."*

| | |
|---|---|
| A Christian nation | 29% |
| A biblical nation | 16 |
| A secular nation | 45 |
| Don't know | 10 |

---

*Note: Newsweek* poll conducted by Princeton Survey Research Associates, June 27–28, 2002; *N* = 1,000 adults nationwide.
*Source:* http://www.thepollingreport.com.

issue. Nevertheless, there probably is considerable overlap between the prolife and pro-prayer sets because both attitudes are
consistent with the ethic of religious traditionalism.
  Gay issues have made their way onto the congressional
agenda only recently. Thus, many members do not have established records and are grappling with this issue for the first time.
If one assumes ideological constraint, legislator and constituent
opinion on abortion probably is a good cue for opinion on gay
issues because they both directly address human sexuality and the
repercussions thereof. Public attitudes on this issue are changing
rapidly, however (Brewer 2003; Wilcox and Norrander 2002), and
public opinion data suggest that open homosexuality is becoming more acceptable and mainstream for many Americans (Wilcox
and Wolpert 2000). As table 1.3 indicates, support for same-sex
marriage has increased slightly over the past few years, although
a majority still opposes such a practice. Support for civil unions
has increased dramatically, however. A majority of CNN/*USA
Today*/Gallup poll respondents (54 percent) indicate that they
would support such a practice, even though 61 percent of respondents in the same poll reject same-sex marriage.[2]
  These poll data suggest that although legislators may be
driven by policy and reelection goals, they may or may not be
certain of the electoral repercussions of position-taking. The level
of district and legislator attitudinal correspondence may vary
from issue to issue. In theory, it should be very high on abortion
but perhaps not as robust with prayer and homosexuality because
the latter issues have not had as enduring and prominent a place
on the agenda of American politics. Nevertheless, because cultural
issues are easy, the correspondence should be reasonably high.
Therefore, when cultural division marks the lines of political conflict, legislators can be expected to be motivated primarily by a
desire to legitimate a set of preferred social relationships through
policy. Their goal is to enact a values-specific policy that promotes
the status of their group values or, alternatively, denigrates a competing group's values.
  Legislator ideology, partisanship, and religion can be expected
to strongly influence legislator decision making on reproductive
policy, gay issues, and school prayer because these phenomena
are reflective of underlying cultural values. Legislators also can
be expected to be responsive to the cultural cues they receive from

**Table 1.3.**  Gay Marriage/Civil Unions Attitudes

*"Do you think marriages between homosexuals should or should not be recognized by the law as valid, with the same rights as traditional marriages?"*

| Date | Should Be Valid | Should Not Be Valid | No Opinion |
|------|-----------------|---------------------|------------|
|      |                 | %                   |            |
| 3/04 | 33 | 61 | 6 |
| 6/03 | 39 | 55 | 6 |
| 1/00 | 34 | 62 | 4 |
| 2/99 | 35 | 62 | 3 |
| 3/96 | 27 | 68 | 5 |

*"Would you favor or oppose a law that would allow homosexual couples to legally form civil unions, giving them some of the legal rights of married couples?"*

| Date | Favor | Oppose | No Opinion |
|------|-------|--------|------------|
|      |       | %      |            |
| 3/04 | 54 | 42 | 4 |
| 5/03 | 49 | 49 | 2 |
| 5/02 | 46 | 51 | 3 |
| 5/01 | 44 | 52 | 4 |

*Note:* CNN/*USA Today*/Gallup polls, conducted most recently March 5–7, 2004; *N* = 1,005 adults nationwide.
*Source:* http://www.thepollingreport.com.

their districts, although legislator and district cultural preferences probably are mutually reinforcing. It also is possible, however, that legislator decision making may be made in the context of cross-pressures—a legislator's own values competing with the values of his or her district. If that is the case, the expectation is that legislators will avail themselves of the many opportunities in the legislative process to assuage their districts while behaving consistently with their own cultural preferences. In particular, a distinction may arise between roll-call voting, on one hand, and sponsorship and cosponsor behavior, on the other.

A first step in understanding the congressional politics of abortion, gay issues, and school prayer—three exemplars of cultural conflict—is to ascertain how legislators approach these issues. Any theory of decision making that treats cultural issues as distinct crumbles if legislators themselves do not perceive the values-based cultural significance of these issues. In the remainder of this chapter I explore the ways in which legislators and staff perceive moral and cultural conflicts generally and reproductive policy, school prayer, and gay rights specifically. I then discuss how legislators decide. My analysis is based on interviews I conducted with House members and staff in summer of 2000 and spring 2002. (Appendix A provides information on the survey instrument and respondents.) The initial results suggest that legislators do perceive moral conflicts in ways that are consistent with the literature. Moreover, decision making seems to be consistent with the expectations I discuss above.

## WHAT IS "MORAL"?

Many respondents had specific ideas about what is and is not a "moral issue."[3] One Democratic legislator indicated that he sees politics, moral or otherwise, through the "race paradigm." Because of the institutionalized racism of American politics (e.g., whites control Congress and the presidency) everything about American politics is "morally suspect." During the course of the interview, this legislator walked to Statuary Hall, pointed to the statue of Jefferson Davis (Mississippi's contribution), and said, "My friend Trent Lott would say, 'Come on now, this statue celebrates limited government and Mississippi history.'" As far as this Democrat was concerned, however, limited government was and continues to be a code for racism.[4]

Other legislators, however, tended not to view moral and cultural conflict, let alone all of American politics, through the lens of race. In fact, another Democratic legislator said unequivocally that "race is not a moral issue. . . . To me race is a constitutional issue. The constitution *gives* us that. It isn't something that I must be morally attached to, but the Constitution says that it [racism] is wrong. I mean, we're all supposed to be equal and have the same rights." Thus, "race is something I take for granted. That is, I take for granted that if you disagree with the Constitution or you feel that you should do things to hurt people based on their race, then as far as I'm concerned you're a racist. And your behavior is racist behavior." This representative's characterization of racial equality issues echoes the discussion of consensus in the policy in the Introduction to this book. Racial equality as a norm is a given and therefore is not a moral issue per se. It is more of a valence issue, for which ends are consensual but instrumentalities are highly debated. On the other hand, this legislator identifies abortion as a profoundly moral issue because when it is considered legislatively, she is forced to struggle with religious themes.[5]

Many legislators and staffers acknowledge that moral issues are "different." That is, they constitute a distinct policy domain. One Republican legislator characterizes the difference between moral and nonmoral issues as a difference in emotion, or passion.

> [T]hey're different because many times the passions run deeper. And [constituents] have formed opinions about it. [With] tax policy or maybe an energy policy, there's a lot of complexities there that the public might have general impressions about or general philosophical bents on, but many times the nuances . . . they just would leave to lawmakers. But when you're looking at the abortion question, if you're looking at something as heartfelt as gay issues, they understand them, they believe deeply, and they express themselves on that.[6]

Again, these issues are easy. As such, they elicit an emotional response. Constituents react to them on a visceral level and do not hesitate to communicate with legislators on these subjects. They form specific opinions; they communicate specific opinions. Thus, legislators receive a great deal of input from the district. It is unclear, however, whether the district-level messages conflict with the legislator's values.

Without describing the distinction between moral and nonmoral issues, many respondents simply identified issues they consider to have a strong moral component. Almost every respondent identified abortion, and many others identified family planning, stem-cell research, school prayer, impeachment, and hate crimes. Several respondents suggested that identification of issues as "moral" is contingent on religion and that the issues that evoke religious themes are the ones they consider to be high-profile moral issues. When one Republican legislator was asked to identify particularly high-profile moral issues, the legislator responded, "I think what you're really talking about is religious issues."[7] A Republican staffer notes, "Whenever you get religious, it becomes a moral debate."[8] Religious themes may not be sufficient for an issue to be considered moral; they may not even be necessary, generally speaking. They are at the core of the cultural conflict I consider here, however.

On the other hand, a Republican Appropriations Committee staffer suggested that most individuals view cultural issues too narrowly, focusing on "social issues from the right of the political spectrum" such as abortion and family planning. Yet culture can incorporate anything from debt relief to world hunger to human rights abuses. As this staffer said, "As soon as you see someone who's a health nut and a vegetarian trying to push free trade organic coffee from a place like East Timor or Columbia, Ethiopia, whatever, you have someone who really is also expressing some deep personal cultural preferences for a view of the world." What connects coffee, debt relief, and international family planning is that in each instance those issues reflect "people's approach to the way they wish to live their lives and they wish other people to be forced to live their lives."[9]

A Democratic representative suggests that although there may be consensus that a few marquee issues are considered moral, there are an array of issues that take on moral significance for some legislators but not for others. What is moral, then, sometimes can be in the eye of the beholder. Thus:

> For me, an ethical policy issue that has been the big one or a big one has been the set of China votes. And yet I know for other people that was a matter of political calculus. Yesterday we had a vote on Internet gambling. . . . [Representative X] and I agree on the China issue, and we have some parallel concerns about gambling, but for me gambling was not the moral imperative. . . . I suspect for [X] they might be, if not equal stature, at least in the same league. Whereas for me, it was a matter of, okay, does this law really work?

On the other hand:

> I think that within any particular cultural context . . . there's more general agreement that this is kind of a moral ethical set of issues. I mean whether that is . . . some of the issues around religion and reproductive rights that have taken on a general

tone of values issues in the United States. . . . [T]he symbolic value of what's done takes on parity, or perhaps is supreme to the functional intent. Where symbolism becomes more important than the function. It might be true of reproductive rights.[10]

The representative makes an important point: Issues are not inherently cultural. In a given context, however, in a given society, there probably is consensus that a handful of issues are culturally significant. These issues evoke a symbolic politics, where the values they engender are as important as the mechanics of specific policies under consideration. In the case of reproductive rights, the values in play are relevant to social cultures already identified in this book. Legislators are not simply debating a medical procedure. One camp vigorously defends—as they see it—the rights of women to make autonomous choices regarding their reproductive capacities, which almost certainly relate to decisions on work and family life. The other camp vigorously defends—again, as they see it—the divinely ordained right to life of human fetuses, which also has repercussions for the health of traditional family and gender arrangements.

In keeping with this characterization, it may be no surprise that when respondents were asked to identify specific issues that stand out as particularly high-profile moral issues, legislators and staff gave various kinds of answers. Some suggested that although certain issues stand out, all issues have some moral component and are cause for reflection. One Democratic legislator notes, "[W]here you're trading interests or balancing interests, there are substantive values we should be tending to. And that suggests that the moral issues are not just the hot-button issues, like abortion or school prayer or whatever people explicitly relate to some religious belief, but it really covers virtually the entire policy spectrum."[11]

A Republican legislative counsel develops this point further:

> Almost everything we end up doing here has some kind of moral component to it or another. And it's just a matter of how polarized people on the other side of the issue are. When you're talking about something like abortion, which is kind of the banner marquee moral issue up here, there isn't much room in the middle. You're either fiercely opposed to it or fiercely in favor of a woman's right to choose, and we used to say that the middle of the road was the surest place to get run over.[12]

Two Democratic staffers note:

> [T]here's the usual, abortion. I think gay/lesbian civil rights
> comes into this. There's a whole, you could make a moral case
> for almost any piece of legislation from environmental legisla-
> tion, God's green earth, to almost anything . . . and campaign
> finance.[13]
>
> Well, I think abortion is the obvious one, particularly with re-
> ligious overtones. I suppose from my point of view you could
> say that providing more aid to poor people has a moral com-
> ponent to it. . . . People tend to look at the issues like the ones
> that come before the Judiciary Committee, like abortion, like
> school prayer.[14]

All law codifies right and wrong. All law has some moral
component. Policy decisions distribute and redistribute resources,
and those kinds of decisions require some calculation about what
and who is good and deserving, what or who is bad. In that sense,
a decision on a tax cut or environmental regulation is as morally
charged as a decision on the gay marriage amendment or the assault weapons ban. What makes cultural conflicts different is that
they represent values—religiously informed values—on which
there is no consensus in the polity. The conflict is over ends, not
instrumentalities, and the public is divided. The Republican counsel makes this point. Moral issues are highly polarized, and just
as there is no overwhelming consensus in the polity, there is no
consensus on Capitol Hill. Moreover, there is very little room, on
the face of it, for compromise. For the legislative process, this situation suggests that these issues may be framed as nonnegotiable,
even if they are not essentially nonnegotiable. As such, compromise becomes difficult. A Democratic representative expresses this
concern precisely, indicating that these issues take on a "right or
wrong, black and white" categorical framing.[15] With regard to
abortion, a Democratic administrative assistant notes, "An issue
like abortion you can't, it's not one that just lends itself to kind
of finding the middle and splitting the difference. Whereas a lot
of other issues at least in theory do lend themselves to that."[16]

   Nevertheless, the importance of framing leaves open the possibility of compromise, according to one Republican legislator.
Reproductive issues, in general, are divisive, and legislative factions around the various reproductive policies tend to overlap.

That is, representatives who oppose abortion often are the same ones who oppose policies advocating contraception. One representative makes the point that by framing contraception as a method of reducing abortions, she has been able to garner support from otherwise prolife representatives.

> [T]here are two or three [of my home state] members that over my years. . . . I have gotten them. You can work with people like on family planning. I've gotten some who didn't quite understand what the issue was and they voted for Title X, where they would have before voted against it. . . . You still have your basic prolife [beliefs], but when you come to understand family planning and what it can do in preventing abortion—you know getting them to be active in the first place—so that's been interesting to watch.[17]

Similar kinds of compromise have been available on "federal employee health benefits and contraception" and international family planning.[18] This analysis suggests that there is room on the margins to frame cultural issues so that new coalitions can be formed because there are some legislators "who you can target, and make the argument that it's not abortion, that it's preventing abortion."[19] The key, of course, is to frame the compromise as consistent with your colleagues' ultimate goal—in this case, ending abortion.[20] It may not work "on the fundamental issues," says the representative, but incremental compromises may be available on related issues, when properly framed.

Willingness to compromise and find common ground may be generational, however. For example, a Democratic staffer notes that although Reps. Nita Lowey (D-N.Y.) and Henry Hyde (R-IL) differ on abortion, they are able to work together on other reproductive issues relating to prenatal care. "I think it's more old-school members . . . who are able to do it. . . . Like Tom Coburn, when he was here, would never compromise at all. I can't imagine him ever working with Nita Lowey on anything." Thus, whereas the more experienced legislators on both sides of the aisle are more likely to "understand the art of compromise and what you need to do" to legislate, the "younger conservatives," from this Democrat's perspective, reject that strategy and remain committed to their ideological positions.[21]

Nevertheless, reproductive policy in particular lends itself to compromise because it is regularly considered in the appropriations process. On the ubiquity of reproductive policy as an appropriations issue, a Republican staffer notes:

> Treasury/Postal because it's contraception coverage, foreign aid bills because it's family planning, HHS because it's counseling and more family planning, let's see, agriculture because of the RU 486. . . . And then the . . . Hyde amendment language that is, you know, versus Mexico City policy—that's in foreign aid bills.[22]

In the context of appropriations, discussions of abortion can be transformed into a discussion about dollars.[23] Ideally, difficult decisions about the direction and substance of policy—whether to fund international family planning, for example—already have been made by authorizers. Appropriators set funding levels. Among Republican and Democratic appropriators, traditionally there has been consensus that their task is to "protect the Federal Treasury" and serve their parent chamber (Fenno 1962, 311). Guided by that consensus, legislators who are otherwise prolife or prochoice may have some flexibility to compromise in committee.

Similarly, when these issues reach the floor, compromise may be facilitated among rank-and-file legislators. According to a Republican staffer,

> My boss has a fairly solid prolife voting record. . . . [A] lot of people, I think, may also have prolife voting records who might not be that dedicated personally to the issue. But rather when it comes down to taxpayer funding on certain things, you'll get more people kind of on board with, "Okay, maybe it is a personal decision as to whether to have a child or not, but certainly this isn't a procedure . . . that people in my district that I'm representing, that may not want to have to pay for it, should not have to use their tax dollars that way." So lots of people kind of hedge the issue . . . , they won't even come right and tell you whether they're personally pro-choice or personally prolife because they look at it as more of a funding issue. And that's about the only way we seem to be able to get at it here is through funding.

The point is that nonnegotiables can be transformed into something decidedly negotiable—in this case, a question of fiscal responsibility. Sometimes gay issues also are dealt with in the context of the appropriations process. The fiscal policy frame may be available for that issue, although by and large it is not. Prayer is not dealt with as an appropriations issue at all.

It is worth noting that the foregoing respondents' comment points to a growing tendency on the part of the Republican majority to use the appropriations process to secure partisan policy goals. The historically consensual task of protecting the Federal Treasury seems to have given way to an era of partisan division, in which policy conflicts are fought not just in the authorization committees but also (and preferably) in the Appropriations Committee. The Republican majority has exerted considerable influence on this committee, with the strategic understanding that appropriations bills must pass; authorization bills do not (Aldrich and Rohde 2000, 2004). Yet although the appropriations process sometimes may provide a useful alternative frame for issues that engender cultural conflict, elevating the level of partisan and cultural rancor in the House Appropriations Committee, as these issues do, probably is not good for the committee, the chamber, or the power of Congress vis-à-vis the executive branch in the long run (Gordon 2004).

The flip side of this observation is that although the appropriations process promotes a nonmoral framing that facilitates the legislative process (in the short run), under certain circumstances issues can take on a moral framing that frustrates the legislative process. Indeed, framing often runs in this direction: nonmoral to moral.[24] According to one Republican legislative counsel, this strategy is an opportune way to win votes:

> [T]here are plenty of members—House, Senate, both—who automatically . . . jump to the moral component of the argument because that's, in their view, the easier way to win votes. They will speak of a bill in terms of . . . if you support my bill it means that you support the rights of minorities, you support the rights of the unborn, you know, goodness, light, mom and apple pie. . . . [Y]ou're making it very, very difficult for anyone to oppose you. Or you're trying to do that. And I am of the opinion that using moral arguments in debate and in Congress for that reason is very, very disingenuous.[25]

Thus, moral framing can be done strategically, and if one can successfully put an issue in a moral frame of reference, opponents are forced to "stand up for sin." This strategy may evidence a great deal of hypocrisy on the part of some legislators, but it is effective. In this sense, the nonnegotiable aspect of cultural conflict produces strategic opportunities, not simply pathologies, in the legislative process.

## JUMPING OFF THE FENCE: MORAL DECISION MAKING

Collectively, the foregoing respondents lend credibility to the argument that certain issues take on a moral quality and therefore have unique characteristics. Such issues are polarizing, subject to framing, and rife with hypocrisy, and they draw on religious—or, at least, values-based—concerns. The question remains: What patterns of politics do these issues produce? Although the literature suggests that legislator decision making will be guided by values-based considerations because the issues themselves draw on status concerns and fundamental values, representatives approach these issues in a variety of ways. One Republican legislator notes that "as a social moderate, I am always caught," but "these are easy votes for most people." They are votes of "principle."[26] Others note that these issues are hard, but not because they do not know what to do. Instead, they understand that these issues are highly symbolic and highly divisive. Although many legislators acknowledge the presence of highly efficacious constituency groups on these issues, they argue that they are guided by their consciences.

Legislators do not always approach cultural issues in a categorical, nonreflective manner. Many legislators have an established record from which it is difficult to deviate, although legislator voting is not necessarily perfunctory. For example, a Republican legislator notes, "I've been a very strong supporter on family planning, and I've been a very strong supporter of choice, but I felt that partial-birth abortion was an unnecessary procedure that simply should not be countenanced. And I think a lot of other members who were prochoice did also."[27] A Democratic legislator argues:

> Those issues are troubling and, I think, should be troubling. So there are ethical dilemmas embedded in these votes. . . . [T]he partial-birth abortion . . . question, for example, required me—and, I think, others—to sort out where we stood on the question of late-term abortions. Where we would draw the line, and how we would, assuming we agreed—as I do with basically the

line the *Roe v. Wade* decision tried to draw. . . . So, it's not totally cut and dry, but . . . sometimes these questions assume a
kind of routinized form around here.[28]

Certain issues at the margins defy black-and-white categorization
and may draw legislators away from their previously established
records. This deviation is not flip-flopping as much as it is reflective nuance. Partial-birth abortions give some prochoice legislators pause, in the same way that stem-cell research has given some
prolife legislators, such as Sen. John McCain (R-AZ), pause.

Again, legislator behavior cannot always be classified in a
bimodal fashion—as for or against abortion, for example. In the
words of a Republican representative:

> There will be another category of members who try to kind of
> walk down the middle. For instance on the abortion issue, there
> are some significant number of members who have articulated
> a formal position which is basically supportive of abortion
> rights, but they will vote for a wide range of prolife measures.
> So they're really trying to go down the middle. . . . But that's a
> minority of members. Most members are either prolife or
> they're straight-out abortion rights advocates.[29]

Some legislators are able to equivocate—or perhaps they simply
adopt positions that are sincerely more complex than the black-
and-white distinctions that often characterize the politics of these
issues. As the foregoing representative notes, however, they are
a minority. Most have straightforward policy positions from
which they do not deviate. "Hardly anybody gets elected to Congress," notes one Democratic legislator, "unless they've planted
their feet one way or the other."[30]

Because some issues are not essentially cultural but may take
on a cultural frame, it should come as no surprise that legislators
sometimes have been known to view moral issues through a gray
lens. Certain policy decisions may challenge their firmly held
beliefs and challenge the categorical framing of an issue such as
abortion. Congressional debate over the partial-birth abortion ban
provides a good example. A prolife Republican representative
notes that "even some people that have a full-blown position in
support of abortion rights, who have had a consistent record in
support of abortion rights, have had some trouble dealing with
partial-birth abortion, and that's why we ended up getting as

many votes for it as we did."[31] Another legislator, though firmly prochoice, reached out to medical experts for guidance on this issue to determine the extent to which women need to have this procedure available to them. The representative did not want to depend solely on the guidance of colleagues because their views can be skewed and extreme. Hence, although the legislator is prochoice, certain issues require additional reflection.[32]

Moreover, some legislators may be reluctant to advance their cultural values legislatively. A Democratic legislator notes that although she is ambivalent about abortion, her constituency is not: They oppose it. Yet the representative has a prochoice voting record.

> Abortion is an issue that I could go either way in terms of my constituency. African Americans, who make up a great part of my constituency, are very conservative people when it comes to abortion and choice and that kind of thing. They would rather not see it happen. On the other hand, I have to think about the fact that as an elected official, particularly a Congressperson, I represent all of the country. I don't just represent my constituency. The entire nation is now my constituency. . . . And I think of my own conviction, and my own conviction regarding that one issue is that abortion is wrong, but I should not be able to say to a woman, "Look, you can't do this because I don't feel that you should do it as a government official." I don't think that I should impose to that extent.[33]

This position is profoundly nuanced—and that characterization is not meant as a pejorative. One expects legislators to promote their cultural values in law. That expectation is an underlying assumption of this research, but this legislator appears to have her feet in two different cultural traditions. She and her district are prolife, so one might expect her to vote in a manner consistent with the culture of religious traditionalism. Yet she votes in a manner consistent with the culture of progressive sexuality. That is, she believes that moral decisions should be made autonomously and that religion should be salient to those decisions only to the extent that individuals choose to reference it.

One Democratic legislator, an attorney by training, notes that although his preferences are clear (there is no ambivalence on his part), legislative consideration of morally controversial issues raises certain difficulties. He compares the distinction between nonmoral and moral issues to the distinction between a commercial case and a slip-and-fall case. The job of litigating, he argues, is more difficult with slip-and-fall cases, just as the job of legislating is more difficult with moral issues. In both instances, the stakes are higher. He notes:

> I prefer commercial cases because it's just money. One way or the other, it's just money. On the face of it, the slip-and-fall case is also about money, but . . . I [am] . . . of the view that in the slip-and-fall you could argue that you were looking for a higher [principle]. . . . Oh my god, you really have to try to do justice in that one, and that's what makes it so hard. And that is somewhat parallel to what I'm thinking. I've only been here a short period of time. Yet there have been things that have come out which are difficult. But they weren't difficult in deciding what I needed to do because as an intellectual matter and as a moral matter I've found that there were imperatives, that it went to my view of the core of doing this job: of being a good citizen and of being a good person. So you make those choices, and then sometimes they are mighty difficult because you think the world might cave in on you, but you know that's what you need to do.

He goes on to say:

> [Moral issues] are emblematic of a set of values. . . . I may be the only person in the world that sees China and education connected. But it all has to do with realization of human potentials and rights, and you know, the only thing on that back wall right there is Jefferson's hand-scribbled version of the Declaration of Independence. And the China vote is emblematic. . . . One of the reasons I consistently voted and spoke out on gay and lesbian rights—I don't care how it polls—is that to me it is like the China issue, and there are a number of other human rights issues. But it's not just human rights; to really achieve human rights, you really need skills, you need empowerment.[34]

These issues are difficult, though not because the legislator himself is conflicted. He is not. The stakes are higher, however, when Congress confronts these kinds of issues. Ethical considerations are at stake, and the representative seems to feel more of an imperative to do the right thing. What makes this situation difficult is that the representative understands that these issues are not simply divisive; they are symbolic of a set of values. Congress is not simply dealing with the issue on the table. Congress is dealing with an array of issues, some of which are fundamentally important and will affect people's way of life. Thus, although the representative is guided by certain imperatives, he recognizes that some issues take on a different kind of significance for many of his constituents and colleagues. He may not agree, but he tries to be cognizant of their frame of reference. Hence, when it comes to voting, the representative notes that:

> whatever the individual issue is for the member, whether it's China or abortion, whatever issue to them is morally controversial, these tend to be conscience votes, and that's how they make up their mind. They draw on themselves as opposed to what kind of mail they're getting or what the leadership wants them to do.

A Republican legislator makes similar points. He notes that when he is considering moral legislation,

> since I have a pretty well-known, established record, there's not a lot of pressure externally. To me, as a person, there's always huge internal pressure when morality becomes part of the decision because you want to do what you think is right in the context of the whole community and the context of the whole environment in which all of us live and work together, which must . . . respect the morality of everyone.[35]

Again, this legislator indicates that these issues are difficult, but not because he is ambivalent. For him, the difficulty lies in doing what is right—following his conscience, as he later indicates—while recognizing and respecting the value of pluralism at work nationally and in the House. These representatives acknowledge the presence of principled disagreement. They have strong feelings and know how they will vote, but they are aware that while they are doing what they think is right, they draw on values that do not resonate with the rest of the chamber. These representatives seem to be a minority. Most representatives did not acknowledge the presence of a morally equivalent opposition.

In any case, these representatives vote their consciences, regardless of external constituent pressures, and this pattern is a common theme. In explaining their decision-making process, other representatives and their staff emphasize that although they may be willing to defer to their district on nonmoral issues, particularly if they do not have strong feelings, that is not the case with moral issues. When they are voting on moral issues, these legislators are guided by their consciences. A Democratic staffer describes his boss's decision-making process as follows:

> [For moral issues], it more comes down to right and wrong because on the other issues he just listens to what people are generally telling him they want. I mean those issues—like whether or not we're going to tax the Internet or something— these things, he listens to kind of what the experts are telling him, maybe some of the companies in his district, things like that that aren't going to affect people's lives in a real serious way. Whereas on these issues that we're talking about, then it's more, "Yeah, those guys are telling me that, but I feel like what's right is this, so I'm going to do this." I think that's generally how he handles it.[36]

A Republican legislative director characterizes his boss's decision-making process in similar terms. When asked if his boss defers to his constituents on some kinds of issues, he notes:

> I'd like to say yeah, but I think on moral issues, I think he's staked out very known, very high-profile positions, at least as far as our constituents are concerned, about how he is going to vote. When you kind of go down a kind of a ladder from moral issues to ones that don't necessarily have a moral component to them, there's more leeway for him to listen and to respond.[37]

A Republican representative makes similar distinctions:

> My decision-making process is as follows. I kind of consider myself the representative—thus our name, . . . I also consider myself as a leader, so I kind of balance those two missions when I'm deciding things. If my district indicates, and I have a pretty good idea that this is a fair representation of my district, if they indicate somewhere between 45 and 55 percent on a certain issue, I vote the way I want to. If it gets between 40 and 45, 55 and 60 percent on an issue I begin to really weight what they think, if it happens to be different than mine. I factor that in. If it's over 60 percent I factor what they think heavily into my decision-making process, and if it's more than that I generally vote with them. Now, obviously I get elected in that district, so I am by that mission a representative of most of their views. So you'll often have differences of opinion. . . . [A]n

example of this would be minimum wage, the increase. I'm not crazy about it from an economic standpoint, but my district overwhelmingly is for it—like 80 percent—so I have voted for those increases, even though I don't think it's good economics. It's not good macroeconomics, I should say anyway. But on moral issues, this is the thing I'm getting to: I decided before I came up here that I was going to vote exactly the way I thought I should vote, regardless of what everyone thought about it, and let the chips fall where they may. . . . And luckily I'm a conservative fellow, and I can fall down exactly how the majority of my district falls down on those issues.[38]

This representative characterizes his decision-making process as highly calculated. The extent to which he considers constituent opinion is positively related to the level and tenor of the district communications he receives. On moral issues, however, he votes his conscience regardless of district opinion—not that this behavior hurts him because by his own account his views are consistent with the majority preferences of his district.

A Republican legislative director makes the point that because his boss is somewhat more conservative than his district, on some issues his boss may be willing to defer to his district—on guns, in particular. On other issues, however, the respondent indicates that his boss and his former boss, another Republican representative, cannot be compelled to vote against their firmly held views. On abortion, he notes, "Both my members, whenever I served with them, they are wholly prolife and very profamily, and therefore no amount of mail, no amount of constituent input, no amount of lobbying by Congress will change their views, no matter what."[39]

Given the pride of place most members seem to give their conscience on moral issues, it is not surprising that many respondents emphasize the importance of personal religiosity in legislator decision making.

[My bosses] seek counsel from other factions, like other members they are close to, just based on facts, I think. . . . [T]hey want to make sure that they are making a conscious decision. But I believe, on moral issues especially, I think it's all based on the member himself and their beliefs and convictions. My boss is the leader of the Prayer Breakfast. And he's a very devout Christian, and he's very family oriented.[40]

> I think he's pretty solid core on that sort of thing, and I don't know if he's ever really torn up that much. And he's a devout Catholic. . . . So that makes it easier votes.[41]

> [My boss] is an Orthodox Jew, so he certainly feels a religious pull on moral issues. And there are some issues where the religious community will call him. But he pretty much came into Congress rock solid and with his beliefs intact, so there isn't a lot of swaying you can do.[42]

According to these respondents, it seems that the values on which legislators draw are explicitly religious. It bears repeating: Cultures provide their adherents with a vision of how we should live with one another and what social relationships are compatible with that vision. Because the cultural dynamic explored in this volume hinges on the ability of religious values to inform culture, it makes perfect sense that respondents reference religion in their (or their bosses') decision-making process.

In theory, reliance on one's conscience (as informed by religious values) in decision making may produce alienation from some part of one's district. In these instances, a Republican representative argues, legislators must lead the district, rather than follow:

> I think ultimately you've got to lead. I'll give you a good example. You just can't sit there and wet your finger and put it up in the air on abortion, or on domestic partners or on any number of things. . . . And my *modus operandi* has always been to listen as much as I can and as long as I can, to think it through myself, and then you reach the point—hopefully prior to the time you actually vote—where you become a spokesman for that way in which you're going to vote. And a lot of the people who don't agree with you, they're gone. But you will influence some; that's what this is all about. . . . You're never going to move all of them. But this business is about ultimately a majority of people determining to do things, whether it's tax themselves or whatever else it is. So I've always kind of taken the role to ultimately come to a decision and then try to be a leader for what I think is the right thing to do.[43]

Thus, this representative casts his votes on the basis of his conscience, not blunt electoral calculations. He hopes that he can move people in one way or another, thereby diminishing any disjunction between himself and his district.

The irony of moral legislation appears to be that although constituents are more likely to form opinions and aggressively promote them with their legislators, these are the very issues on which legislators are least likely to be responsive, by their own account. Respondent after respondent suggests that representatives take up the trustee mantle in considering moral issues. Again and again, legislators and staff indicate that however they vote on other issues, on moral issues their conscience is their guide. They develop positions on the basis of deeply held values, and they cannot easily be moved. In the words of one Republican representative:

> I will say that on many of these issues that are identified as moral issues, many members don't feel much pressure at all because they've already staked out a position. They really have no interest in changing their position.[44]

A Democratic legislative director echoes this sentiment:

> [My boss] is a pretty firm person in what she believes in. Her state and local career in elected politics I think helps her formulate those ideas already. But she doesn't usually bend to the will of the votership. . . . I think they're conscience votes, and she also has a legislative record from back home. And she doesn't go against it: She formulated her conscience votes back then and is firmly prochoice, and she's been that way since she's been an elected official.[45]

A Democratic administrative assistant makes the point that—in principle, at least—this approach can mean voting against one's district, though the danger is not very great.

> I think for members of Congress who are elected officials, for issues on which there is a strong moral component, members may be less able to be swayed by letters from constituents or by presentations from lobbyists or other activist organizations or from their leadership. . . . [T]hey've got a position, and I think that most people wouldn't like to think that if you took a particular position on abortion and then your mail started to come in and you know, it was 10 to 1 against that then you would just switch. . . . [T]hey ultimately decide based on what they think personally is the right thing to do, and they hope that you're a reasonable representative of your district to begin with, or you wouldn't have gotten elected, and you've also

given them as broad a sense as you can, as detailed sense as you can, of where you are in these issues. So when you take a position, it's not a complete surprise. [46]

The hope and expectation of the legislator is that one's district supports the legislator—but either way, legislators do what they think is right. They are profiles in courage, if you will.

Again, however, these votes may not be high-risk votes. One reason legislators can be profiles in courage is that they probably are in line with the modal position of their districts on these high-salience issues—abortion in particular. A Democratic legislative director notes that "[the district is] a very progressive place, and I think she is in line with the vast majority of constituents."[47] According to a Republican representative, "I think I'm pretty much in sync with my district on a wide range of issues, both of moral and economic and whatever. . . . But I don't view myself as kind of a missionary for that issue in my district."[48] These two respondents emphasize, as many others have, that legislators do what they think is right, regardless of mail or other external pressures. The truth, however, is that many legislators find themselves supported by their districts on these issues. Thus, there is no electoral risk in being a trustee because there is no great disjunction between members and their districts. This theme is common, and it suggests that trustee/delegate distinctions are not very useful in this policy domain.

On the other hand, one former Republican representative discussed a specific instance in which he did vote contrary to the preferences of his district, on the issue of civil rights. In this case, religion was an important guide.

> [I experienced] the struggle of conscience . . . within me when the civil rights battles were raging in the 1960s over the passage of the initial Civil Rights Act of 1964 and the Voting Rights Act of 1965 and the Housing Act . . . in 1968. And for me it was a matter of religious conviction. I listened very carefully to the clergy who came to my office and were part of the broad civil rights coalition, the leadership conference on civil rights. . . . And the moral arguments, the religious convictions that I had from my own personal faith . . . weighed very heavily in my mind. They were supervening as far as I was concerned. . . . I think there are supremely transcendent moral convictions that you can have that enable you to take positions and stands that

are not always politically popular, and you have to assume the role of trying to be an educator and hope that you can be sufficiently persuasive with your arguments, that you can win over at least some—not all: There's some that are just absolutely beyond your help.[49]

When this former representative was asked if he thinks his district supported his positions on moral issues, he raised the issues of race and gay rights and noted:

Not on the open housing bill, I don't think. I think initially I had the laboring order to bring them around on the grounds that this was not an invasion of property rights—to tell landlords to turn somebody down and if you do, you're going to be subject to the penalties provided for in the law that was passed on discrimination against people on the basis of race, color, ethnic background for housing. I think I supported gay rights back in the 1960s when the gay and lesbian alliance had far less power than they do today. Now it seems to me they are one of the most powerful lobbying organizations. They have made enormous strides. And I think it turned around a lot of thinking. But back when I voted on an amendment to a bill that had been offered to deny representation to gays or lesbians from the Corporation for Legal Services, . . . I remember a fellow by the name of Bob Bauman[50]—who later disclosed he was gay himself, but closeted—offered an amendment on the floor that would severely restrict the ability of any attorneys hired through the Corporation for Legal Services to render legal services to people in that group. And I voted against his amendment. I thought it was unfair and discriminatory, and it became an issue in the last primary contest I had, which was more severely fought than any other since the first one I fought when I was first elected. That was an issue that I had voted to support, gay rights.

When this former legislator was confronted with moral issues, he voted in accordance with his own moral and religious convictions. For many legislators, such behavior does not present an electoral risk because they reflect their district's dominant preferences. As a moderate Republican, however, this legislator was on the opposite side of the moral divide from his constituents on several highly salient issues. By his own account, in voting on the basis of his true (religiously informed) preferences, he was voting against his district and inviting challenges from the right in his own party. Thus, even when the costs were potentially high, his voting behavior was guided by policy—by a desire to affirm a particular set of social relationships.

## CONCLUSION

Legislators perceive a distinction between moral and nonmoral issues. Some identify religion as the source of the distinction. Others simply suggest that these are the issues on which they vote their conscience. They cast votes with an eye toward specific policy outcomes, based on their fundamental values, and cannot easily be moved by external pressures. Yet some legislators concede that there really is not that much external pressure. Constituents write, and in some instances legislators must truly lead, but legislators generally have adopted positions consistent with the modal preferences of their district, as far as they are concerned. Yet even though legislators and staff indicate that on moral issues legislators take positions from which they cannot be swayed, it is worth noting that the politics of cultural conflict in the House can be structured and restructured by employing different frames of reference. That restructuring can transform absolutist cultural conflict into incremental distributive politics.

# 2

# The Culture of
# Progressive Sexuality

The government has an absolute overriding duty to enforce
morality in interpersonal relations. We have a moral duty to
protect innocent people from those who would impose on
them. That is a very important moral duty. But is it the
government's duty to say divorce is wrong and there are
strong biblical arguments that say if you are divorced, you
should not remarry? And should the government then put
obstacles in the way? No.
                                        —Rep. Barney Frank (D-MA)

Representative Barney Frank envisions a role for government
as the protector of public morality. The moral vision he
advocates, however, is not informed by religious values.
The moral vision Frank seems to promote is one in which government carves out and defends individual autonomy, directed
toward making private moral decisions pertaining to families,
marriage, and sexuality. Religion informs these decisions only to
the extent that individuals wish. This moral vision, or culture,
competes in the public space with the culture of religious traditionalism discussed in chapter 3. Given their autonomous vision
of society, advocates of progressive sexuality regard an array of
previously unconventional social relationships as appropriate:
Gay relationships, for example, and relationships in which women
are equal economic partners with men and control their reproductive capacities are considered consistent with a vision of progressive sexuality.[1] In this chapter I trace the politics of two social

51

movements within the culture of progressive sexuality: feminism and the gay rights movement. I devote special attention to the efforts of Congress to cope with the demands of these movements, both of which call on government to enact policies that legitimate their culture. Abstract normative debates are well and good, but in a practical sense, cultures compete over concrete issues—such as abortion and gay marriage. They compete not just for the rhetorical high ground but also for policy.

## FEMINISM AND FERTILITY

The feminist movement has advanced on the economic, political, and social fronts. Even before the 1920 ratification of the Nineteenth Amendment, which gave women the right to vote, both political parties soberly regarded women as a potential source of electoral support—although the parties had a very narrow concept of what issues were important to women. While the parties set up organizational offices to reach out to women, women's issues were defined domestically: Pay equity and reproductive health were many years off. As women's issues were institutionalized in party organizations, "women's unique policy interests were co-opted, independent women's organizations were diminished, and few policy concessions were granted" (Leege et al. 2002, 119; see also Harvey 1998).

As Leege et al. (2002, 120) note, in the years after the Nineteenth Amendment was ratified, Republicans quickly reached out to women and tried to incorporate them into their coalition. After suffering national electoral defeats in 1932, 1934, and 1936, the party began to compete for women's votes, rather than simply assuming that women would vote in the same manner as their husbands. Later, Dwight Eisenhower advanced the idea of pay equity and even appointed women to high-profile positions in government (Melich 1996, 10). As a result, there was an electoral "gender gap" in the 1950s: Women supported Eisenhower at higher levels than men did. In 1952, 58 percent of women supported Eisenhower, compared to only 53 percent of men. The gap widened in 1956, with 61 percent of women supporting Eisenhower, compared to 55 percent of men (Costain 1992, 33). Practically speaking, early feminists did not really have alternatives. The Democratic Party at that time was dominated by

"Southern traditionalists and evangelicals, Northern ethnic Catholics, and organized labor"—none of whom were eager to carry water for gender equality (Leege et al. 2002, 119).

By the 1960s, however, the Depression had been replaced by the civil rights movement for African Americans and the Vietnam War as the defining events of political socialization for a new generation of young Democrats. The New Deal coalition began to show cracks. In the realm of congressional politics, this period produced reform as liberal Yankee Democrats demanded power from their intraparty rivals, the conservative southern Democrats. How did stress within the New Deal coalition affect the treatment of women's issues by the parties? Leege et al. (2002) argue that Democratic leaders sought the support of women to shore up the fragmenting party. President Kennedy signed equal pay legislation, and left-leaning congressional Democrats started to promote issues of gender and racial equality. "Many Democrats and many Republicans . . . introduced equal rights amendments to the U.S. Constitution," as "Democrats contested the traditional Republican ownership of the gender equality issue" (Leege et al. 2002, 120).

It is worth noting that even before women achieved the right to vote, they were an influential political force. They used their influence to promote the establishment of a "maternalist welfare state" (Skocpol 1994a, 1994b, 1992; Skocpol et al. 1993), which was designed to protect women against poor labor conditions and provide women with financial benefits necessary to raise their families. Indeed, "America's first publicly funded social benefits other than military pensions and poor relief were mothers' pensions" (Skocpol 1992, 10). These welfare programs spread at the state level and were enacted by Congress in the early 1900s. These programs were in marked contrast to the "paternalistic" welfare systems of Western Europe, which tended to focus benefits on men, the family breadwinners. Explanations for America's unique welfare state are numerous. To no small extent, however, the development of the maternalist welfare state is a result of the perceived rampant corruption of the paternalistic Civil War pension system—America's first social welfare system—and the efforts of the vast number of federations of women's clubs across the country (Skocpol 1992).

A full-fledged maternalist welfare state never did develop. Congress eliminated some programs, and the Supreme Court struck others down. Before the Depression, however, the United States was developing a unique welfare regime. According to Skocpol (1992, 526), "With the coming of the Great Depression and the new Deal of the 1930s, the nation took new paths. Earlier experiences with the Civil War benefits and maternalist policies of course influenced the Social Security Act and subsequent U.S. social policymaking. But from the 1930s onward, new political actors, policy proposals, and principles of legitimation for public social provision came to the fore."

Congress continued to address women's social welfare with the Aid to Families with Dependent Children (AFDC) portion of the Social Security Act of 1935 (P.L. 74-271). Although aspects of the maternalist welfare state were preserved, they were "subordinated and pushed to the side" (Skocpol 1992, 535). Men dominated the Social Security board, which supervised AFDC and emphasized contributory forms of public assistance. This approach was a departure from the time when women's social programs were managed by the autonomous, female-dominated Children's Bureau (Skocpol 1992, 536). In 1996 the welfare regime in the United States moved even further away from the original maternalist programs. Democratic President Bill Clinton and the Republican-controlled Congress collaborated to enact the Personal Responsibility and Work Opportunity Reconciliation Act of 1996 (P.L. 104-193), which went into effect in 1997. AFDC and the system of federal welfare entitlements were eliminated, as such, and replaced with a new program, Temporary Assistance to Needy Families (TANF). With funding from federal block grants, TANF gives the states a great deal of flexibility in designing their own assistance programs. Moreover, as the name suggests, the assistance is temporary.

The maternalist agenda still finds voice in groups such as the Children's Defense Fund and the National Forum on the Future of Children. These contemporary advocates of women's social welfare act under the premise that women and children are ill-served or inadequately served by the system of benefits that currently exists in the United States (Skocpol 1992, 536). Yet social welfare issues, though important to contemporary feminists, do not swing on the axis of cultural conflict in the same way reproductive issues do. In any discussion of pay equity, workplace sexual harassment, or maternity leave, the role of women in society and the fallout from the entrance of women into the workforce provide an implicit subtext. As I note in the Introduction to this volume, however, cultural conflict refers more to a rhetorical style than a concrete set of issues. In current politics, economic feminism tends not to be framed by elites—progressives or religious traditionalists—in explicitly moral or cultural terms. When Pat Buchanan refers to the role of radical feminism in the culture war, he is not talking about the Family and Medical Leave Act; he is referring to changing sexual norms and reproductive policy. This aspect of the feminist agenda—progressive sexuality, broadly construed—has roots that go back more than 100 years and revolve around issues of contraception and abortion.

## CONTRACEPTION

Women have made attempts to regulate their reproductive capacities for thousands of years. While states were beginning to criminalize abortion in the mid-nineteenth century, many women's rights advocates "supported the idea of voluntary motherhood, a woman's right to limit the size of her family by natural means" (O'Connor 1996, 21). Without this right, women would not be able to attain full equality. Given the political and Victorian moral tenor, these advocates did not aggressively pursue abortion rights. Instead, they pushed for access to contraception.[2] "Birth control advocates could still claim to favor strong, healthy families while objecting to abortion" (O'Connor 1996, 22). Although this strategy may have kept early feminists from being demonized or cast as antifamily, birth control was still a controversial topic. In the Comstock Act of 1873 (42 Cong. 258), Congress prohibited interstate distribution of "obscene" materials having to do with contraception or abortion. Before this legislation, there was no federal involvement in contraception; after this legislation, little information about this topic was available to women (McFarlane and Meier 2001, 30; O'Connor 1996, 22).

By the early twentieth century, social structural changes were giving way to reform in the area of contraception. As McFarlane and Meier (2001, 32) note, the hold that traditional morals had on

society was weakening as a result of urbanization, industrialization, growing affluence, and the emergence of women in the
workforce. According to Alfred Kinsey, 36 percent of upper-
middle class "women born between 1900 and 1909 reported having premarital intercourse" (McFarlane and Meier 2001, 32). This
figure represented a significant jump from previous generations,
suggesting that the need for contraception and the willingness to
use contraception probably was increasing among many women.
There also was a burgeoning Progressive movement that demanded political reform in the face of the structural changes
American society was experiencing (O'Connor 1996, 23).

Among other things, the Progressives and their ilk noticed
that poor Americans were having large families that they could
ill afford, while upper-middle class families were not. This pattern suggested that regardless of "Comstockery," upper-middle
class women were using some form of birth control, and poor
women were not. Progressives such as Margaret Sanger (1879–
1966) found this gap troubling because they believed that contraception "was the only way out of poverty for many" women
(O'Connor 1996, 23). Sanger was one of the most outspoken advocates of family planning. Under her leadership, the American
Birth Control League successfully weakened state-level Comstock
laws (McFarlane and Meier 2001, 32).

A federal appellate court "largely invalidated" the original 1873
federal statute in *U.S. v. One Package*, 86 F. 2d 737 (1937). In the
opinion of the court, had policymakers been aware of the health
risks inherent in pregnancy and the therapeutic value of contraception, they might not have deemed contraception obscene
(McFarlane and Meier 2001, 33; see also O'Connor 1996, 23; Dienes
1972). State laws prohibiting dissemination of contraception or information about contraception were not struck down until 1965,
however, with the Supreme Court's ruling in *Griswold v.
Connecticut*, 381 U.S. 479. As a challenge to a Connecticut law,
Estelle Griswold—who at the time was executive director of Planned
Parenthood—set up a clinic that provided counseling to married
couples concerning birth control. She was convicted under Connecticut law. The U.S. Supreme Court heard her appeal and overturned the Connecticut statute, ruling that the law violated the
privacy rights of married couples to plan their families.

McFarlane and Meier (2001, 33) note that in the same year as the *U.S. v. One Package* decision, survey data indicate that "71% of Americans were in favor of birth control," and the American Medical Association (AMA) "recognized birth control as an integral part of the medical practice." Yet the U.S. Congress and state legislatures were essentially silent on this issue. Even after the federal Comstock Act was overturned and state-level Comstock Acts were weakened, Congress was reluctant to involve itself in this area because it was still controversial. Congress did not directly involve itself in contraception until the mid-1960s, in the context of President Johnson's Great Society War on Poverty and the Civil Rights movement. With increased attention being paid to the family planning needs of poor women, Congress created an array of family planning programs. This development was a remarkable about-face: "In less than 100 years, the Congress of the United States had moved from prohibiting birth control to promoting it" (McFarlane and Meier 2001, 34).

Congress continued to promote family planning through the 1970s, with the support of Presidents Johnson, Nixon, and Carter. In the 1980s, support for family planning became less consensual. The Democratic-controlled Congress supported it, but it received diminishing support from Republican Presidents Reagan and George H. W. Bush. President Clinton supported family planning assistance, but the 1994 ascendance of Republicans as the majority party in Congress blocked his agenda in this area. For Clinton, the emphasis was an effort to promote feminist values and progressive sexual norms. For the Republican Congress, the focus was an effort to promote profamily, conservative Christian values.

McFarlane and Meier (2001, 39–54) superbly catalog relevant post-*Griswold* federal legislation pertaining to family planning. In 1965, for example, the Office of Economic Opportunity started to fund family planning. For the first few years, however, it did so without a specific statutory requirement. Also in 1965, Congress enacted Title XIX of the Social Security Act (P.L. 89-97), which created Medicaid. Medicaid was designed to provide assistance to people who could not afford medical care. "Family planning services were not included in the statute, but they were mentioned in the Title XIX regulations published in the Federal Register" (McFarlane and Meier 2001, 41). In 1967 Congress enhanced federal resources available to fund family planning services for poor Americans under the auspices of two existing federal programs: Titles IV-A and V of the Social Security Act. Title IV-A's original goal was to strengthen families through provision of social services under the welfare rubric. The 1967 statutes included family planning among those services. The 1967 statute also made family planning a "required Title V service" (McFarlane and Meier 2001, 41).

Congress continued down this path in the 1970s. In 1970 it passed Title X of the Public Health Service Act, which provided categorical grants to the states. Again, the legislation focused on providing family planning services for poor Americans (McFarlane and Meier 2001, 42). Title IV-A and Title XIX programs were expanded in 1972. Some states were not making family planning assistance easily available, even though such assistance was permissible and in some cases required by law. Congress created "family planning incentives," and reimbursements "increased to 90 percent." In 1975 Congress enacted Title XX of the Social Security Act. This statute created social service block grants that, among other things, pertained to family planning. Although Title XX incorporated aspects of Title IV-A, the legislation "revised" some of the programmatic requirement (McFarlane and Meier 2001, 44).

The Title V, X, XIX, and XX family planning programs "survived the budgetary politics" of the early Reagan years (McFarlane and Meier 2001, 47). President Reagan came to office in 1981 with the goal of creating a more modest family planning regime because he was an advocate of smaller government in the area of domestic politics. At the same time, his efforts to scale back family planning services no doubt were a response to an important constituency group that had aided his election—the conservative coalition, which opposed family planning not just on economic grounds but also on moral grounds (McFarlane and Meier 2001, 46). The matching rate of federal dollars to state dollars under Title V was changed from 1:1 to 3:4, and the requirement that 6 percent of funds be directed toward family planning assistance was eliminated (McFarlane and Meier 2001, 47). The Title X block grant program was reauthorized, but its funding was cut. The overall level of federal reimbursement to states under the Title XIX Medicaid program was reduced, although Congress "retained the 90 percent federal match for family planning" (McFarlane and Meier 2001, 49). Funding for Title XX block grant programs was reduced, and the requirement that states match funds for services was eliminated. Thus, states did not have an incentive to spend money on contraception. McFarlane and Meier (2001, 49) also note that in 1981 Congress passed the Adolescent Family Life Act (Title XX of the Public Health Services Act), which directed family planning efforts at curtailing sexual activity among adolescents. More bluntly, it funded abstinence education, and it replaced previous legislation that funded "pregnancy-prevention and pregnancy-related services . . . including . . . sex education."

Family planning came under siege during the Reagan and George H. W. Bush administrations. President Clinton's election in 1992 provided a brief respite, however (McFarlane and Meier 2001, 51)—"brief" being the operative word. "Any consideration of further expanding family planning programs came to a screeching halt with the 1994 midterm elections" (McFarlane and Meier 2001, 51). The Republicans won control of both chambers of Congress, and the new majority wished to collapse various social service categorical grant programs into block grants. Furthermore, the Republicans wanted to transform federal entitlement programs into block grants. Block grants provide money to states for spending in a broad policy area, with few strings attached (McFarlane and Meier 2001, 51). Block grants would allow the federal government to provide money to the states for public health, for example, without the requirement that money be spent on family planning.

Although Republicans were successful in their efforts to transform the welfare regime in the United States, Medicaid—"the largest intergovernmental entitlement"—was left intact, for the most part. Hence, family planning assistance under the auspices of Medicaid also was left intact (McFarlane and Meier 2001, 52). The Personal Responsibility and Work Opportunity Reconciliation Act of 1996 (PRWORA) did eliminate, however, the longstanding requirement that states "provide family planning services to welfare recipients" (McFarlane and Meier 2001, 52). In this new era, the efforts of the Republican-controlled Congress in the area of family planning focused on reducing illegitimacy, teen pregnancy, and underage sexual activity and increasing abstinence education.

In fact, PRWORA provided a bonus of $20 million per state to "the five states showing the greatest decrease in out-of-wedlock births" (McFarlane and Meier 2001, 53).

## ABORTION

As with contraception, abortion restrictions tightened in the nineteenth century and loosened in the twentieth century. The timetable and the path were different, however. In the early years of the republic, government made no effort to control women's reproductive capacities. Until Connecticut criminalized postquickening[3] abortions in 1821, there were no abortion restrictions (O'Connor 1996, 19). This legislation marked the beginning of the first wave of antiabortion law. Ten states placed restrictions on abortion out of concern for women's health. Lacking popular support, these laws were neither noticed nor enforced to any great extent (McFarlane and Meier 2001, 35; see also Rosenblatt 1992 and Sheeran 1987). Massachusetts launched a second wave of antiabortion statutes in 1846; New York followed closely behind. Forty new state-level antiabortion statutes were enacted between 1860 and 1880. What made this second wave distinct from the first was that many of these new statutes eschewed the distinction between prequickening and postquickening. Abortion at any stage of fetal development was criminalized (McFarlane and Meier 2001, 35; Tatalovich 1997, 27).

The newly created AMA strongly supported these new laws, as did the Catholic Church. O'Connor (1996) suggests that the AMA was motivated by desires to drive midwives out of business, increase birthrates, and encourage chastity among women (O'Connor 1996, 20–21). The AMA undoubtedly was motivated by concern for maternal health as well. In an era when antiseptic techniques were little understood, surgery for any reason was extraordinarily dangerous. In the mid-nineteenth century, New York had "*a 30 percent death rate* from infection after abdominal surgery even when performed in hospitals" (Tribe 1992, 29, quoted in McFarlane and Meier 2001, 35; emphasis in original). The problem was so dire that the state of New York prohibited all surgeries "unless two physicians could attest that it was essential to the life of the patient" (O'Connor 1996, 20).

At the same time, the teaching of the Catholic Church on abortions evolved. Historically, the church had not been active in antiabortion politics and had adopted the stance that prequickening abortions were permissible. In 1869 Pope Pius IX rejected the prequickening/postquickening distinction; he prohibited abortion completely (McFarlane and Meier 2001, 36) and set excommunication as the punishment "for physicians who performed abortions" (O'Connor 1996, 20).

Although the Catholic Church was unequivocal in its rejection of abortion on moral grounds, the second round of antiabortion statutes was advanced by physicians and grounded in concerns about maternal health. Certainly, many legislators regarded abortion as morally wrong, and they adopted statutes consistent with the stated position of the Catholic Church and some Protestant churches that stepped into the fray on the issue (O'Connor 1996, 20–21). Nevertheless, "the Roman Catholic Church did not take an *active* role in the abortion debate until the 1950s (O'Connor 1996, 21; emphasis in original). "Physicians, not clergy, were the driving force" on abortion restrictions (McFarlane and Meier 2001, 36). By 1910, the movement to restrict abortion was almost complete. Only Kentucky had failed to criminalize abortion "at any stage" during pregnancy, although many states permitted therapeutic abortions to save the life of the mother (McFarlane and Meier 2001, 36).

Regardless of state-level restrictions, abortion remained a common practice in the first half of the twentieth century; abortions occurred in one in three pregnancies (McFarlane and Meier 2001, 36). While the number of legal therapeutic abortions was increasing,[4] so too was the number of illegal, unregulated, so-called back-alley abortions. This criminal behavior was rampant, and the mortality rate for these illegal procedures was very high (McFarlane and Meier 2001, 36). Although doctors had championed abortion restrictions for years, they began to support decriminalization. Moreover, the once-private decisions of doctors to perform therapeutic abortions was coming under increased scrutiny by hospitals. For its part, the American Law Institute revised its Model Penal Code to permit legal abortions under a variety of circumstances, such as when carrying the pregnancy to term would threaten the health of the mother, when the baby would have severe "physical or mental defects," and when the pregnancy had occurred "as a result of rape or incest" (McFarlane and Meier 2001, 37; see also O'Connor 1996, 27;

Tatalovich 1997, 28). The thalidomide controversy and a German measles outbreak, which caused tens of thousands of birth defects, focused the attention of the American people and policymakers on this procedure. The medical profession continued to advocate for liberalized abortion laws, and between 1967 and 1972 nineteen states passed less restrictive abortion laws (McFarlane and Meier 2001, 37).

Just as Congress had been reluctant to involve itself in earlier controversies involving birth control, so too was it unwilling to enter the abortion fray as states began to relax their restrictions. Abortion rights advocates used the federal courts to advance their agenda and challenge state-level restrictions. On January 22, 1973, the U.S. Supreme Court issued its decision in *Roe v. Wade*, 410 U.S. 113, striking down all abortion restrictions and basing its decision on the right to privacy, as it had in *Griswold v. Connecticut* eight years earlier. Interestingly, the Court issued this decision without the input of the executive branch. In spite of President Nixon's stated opposition to abortion, the U.S. Solicitor General's office failed even to file an *amicus curiae* brief on the matter (O'Connor 1996, 44).

The Supreme Court's decision did not resolve this policy issue. If anything, the Court's *Roe* decision accelerated the politicization of religious traditionalism. After *Roe*, abortion was framed "as a question of a woman's right to bodily integrity and privacy versus a fetus's right to life." This framework made establishment of "common ground and compromise in the political arena . . . almost impossible to attain" (Strickland 1998, 4). As long as the public remains polarized, judicial and legislative actions cannot remedy the cultural divide. Congress and state governments continue to legislate on this issue, and the U.S. Supreme Court continues to hear cases that test the limits of *Roe*. Although the justices have never overturned their 1973 decision, they are increasingly willing to allow some restrictions on abortion. Most notably, in *Webster v. Reproductive Health Services*, 492 U.S. 490 (1989), the Court upheld a Missouri statute that prohibited abortions in state hospitals and required fetal viability tests under certain circumstances. In *Planned Parenthood v. Casey*, 505 U.S. 833 (1992), the Court upheld a Pennsylvania statute that introduced a twenty-four-hour waiting period for abortions and required minors seeking an abortion to obtain the consent of a parent or guardian.

In the wake of *Roe*, prolife advocates have lobbied Congress for a Human Life Amendment to the U.S. Constitution that would prohibit abortions. In fact, many constitutional amendments have been offered on this subject; some would ban abortion, others would constitutionally enshrine the *Roe* decision. None of these amendments has achieved the two-thirds vote in each chamber of Congress required to send them to the states for ratification (O'Connor 1996, 67).

In the absence of that kind of profound action, both sides of the abortion issue continue to dicker over federal money for abortion in the annual appropriations process (see chapter 1). Including and in addition to funding issues, Congress considers the abortion issue on a regular, even routinized, basis. According to Tatalovich (1997, 95), "the first abortion bill introduced in Congress was in 1970, with six more in 1971 and three more in 1972. . . . There had been a surge in legislative activity as the number of bills sponsored rose to 571 through 1988." Moreover, 94 percent of these bills were prolife bills. "[P]ro-choice forces in Congress have fought a rearguard battle" against their prolife colleagues (Tatalovich 1997, 98). Although most of these bills died in committee, "some enactments imposed substantial restrictions on abortion policy. The pro-life agenda targeted a broad range of federal programs. The Family Planning Services and Population Research Act of 1970 (P.L. 91-572) . . . prohibited the use of federal funds for programs where abortion is a method of family planning. Under the Health Programs Extension Act of 1973 (P.L. 93-45), judges and public officials were barred from ordering recipients of federal funds to perform abortions . . . where the moral convictions or religious beliefs of these persons are violated" (Tatalovich 1997, 96). Congress also enacted legislation in 1977 stating that "employers are not required" to pay for abortions through their health insurance plans unless the life of the mother is in danger,[5] and legislation in 1979 mandated that healthcare providers should not face discrimination because of an unwillingness to perform abortions[6] (Tatalovich 1997, 96–97).

For the most part, the myriad appropriations riders have curtailed abortion-related spending. Tatalovich (1997, 97) notes that instances of "antiabortion riders are too numerous to mention." Through this process, abortion foes have been able to limit abortion-related foreign aid and funding for abortions in the District of Columbia and limit abortions in military hospitals. The rider with the most widespread impact on domestic policy has been the Hyde Amendment, which originally amended the 1976 Labor, Health, Education, and Welfare Act. According to O'Connor (1996), "One possibly unintended policy consequence of *Roe* . . . was that poor women, already eligible for free medical assistance under the Medicaid program, could qualify for federal funds to cover the cost of their abortions so long as they were deemed 'medically necessary'" (O'Connor 1996, 67–68). After *Roe*, the number of abortions and the number paid for by the government both increased. Representative Henry Hyde (R-IL) calculated that the federal government was paying for 250,000 to 300,000 abortions per year through the Medicaid program (Tatalovich 1997, 97). In an effort to control the effects of *Roe*, Hyde's amendment prohibited the use of federal Medicaid funds to pay for abortions.[7] Congress might not be able to overturn *Roe*, but it could limit access to abortions by poor women. Because the Hyde Amendment was part of an appropriations bill, it must be renewed annually, guaranteeing contentious debate on this issue in every session. The amendment always passes, though its language varies. In 1981 Congress agreed to a Hyde Amendment that permitted Medicaid funds to be used for abortions only if the life of the mother was endangered. In 1994 Congress agreed to language that permitted funding in cases of rape and incest (O'Connor 1996, 68–69, 75; Tatalovich 1997, 97).

In the wake of the 1989 *Webster* decision, prochoice advocates in Congress introduced the Freedom of Choice Act, which would have codified the *Roe* decision. The bill never made it to the floor for consideration. It was reintroduced in 1993 after the murder of abortion provider Dr. David Gunn and the election of Democratic President Clinton. The Freedom of Choice Act seemed to have a better chance of passage at that time, but it suffered the same fate as the 1989 version of the bill and never made it to the floor of either chamber. Nevertheless, the news in the 1990s was not all bad for prochoice advocates. In 1994 Congress passed the Freedom of Access to Clinic Entrances Act (P.L. 103-259). This legislation "proposed to make it illegal, and punishable by civil and criminal penalties, to physically impede access to a medical facility" (McFarlane and Meier 2001, 73; see also O'Connor 1996, 138–39, 166–68).

When the Republicans won control of the House of Representatives in the 1994 midterm elections, the new majority attempted to place new restrictions on abortions. Among other things, they tried to reinstitute the Mexico City policy. Originally a Reagan administration policy, the Mexico City language determined that nongovernmental organizations (NGOs) that used their own funds to provide or advocate for abortion services would no longer be eligible for family planning funds distributed by the U.S. Agency for International Development (USAID). Days after taking office in 1993, President Clinton had reversed this policy. Although the Republican Congress was unsuccessful in reinstituting Mexico City, the Republicans reduced the amount of money spent by the United States on international family planning assistance. In 2001 President George W. Bush reversed President Clinton's policy, signing an executive order on the anniversary of the *Roe* decision that prohibits federal funds from being directed to international family planning groups that provide abortion services or abortion counseling. Congress also reinstated the abortion ban in overseas military hospitals—another Reagan administration policy that had been overturned by President Clinton. The policy forbade the performing of abortions in overseas military hospitals even if the services were paid for in full by the patient, unless the patient's life was in danger (McFarlane and Meier 2001, 71, 74–75).

Legislative consideration of the Partial Birth Abortion Ban Act of 1995 marked the most high-profile abortion battle of the 104th Congress (1995–1996). This legislation would have prohibited the procedure whereby a fetus is partially delivered vaginally, the fetus's head is deflated, and the delivery is completed, unless the life of the mother was in danger. The legislation had bipartisan support, but President Clinton indicated that he would veto the bill unless it included an exception for the health of the mother. Republican leaders kept the amendment that would have provided for such an exception off the floor, fearing that it would be passed and would provide an enormous loophole for people trying to get around the legislation. Because the amendment was never considered and never agreed to,

President Clinton eventually vetoed the legislation. As the outcome of this bill suggests, prolife activists in the 104th and 105th
Congresses found it difficult to pass sweeping prolife legislation
when compromise was necessitated by a Democrat in the White
House.

With the election of President George W. Bush and a Republican House and Senate in 2000, the possibility of banning this
procedure gained new life. The defection of Senator James Jeffords
(VT) from the Republican Party, however, threw control of the
Senate to the Democrats, and the Senate ignored the many prolife
bills approved by the House. The House passed a ban on partial-
birth abortion in the 107th Congress (2001–2002), but the bill did
not get a vote in the Democratic-controlled Senate. Nevertheless,
prolife activists did score a legislative victory with the Born-Alive
Infants Protection Act of 2002 (P.L. 107-207), which classifies as a
"person" any human born alive, at any stage of development. In
an incredible show of consensus, this bill passed on a voice vote
in the House and under unanimous consent in the Senate. With
unified Republican control of Congress after the 2002 midterm
elections, the Partial-Birth Abortion Ban Act of 2003 (P.L. 108-105)
was passed and signed into law by President George W. Bush on
November 5, 2003. Notably, in a 5–4 decision the U.S. Supreme
Court struck down a similar Nebraska statute in 2000,[8] finding
that the law placed an "undue burden" on a woman's right to an
abortion. To date, the Supreme Court has not assessed the con-
stitutionality of the 2003 federal statute, although it continues to
hear other abortion-related cases. In May 2005, for example, the
Supreme Court agreed to review a lower federal court's decision
that repealed a New Hampshire parental consent law. Prolife advocates were pleased by this development, believing that the
Supreme Court is likely to reverse the lower court's decision.[9]

## THE MODERN GAY RIGHTS MOVEMENT

The modern gay rights movement developed in Germany even
before the rise of the Third Reich. Most of the scientific research
into the nature of homosexuality was taking place in Germany.
In the late nineteenth century, German men who identified themselves as homosexual developed politically significant groups
designed to challenge Germany's antisodomy laws (Faderman

1991, 188). Development of gay rights as a culturally salient issue in the United States is not as old as development of reproductive politics. Although some historians have traced the roots of the gay rights movement to the late nineteenth century (see Cruikshank 1992), the modern gay rights movement, as a social movement, did not exist fifty years ago. Homosexuality certainly existed in the nineteenth century, and some historians have found evidence of gays and lesbians in American history dating back as far as the sixteenth century (Katz 1976). Pervasive Judeo-Christian values considered homosexuality to be sinful, however, and so did larger American society. "Throughout much of American history gay identity has remained hidden because of an atmosphere of pervasive hostility to homosexual expression" (Button, Rienzo, and Wald 1997, 23). This hiddenness inhibited the development of a political or cultural gay identity.

In the United States, the emergence of industrialization in the nineteenth century facilitated development of a communal or social gay identity. The agrarian lifestyle, with its emphasis on the localized family unit, was giving way to a new lifestyle in which people were more mobile and better able to pursue their individual pleasures. World War II accelerated the development of a communal gay identity. What was originally called the "homophile" movement developed in the wake of World War II because the war disrupted the traditional American social structure. Many people were uprooted from their families and suburban lives and joined the armed forces or the civilian workforce. This trend brought previously isolated gays and lesbians into contact with each other. Rather than return home after the war, many of these newly self-aware gays migrated to major cities such as San Francisco, Boston, and New York. Society at large considered gays perverse and deviant (Rimmerman 2002, 20), but in these major cities gays and lesbians developed their own subculture and sense of community (Button, Rienzo, and Wald 1997, 23–24). In this context, the number of gay bars increased, gay themes emerged in some novels, and Kinsey's findings on homosexual behavior (Kinsey, Pomeroy, and Martin 1948) were publicized (D'Emilio 2000, 32).

In the 1950s McCarthyism created a backlash against this brief period of incremental liberation. Directed at gays, among others, McCarthyism refers to investigations of and attacks on perceived enemies of the state during the cold war. "The Senate investigated the employment of 'sexual perverts' by the government; the military conducted witch hunts against gays and lesbians; the FBI began surveillance of the gay community; postal authorities opened the mail of suspected homosexuals." Around the country, gays were subject to arrest and harassment (D'Emilio 2000, 33). Although this treatment persecuted gays and lesbians, it fostered political self-awareness (Button, Rienzo, and Wald 1997, 24; Faderman 1991, 190). Few homosexuals were organized for political action, but that situation was about to change. In 1951 gay leftist Harry Hay founded the Mattachine Society, the goal of which was to organize and mobilize gays for political action (D'Emilio 2000, 33). In 1955 lesbians formed their own group, the Daughters of Bilitis.

Early political activists defined homosexuals as a sexual minority similar to racial and ethnic minorities and entitled to the same rights. This self-definition made development of a gay civil rights movement easier to attain and more likely to engender support (Button, Rienzo, and Wald 1997, 25). Rimmerman (2002) refers to this strategy as assimilationist. Assimilationists work within pluralist, liberal democratic systems to secure politics rights. Other early activists, such as the Mattachine founders, adopted liberationist rhetoric. That is, they operated from outside the political mainstream and made efforts to change the society and the dominant culture to be accepting of gays and lesbians (Rimmerman 2002, 2). The conservative tenor of the times produced more moderate behaviors, however. Mattachine was not the radical group Hay envisioned. Although the moderate approach allowed early gay rights groups to "take root," it did not produce change. In the 1960s gay rights activists became more aggressive, challenging the notion that homosexuality was an illness and challenging the ban on gays and lesbians in the federal workforce (D'Emilio 2000, 33–34).

The 1969 Stonewall riots marked a turning point in the modern gay rights movement in the United States (Button, Rienzo, and Wald 1997, 25; Faderman 1991). Stonewall was a gay bar in Greenwich Village. On June 28, 1969, police raided the bar, and patrons resisted what they considered police oppression: "Instead of scampering off in relief when the police booted them out onto the street after questioning them, the 200 working-class patrons—

drag queens, third-world gay men, and a handful of butch lesbians—congregated in front of Stonewall and, as blacks and other oppressed groups had done before them in the course of the decade, commenced to stage a riot" (Faderman 1991, 194). Within a year, hundreds of gay and lesbian publications and organizations were founded. Stonewall was a rallying cry for gays and lesbians. Many new gay rights organizations were created. Prior to Stonewall, there were fewer than fifty such organizations; by 1973 there were more than 800 (Button, Rienzo, and Wald 1997, 25; D'Emilio 2000, 35).

The timing could not have been better. In the late 1960s and early 1970s many aggrieved groups, such as women and racial and ethnic minorities, were asserting themselves and demanding civil rights. The number of issue-oriented social movements also seemed to be increasing—for example, during this period the antiwar movement, the environmental movement, and nuclear weapons and energy protesters became highly visible. Many Americans were engaging in unconventional political behavior in an effort to achieve postmaterial goals (Inglehart 1990). The gay rights movement also developed a strong liberationist, radical, and anarchic strain, consistent with the other radical protests groups of the day, such as the Black Power movement and the New Left. Rather than trying to educate the public, they adopted the strategies of outsiders, such as sit-ins and public protests (D'Emilio 2000, 35).

Although many of the aggrieved groups represented by these social movements have made great progress since the 1960s and are now mainstream political interests (Wald 2000, 25), the gay rights movement faltered; it failed to become mainstream or receive mass support. In spite of the progress of the gay rights movement, homophobia remains widespread and socially acceptable (Button, Rienzo, and Wald 1997, 2). Nevertheless, the early gay rights movement achieved some success. In the wake of Stonewall, the American Psychiatric Association ceased to classify homosexuality as a mental disorder. In addition, "[N]umerous states repealed their sodomy laws, the U.S. Civil Service Commission eliminated its ban on the employment of gays, and the National Education Association amended its nondiscrimination statement to include protection for 'sexual preference' . . . and in 1980 the Democratic Party included gay rights in its national platform" (Button, Rienzo, and Wald 1997, 26). Moreover, although the prominence of the more radical elements of the gay rights movement may have dissipated in the current era, the liberationists did leave an imprint on the mainstream gay rights movement. The liberationists embraced gay pride and believed that coming out was the key to progress—two ideas that contemporary gay rights activists still embrace (Rimmerman 2002, 27).

The primary goal of the movement, however, was to amend federal civil rights laws to include homosexuality as a protected class, like race, gender, and religious preference. The movement has failed on that account. Progay legislators in Congress have tried to amend the 1964 Civil Rights Act to include sexual orientation as a protected category. Over the years many such efforts have been made, but they have all failed (Button, Rienzo, and Wald 1997, 26). Although the late 1970s saw progress in the area of gay rights, progress ground to a halt in the 1980s. In 1980 conservative Republican Ronald Reagan was elected to the first of his two terms, and Republicans won control of the Senate. The rate of passage for state and local civil rights legislation slowed, as did the rate at which states repealed their sodomy laws. At the same time, the social movement of conservative Christians and their efforts against progressive sexuality, feminism, and gay rights was gaining steam. The 1986 Supreme Court decision in *Bowers v. Hardwick*, 478 U.S. 186, in which the Court upheld Georgia's antisodomy law, was regarded as a significant setback. As progress slowed, the movement once again started to splinter (D'Emilio 2000, 37–38; Button, Rienzo, and Wald 1997, 27).

Although the 1980s brought splintering and stunted progress for supporters of gay rights, the decade also brought the prospect of reinvigoration. The AIDS epidemic entered the national consciousness in the early 1980s with a report by the U.S. Centers for Disease Control and Prevention (CDC) of a "mysterious outbreak of a fatal illness among clusters of gay men in a few major urban areas." Although gay rights activists acknowledged the tragedy wrought by this disease, the epidemic also unleashed "new constructive energy." The epidemic was regarded largely as a gay disease. The media gave it little attention, and policymakers were unwilling to direct scarce resources—this was the 1980s, after all— toward combating the disease. Gays and lesbians gained an appreciation of how politically weak they were, so the epidemic served as a rallying point (D'Emilio 2000, 38; Schroedel and Fiber 2000, 100). More gays and lesbians came out of the closet, disparate parts of the gay community began to cooperate, and gay organizations were built up. Gays and lesbians, using these organizations, lobbied policymakers on AIDS issues. As D'Emilio (2000, 39) notes, once the door was open, "it became easier for activists to use their new access to address issues of homophobia and gay oppression."

Because public attitudes on gay issues are changing rapidly and vary across social groups (Brewer 2003; Lewis and Edelson 2000, 194; Wilcox and Norrander 2002), legislators may not be certain of the electoral repercussions of position-taking on this issue. Thus, supporting gay rights rarely has been politically palatable for politicians. Not surprisingly, gay rights have received little attention from the institutions of government. In the past thirty years, the *modus operandi* typically has been to ignore the issue. Campbell and Davidson (2000) note that "[o]f the ten thousand or so bills introduced in each Congress, a preliminary search of workload for the years 1975 through 1999 (94th through 105th Congresses) suggests that in each Congress only a very small proportion of bills—ten to twenty—deal overtly with gay rights" (Campbell and Davidson 2000, 350). Moreover, to the extent that Congress has taken up gay issues, it has tended to be hostile (Campbell and Davidson 2000, 350; Ellis 1998). Alternatively, Congress has engaged in purely symbolic supportive actions. For example, Congress might express support for tolerance of gays and lesbians in a resolution, without actually enacting statutes that legitimate or mandate such toleration. In the 1980s Congress appropriated money for AIDS research, prevention, and education without actually confronting the "politically profound policy issues surrounding the disease" (Campbell and Davidson 2000, 349).

Many Americans regarded AIDS as a gay disease, largely confined to gay men and intravenous drug users, neither of which are politically powerful constituency groups. Legislators could safely ignore the disease. In fact, confronting the disease might be regarded as an electoral liability. As the medical community and as policymakers came to understand that AIDS affected other, more mainstream segments of the population, and as policymakers came to appreciate the magnitude of the public health crisis produced by AIDS, Congress became more "proactive" in its concern for the disease. Unfortunately, the institution found itself unable to come to a policy consensus for coping with the epidemic. Campbell and Davidson (2000, 353) attribute this inability to a lack of specialization on the part of legislators. They did not know enough to know what to do. Thus, when Congress created a fifteen-member National Commission on AIDS, the original House legislation, HR 2881, passed with overwhelming support. Even some of the House's most conservative members—legislators such as Bob Dornan (R-CA), Newt Gingrich (R-GA), and Dan Burton (R-IL)—were among the proponents of this bill. Eventually it was included in a larger Senate public health bill, S. 2889, and was enacted as part of P.L. 100-607, which provided the first significant federal response to AIDS. The Commission provided Congress with a way of dealing with AIDS without having to confront it themselves. AIDS activists were supportive of the Commission, hoping that it would be a source of unbiased, bipartisan information. Of course, complicating congressional debate over AIDS was the fact that although some members framed the issue as a public health problem, others regarded it as a moral problem (Campbell and Davidson 2000, 352–58).

Supporters of gay rights scored two more legislative victories in 1990. After receiving overwhelming House and Senate support, the Hate Crime Statistics Act of 1990 (P.L. 101-275) was signed into law by President George H. W. Bush on April 23, 1990. The law requires the Department of Justice to gather statistics on the incidence of crimes motivated by religious, racial, or sexual orientation bias. On July 26, 1990, Bush signed into law the Americans with Disabilities Act of 1990 (P.L. 101-336), which prohibits discrimination on the basis of disability, including HIV status (D'Emilio 2000, 39). Both legislative victories were possible, however, because the statutes in question were not single-issue gay rights bills. They addressed issues that were important to the gay community, but they did so in the context of broader legislation.

Although the 1990s began with promise, the decade turned out to be a time of mixed results for supporters of gay rights. Gay culture seemed to be moving into the entertainment mainstream. In the 1992 campaign for the presidency, Bill Clinton actively courted gay and lesbian voters and promised to lift the ban on gays in the military. Once elected, Clinton appointed the first presidential liaison to the gay and lesbian community. Clinton may have supported gay rights and openly gay military integration more than any other major party candidate ever had, but the issue was not at the top of his agenda. Clinton had run on the economy, but he was forced to expend early attention and political capital on an issue that was of marginal importance to many Americans;[10] the issue was forced onto the agenda by political opponents looking to damage the new president. A bipartisan coalition in Congress took the issue out of his hands, and Clinton ultimately settled for the "don't ask, don't tell" compromise (D'Emilio 2000, 40).

Then, in 1993, one of the most enduring gay rights issues emerged. The Hawaii Supreme Court ruled that the state's failure to issue marriage licenses to same-sex couples constituted sex discrimination under Hawaii's constitution. This decision created the very real possibility that one of the fifty states would institute gay marriage or some equivalent union. Because the "full faith and credit" clause of the U.S. Constitution traditionally has been interpreted to mean that states must recognize marriages conducted in other states, the ramifications of this possibility would be felt all over the country. The Hawaii court's decision created the possibility that same-sex couples could marry in Hawaii and then return to their home states or move out of Hawaii and demand that another state recognize their marriage or union. Gay rights—specifically, gay marriage—was now a federal issue demanding a federal solution. The issue was on the political agenda, and Congress could no longer ignore it. Several states quickly passed laws prohibiting recognition of same-sex marriages performed in other states.

In 1996 Congress passed and President Clinton signed the Defense of Marriage Act (P.L. 104-199) (DOMA). "DOMA shifted the argument from an issue of sex discrimination in a courtroom in a gay friendly state to a debate on a fundamental pillar of Western Civilization in the Republican controlled Congress" (Lewis and Edelson 2000, 193). DOMA defined marriage for federal purposes as a union between a man and a woman. Same-sex partners would not be able to file their taxes jointly, nor would a female partner be eligible for her "wife's" social security benefits. DOMA also permitted states to refuse to recognize same-sex marriages performed in other states.

In a strange role reversal, Republicans argued for the need for national standards, and Democrats argued for states' rights.

Republicans argued that they were upholding a sacred institution while saving the government money—in that the government would not have to provide benefits to same-sex couples. Furthermore, they argued that the country should not be bound by the actions of a single state and that judicial policymaking in this area is undemocratic. Democrats argued that DOMA was simply election year saber rattling, that the legislation was unconstitutional, and that by involving itself in marriage issues, Congress intruded on states' rights (Campbell and Davidson 2000, 361; Lewis and Edelson 2000, 201–2).

Rhetoric aside, Campbell and Davidson (2000, 361) note that "[u]nderneath the concerns about states' rights lay a fundamental disagreement about the proper definition of marriage that involved an emotional clash over religious conviction and public morality." The cultures I address in this book—progressive sexuality and religious traditionalism—came into and remain in direct conflict over this issue. The debate over DOMA, as documented in the *Congressional Record*, provides overwhelming evidence of this cultural conflict: Sexual progressives made an argument for civil rights and fair treatment of alternative lifestyles, and religious traditionalists made an argument for traditional values. Following are two excerpts from July 12, 1996, debate on DOMA.[11]

> Rep. Mink (D-HI): Now, this is not a debate about religion. It is a debate about a State process that has been in place in all of the 50 States, granting to the States the right to issue licenses. It is not a matter of invasion of the prerogatives of religion or the churches because long ago judges and justices of the peace were granted the power to also ordain a marriage. . . . But the further gravity of this situation is that this body is being asked, beyond that, this body is being asked to take away rights that are accorded every other citizen by Federal law in determining retirement benefits, health benefits, the rights to burial in a Federal cemetery, the rights to privilege in a Federal trial which is accorded married couples not to have to provide testimony against each other. It is defining in a way contrary to the citizens of my State rights that will be accorded to every other citizen in this country. It is a deprivation of the concept of equal protection. . . .
>
> Rep. DeLay (R-TX): As a father and an observer of this culture, I look ahead to the future of my daughter and wonder what

building a family will be like for her. We saw startling statistics in 1992 that told us that Dan Quayle was right. Children do best in a family with a mom and a dad. We need to protect our social and moral foundations. We should not be forced to send a message to our children that undermines the definition of marriage as the union between one man and one woman. Such attacks on the institution of marriage will only take us further down the road of social deterioration.

Campbell and Davison (2000, 361) note portions of the debate during which Rep. John Lewis (D-GA), a veteran of the civil rights movement, referred to the bill as a "repudiation of the Declaration of Independence's guarantee of the pursuit of happiness." On the other hand, Rep. Tom Coburn (R-OK) declared, "The fact is, [gay marriage] is morally wrong." In the end, DOMA was an easy victory for the Republican leadership. It won bipartisan support and was signed by Bill Clinton, the most progay president to date.

The possibility of gay marriage seemed to legitimize concerns about "the dangers of the 'gay agenda.'" It also presented a problem for Democrats—Clinton in particular. He was put in the position of either signing the legislation and thereby alienating an important Democratic voting block[12] or not signing it and being painted as an extremist (Lewis and Edelson 2000, 200).

Although DOMA was a disappointment for advocates of gay rights, it very nearly gave way to an unexpected and critically important victory (Lewis and Edelson 2000, 193). When the bill reached the floor of both chambers, legislators sympathetic to gay rights tried to amend the legislation so that it would include protections against employment discrimination. If these amendments had been successful, legislators would have struck a blow to gay marriage while providing an important civil rights victory to the gay community. "The House disqualified the amendment as not germane, but Senate proponents and opponents reached a compromise to allow a freestanding vote on ENDA [the Employment Non-Discrimination Act]" (Lewis and Edelson 2000, 203). ENDA was and continues to be less emotionally charged than DOMA. It does not represent an assault on western civilization because proponents have framed it as an issue of basic fairness. Many Americans consider marriage to be a cornerstone of American families and appropriate sexual relationships. Thus, it is an important cultural symbol. Employment is not. Nevertheless, ENDA was defeated in the Senate, albeit by a razor-thin margin of 49–50. DOMA, on the other hand, passed easily in the Senate with overwhelming bipartisan support by a vote of 85–14. Although DOMA remains the law of the land, the issue of gay marriage is unsettled. Hawaii never did institute gay marriage. Vermont came close, instituting a system of civil unions that provides same-sex couples with the rights and privileges of marriage. On November 18, 2003, the Supreme Judicial Court (SJC) of Massachusetts ruled that same-sex marriages are legal, based on the Massachusetts constitution. It ordered the legislature to institute a system of gay marriage. On February 4, 2004, the court issued an advisory opinion indicating that a system of civil unions, similar to the system in Vermont, would be an inadequate compromise. In the opinion of the majority, "For no rational reason the marriage laws of the Commonwealth discriminate against a defined class; no amount of tinkering with language will eradicate that stain, . . . The [civil unions] bill would have the effect of maintaining and fostering a stigma of exclusion that the Constitution prohibits."[13] Governor Mitt Romney (R) supported an amendment to the Massachusetts constitution that would have banned gay marriage, but the legislature rejected three such proposals. On May 17, 2004, the Commonwealth of Massachusetts lifted its ban on gay marriage, and in the first week 2,500 couples sought marriage licenses.[14] One year later, "some 6,200 [marriage licenses] have been handed out to same-sex couples."[15] With the election of additional pro–gay-marriage legislators to the statehouse, the effort toward a compromise that would amend the Commonwealth's constitution to forbid gay marriage but allow civil unions appears to have lost momentum.[16] Opponents of gay marriage, for their part, are pursuing an outright constitutional ban on both gay marriage and civil unions.[17]

To prevent gays and lesbians from outside Massachusetts from flocking to the Commonwealth to be married and then returning to their home states looking for recognition, Governor Romney barred the state from issuing marriage licenses to non-Massachusetts residents. Romney's ban is based on a 1913 Massachusetts law, originally enacted to prevent interracial marriages, "that forbids Massachusetts to marry a couple if their marriage would be 'void' in their home state. . . . [S]ince no other state permits gay marriages within its borders, only Massachusetts residents, or people who intend to move to Massachusetts, can get Massachusetts marriage licenses."[18] As of this writing the governor's application of this law had not yet been reviewed by a Massachusetts court, but a state Superior Court judge declined to issue an injunction against its enforcement,[19] and in February 2005 the Commonwealth's highest court, the SJC, agreed to hear a challenge to the 1913 statute.[20] Assuming that the SJC upholds the application of the law, non-Massachusetts residents will be denied standing to challenge DOMA. The possibility remains, however, that gay couples who reside in Massachusetts and are married in Massachusetts could change their state of residence and demand that their new state recognize their union, based on the "full faith and credit" clause of the Constitution. This possibility would allow for a challenge to DOMA.

One such challenge already has been decided. In January 2005 a federal judge struck down a lawsuit filed by two women who were married in Provincetown, Massachusetts, in July 2004. They tried to secure recognition of their union in the state of Florida, but a "local clerk of the court . . . refused to accept the couple's Massachusetts marriage license."[21] DOMA has been in force since 1996, but because no state married same-sex couples until 2004, no one had ever had standing to challenge the law. Now, continued challenges to DOMA seem almost certain. Although the law may stand up to judicial scrutiny,[22] opponents of gay marriage do not appear to be willing to take a chance. In his January 20, 2004, State of the Union address, President George W. Bush indicated his support for a constitutional amendment banning gay marriage: "If judges insist on forcing their arbitrary will upon the people, the only alternative left to the people would be the constitutional process. Our nation must defend the sanctity of marriage."[23] President Bush reiterated this sentiment in his 2005 State of the Union address.

Fearing that the U.S. Supreme Court eventually could overturn DOMA, legislators in the 108th Congress (2003–2004) took preemptive steps to codify the definition of marriage. Legislators in both chambers offered constitutional amendments that would define marriage as a union between a man and a woman. No action was taken on the initial House measure, H.J.Res. 56, which was introduced by Rep. Marilyn Musgrave (R-CO) on May 21,

2003, and languished in the Judiciary Committee thereafter. Rep. Musgrave introduced a slightly amended version of her original measure on September 23, 2004, H.J.Res. 106. The language of this new amendment corresponded with that of the Senate measure, S.J.Res. 40, which was introduced by Sen. Wayne Allard (R-CO) in July 2004. It read as follows: "Marriage in the United States shall consist only of the union of a man and a woman. Neither this Constitution, nor the constitution of any State, shall be construed to require that marriage or the legal incidents thereof be conferred upon any union other than the union of a man and a woman."

The issue of gay marriage would be taken out of the hands of states if this amendment were to be ratified. Opponents of the amendment staged a filibuster, and on July 14, 2004, the Senate voted on a motion to invoke cloture. Cloture was defeated by a vote of 48–50—12 votes short of the 60 required to keep the amendment alive. Not even half the Senate wished to proceed with the amendment, and the motion to proceed with consideration of S.J. Res. 40 was withdrawn on July 15.

Six Republicans—Senators Sununu (N.H.), Collins and Snowe of Maine, Campbell (Colo.), Chafee (R.I.), and McCain (Ariz.)— and Senator Jeffords (I-Vt.) joined with Democrats in defeating the amendment. Democratic Senators Byrd (W.Va.), Miller (Ga.), and Nelson (Nebr.) voted with the Republicans. Senators Kerry (Mass.) and Edwards (N.C.) missed the vote, though their votes would not have affected the outcome. Some observers projected that House Republican leaders might try to bring a marriage amendment to the floor in the fall just prior to the 2004 presidential election, and they did.[24] On September 30, 2004, the House voted on H.J.Res. 106. It received 227 yea and 186 nay votes, but it did not secure the two-thirds majority required to pass a constitutional amendment. Thirty-six Democrats voted for the amendment, and 27 Republicans voted against it.

In the 108th Congress, at least, a marriage amendment was "an issue whose time has not come," according to Senator Richard Durbin (D-IL).[25] Nevertheless, the House tried to take other steps to protect the status of DOMA. On October 16, 2003, Rep. John Hostettler (R-IND) introduced H.R. 3313, the Marriage Protection Act, which if passed would remove DOMA from the jurisdiction of the federal courts. This bill sat dormant in the Judiciary Committee for many months. After the Senate was unable to invoke cloture on S.J. Res. 40, however, it became apparent that House and Senate Republican majorities would be unable to propose a marriage amendment. With that, the House leadership took a different tack, and H.R. 3313 moved.[26] It was reported out of committee on July 19, 2004, and was passed in the House on July 22, 2004. Seventeen Republicans defected, voting against the legislation, and 27 Democrats defected, voting for the bill. It was referred to committee in the Senate but did not receive additional consideration. Various gay marriage bills and amendments have been offered in the 109th Congress (2005–2006), but as of this writing all remain in committee.[27]

Gay marriage in Massachusetts has been a significant victory for advocates of gay rights, although it is not clear how long that victory will last or how widespread its effects will be. Connecticut, for example, joined Vermont by instituting a system of civil unions in 2005. "California, Hawaii, and New Jersey . . . allow for domestic partnerships."[28] In May 2005 a federal judge overturned Nebraska's gay-marriage ban, which passed in 2000 with 70 percent of the popular vote, and the American Psychiatric Association issued a proclamation supporting gay marriage.[29] However, opponents of gay marriage have redoubled their efforts to amend state constitutions in the wake of the July 2004 U.S. Senate vote.[30] Eighteen states constitutionally ban gay marriage, as of this writing, and more are likely to follow. In 2005 the legislatures in Alabama, South Dakota, Tennessee, Texas, and Virginia all approved constitutional bans on gay marriage that now await ratification by the voters, and the existing marriage bans in New York and California currently face judicial scrutiny.[31]

Finally, it is worth noting that the Massachusetts victory for supporters of gay rights was preceded and followed by two significant legal victories. In 1996 the U.S. Supreme Court struck down Amendment 2 to Colorado's constitution, which had been adopted by Colorado voters and forbade government officials from taking actions to protect gays from discrimination. In *Romer v. Evans*, 517 U.S. 620, the Court ruled that this amendment violated the Equal Protection clause of the Fourteenth Amendment to the U.S. Constitution. In 2003 the Supreme Court issued a decision in *Lawrence et al. v. Texas*, 539 U.S. 558, that struck down all state sodomy laws. Just sixteen years earlier, in *Bowers v. Hardwick,*

478 U.S. 186 (1986), the Court had ruled that individual discretion
in private sexual contact is not a fundamental right protected by
the right to privacy and therefore is not insulated from state regulation. *Lawrence*, which arose from a challenge to Texas's sodomy
law, reversed that precedent.

Although the *Lawrence* decision does not have anything to say
directly about the status of same-sex marriages, Justice Scalia in
his dissenting opinion makes clear his belief that the Court's decision in *Lawrence* lays the groundwork for judicially imposed gay
marriage. He writes:

> One of the benefits of leaving regulation of this matter to the
> people rather than to the courts is that the people, unlike
> judges, need not carry things to their logical conclusion. The
> people may feel that their disapprobation of homosexual con-
> duct is strong enough to disallow homosexual marriage, but
> not strong enough to criminalize private homosexual acts—
> and may legislate accordingly. The Court today pretends that
> it possesses a similar freedom of action, so that we need not
> fear judicial imposition of homosexual marriage, as has re-
> cently occurred in Canada. . . . At the end of its opinion—after
> having laid waste the foundations of our rational-basis juris-
> prudence—the Court says that the present case "does not in-
> volve whether the government must give formal recognition
> to any relationship that homosexual persons seek to enter."
> . . . Do not believe it.[32]

## CONCLUSION

For more than 100 years the nation has been coping with an evolution in sexual norms and the growth of progressive sexuality.
The feminist movement is one important aspect of progressive
sexuality, and it has given way to values-based disagreement over
gender roles and family. Although this disagreement is well documented in the battle over the Equal Rights Amendment and passage of Title IX of the Education Amendments of 1972, among
other significant measures, it culminated with the twentieth-century struggle for and against reproductive rights. In assessing the
status of women in American society, it is not useful and probably impossible to separate issues of economic and bodily integrity. Abortion, more than any other issue, has something to do

with both. Indeed, many feminists would argue that only if women have control over their reproductive capacities can they really possess bodily integrity and therefore control other aspects of their lives, become autonomous, and acquire full and equal citizenship (Stetson 1997, chapter 4).

Issues of bodily integrity and economic security appear to be inextricably linked. In considering why women are poorer than men, in the aggregate, Virginia Woolf observed, "They [women] were having children." Echoing Woolf's sentiment, many late-twentieth-century feminists argued that "women are poor because of the effect of traditional gender roles on their ability to accumulate economic resources" (Stetson 1997, 333–34). Therefore, the struggle for reproductive rights is more than the struggle for reproductive rights alone. It is part of a larger cultural agenda that eschews traditional gender roles and regards control over reproductive decisions as critical to that vision. Congress sometimes has been reluctant to involve itself in abortion politics because the issue has taken on a moral dimension that complicates effective governing. Yet Congress has been pushed to legislate abortion regulations and funding levels, and it is now very much involved in the issue in every session. Sometimes Congress has addressed this issue in a regulatory manner, sometimes in a redistributive manner—but it is always on the agenda, with no resolution in sight.

The gay rights movement represents a different strain of the same cultural conflict. The culture of religious traditionalism—arguably the dominant culture in American society—regards two-parent families with parents of different sexes as supreme among social relationships. Gay relationships are deemed inconsistent with this vision of society. Therefore, activists in the gay rights movement spent the better part of the twentieth century trying to achieve some recognition or affirmation of their status. Challenging William Graham Sumner's aphorism that "stateways cannot change folkways," they demand that "stateways" change and hope that "folkways" follow. Initial attention to gay issues on the part of Congress was confined, for the most part, to its efforts to cope with the AIDS epidemic. In the past decade, however, gay rights issues have made their way onto the legislative agenda with greater prominence, as Congress has considered hate crimes, gays in the military, same-sex marriage, and employment discrimination. Supporters of gay rights have achieved significant victories (e.g., gay marriage in Massachusetts and the striking down of state-level sodomy laws). Congress, as the national arena for cultural conflict, now finds itself in a position to respond to these victories in ways that either affirm or rescind them.

# 3

# The Culture of Religious Traditionalism

> My friends, this election is about much more than who gets
> what. It is about who we are. It is about what we believe. It is
> about what we stand for as Americans. There is a religious war
> going on in our country for the soul of America. It is a cultural
> war, as critical to the kind of nation we will one day be as was
> the cold war itself.
>
> —Patrick J. Buchanan

On August 17, 1992, Pat Buchanan took the podium in
prime time at the Republican National Convention and
characterized the presidential election as a choice between President George H. W. Bush, a " champion of the Judeo-
Christian values," and Governor Bill Clinton, a champion of
"radical feminism . . . abortion on demand, . . . homosexual rights,
discrimination against religious schools, women in combat."
Buchanan's speech served to rally the evangelical base of the Republican Party.[1] His effort to frame the election as a cultural conflict is nothing new. This strategy has been effective since the New
Deal (Leege et al. 2002). Buchanan captured an axis of cultural
conflict that has been relevant in American politics for decades—
the conflict between religious traditionalism and progressive sexuality. Of course, Buchanan would be very likely to characterize the
conflict as one between Christianity and secular humanism.

In chapter 2 I discuss the development of progressive
sexuality and the efforts of certain cultural groups to achieve

legitimacy from government. Feminists spent the better part of the twentieth century trying to secure reproductive rights, and gay rights activists sought recognition of their relationships. These two subcultural movements have in common an affinity for autonomy in moral decision making. Religious traditionalists have been equally assertive in their efforts to achieve government legitimacy for their values. They have fought the culture of progressive sexuality over issues such as abortion and gay marriage, and they have waged their own offensive battle over the issue of religion in schools. More than any others, these issues were politicized by the Christian Right in the early 1980s at the national level (Liebman 1983; Moen 1989, 1992). In fact, religious traditionalists probably would argue that feminism and the gay rights movements have flourished as a result of a *lack* of religion in schools. What animates adherents of this culture is the belief that appropriate social relationships are defined by Christian values, and moral decisions should be made in that context. Thus, religious traditionalists are more supportive of the view that public policy should be grounded in Christian values, and schools should certainly have a role in spreading those values. In this chapter I discuss efforts by religious traditionalists to promote their culture.

## CONSERVATIVE PROTESTANTISM AND PUBLIC LIFE

Politicization of progressive sexuality and religious traditionalism comports well with Tatalovich and Smith's (2001) suggestion that moral conflicts arise out of competing concerns for social status. One group, typically on the left, fights for equality and recognition of their social status. Another group, typically on the right, perceives the status claims of this new group as a threat to its status and joins the battle to fight for "preservationist" policies. In that sense, the mobilization of Christian conservatives was driven, to some extent, by the growth of feminist and gay rights groups. Button, Rienzo, and Wald (1997) argue that early successes on the part of gay rights activists were partly a result of a lack of mobilization by Christian conservatives.

It was not long, however, before religious traditionalists entered the political realm to fight what they perceived to be a moral battle. By the 1970s homosexuals were politically self-aware and beginning to demand citizenship rights. As such, they engaged the political system. At the same time, a proactive feminist movement was growing, out of concern for economic justice and bodily autonomy. Women were working outside the home, the culture was liberalizing, and a variety of groups were demanding recognition of their civil rights. Against this backdrop, Christian conservatives became politicized, and their efforts to secure public policy consistent with their vision should not be underestimated. With the politicization of these two cultural groups, one cultural group came to the public square demanding an "'immoral' good," and the other came demanding its elimination (Meier and McFarlane 1993, 85).

Wilcox (2000, 5) characterizes the Christian Right as "a social movement that attempts to mobilize evangelical Protestants and other orthodox Christians into conservative political action." Their motivation for politics is a response to what they perceive as rampant immorality and an environment that is hostile to their values and beliefs (Fowler, Hertzke, and Olson 1999, 137). The movement is composed mainly of white evangelicals and fundamentalists.[2] Not all fundamentalist and evangelical Protestants are part of the Christian Right, however. Like all social movements, it comprises a diverse set of factions that do not necessarily operate in coordination with one another. Some individuals who identify as Christian Right are concerned primarily with single-issue activism, such as fighting abortions or the radical gay agenda and supporting home schooling or prayer in public schools. Others are more concerned with an array of issues having to do with family values (Wilcox 2000, 7).

Although the Christian Right emerged in the late 1970s, the roots of the movement go back many decades. In the twentieth century, conservative Protestants have had an on again, off again history of engagement with the politics of the secular world. Until the 1920s, Wald (2003) notes, evangelical Protestants had been an important force in American political life; they can even be attributed with stirring up antislavery sentiments in the North. Prior to World War I, evangelicals championed an array of progressive causes, including currency reform, women's suffrage, and corporate reform—all in an effort to "defend the economic interests and social values of traditional Protestantism" (Wald 2003, 201–2). After World War I, these evangelicals were confronted with the realities of modernism. Partly as a result of urbanization and a growth in the birthrate among non-Protestants, evangelicals saw their hold on the cultural fabric of the country loosening. With that, they saw a relaxation of sexual norms and an increased level of reverence for and deference to science. Some people in the Protestant camp—the early mainliners—questioned literalist interpretations of the Bible (Wald 2003, 201–2).

The evangelicals reacted to these phenomena defensively. They believed that orthodox Christianity was under attack, and they were determined to turn the cultural tide back in their favor and purify the nation. They fought to restrict alcohol consumption and replace the teaching of evolution in schools with the Genesis creation narrative (Gusfield 1963; Wilcox 2000, 30–31; Wald 1997, 219). The Ku Klux Klan, for example, framed its raison d'être in the 1920s as an effort to "preserve Christian values," and it attracted many evangelicals for its membership. In addition to African Americans, the Klan fought against the burgeoning Catholic and Jewish immigrant populations, believing that they polluted "the moral environment" in America (Wald 2003, 202–3).

These Protestants met with mixed success. In 1919, for example, they strongly supported the ratification of the Eighteenth Amendment to the Constitution, which prohibited the manufacture, sale, or transportation of alcohol. Of course, this amendment did not eliminate alcohol within the nation's borders. Instead, it drove the alcohol industry underground and onto the black market, producing widespread organized crime. In 1933 the Eighteenth Amendment was repealed by the Twenty-First Amendment. Thus, Prohibition did not represent real success in the short run or the long run.

As with Prohibition, evangelicals both won and lost in the battle over evolution in schools. Organizations such as the Bible League of North America, the Defenders of the Christian Faith, and the Flying Fundamentalists were founded to fight for the replacement of evolution with the Genesis creation story in schools. These groups had mixed success in lobbying state legislatures to pass antievolution laws. Wilcox (2000, 31) notes that "thirty-seven antievolution bill were introduced in twenty state legislatures, but most failed to pass." The antievolution movement fought its most high-profile battle in the so-called Scopes monkey trial of 1925. Teacher John Scopes was charged with violating a Tennessee law that prohibited the teaching of evolution. Three-time Democratic presidential candidate and evolution opponent William Jennings Bryan prosecuted the case. Bryan took the stand to be cross-examined about his own fundamentalist beliefs and was "humiliated" by noted defense attorney Clarence Darrow. Ultimately, Scopes was convicted, and in that sense, the case was a victory for evangelicals. On the other hand, Scopes was fined only a token $100. Moreover, the state Supreme Court quickly overturned his conviction on a technicality (Wilcox 2000, 31).

Not only was Scopes' conviction overturned, but opponents of evolution were lampooned before the nation. The trial received a great deal of national attention, and the public received all their news about this event from onsite reporters. *Baltimore Sun* editorial writer H. L. Mencken famously covered the trial and derided opponents of evolution as "morons" and "hillbillies."[3] This characterization stuck for many years, and evangelicals were humiliated. Bryan died in Tennessee soon after the trial, and with his death, the antievolution movement died as well, at least for the time being. Seventy-three years after the Scopes trail, the Kansas Board of Education removed the teaching of evolution from its mandatory science curriculum, although the board reversed itself after several antievolution board members were defeated in their reelection bids. In summer 2005, however, the Kansas State Board of Education plans to assess and revise public school science curricula.[4] The issue of evolution is a major sticking point. Indeed, efforts by the Christian Right to make public schools more amenable to their teachings have endured. In addition to disputes over evolution, vigorous battles are routinely waged by conservative Protestants to restrict sex education classes to teaching abstinence only, to have the Bible taught as literature, and to allow prayer in schools and at school events.

After Scopes, many conservative Protestants became disillusioned. Having been failed by the political system, they restricted their engagement with politics and focused their energies on their spirituality (Moen 1992, 2). This experience of disillusionment was reinforced by the theological underpinnings of fundamentalist Christian premillinarian eschatological theology. In preparation for the end times, fundamentalists believe that Christians should focus their energy on otherworldly concerns, such as saving souls—theirs and others. To concentrate on the things of this world is to lose sight of the prize (Wilcox 2000, 26–27; 1996, 1988).

For example, when more liberal churches took an active role in the civil rights movement in the 1960s, many conservative Christian denominations eschewed such political involvement. No less than the Rev. Jerry Falwell spoke out against such forays into the political world (Moen 1989, 9; White 1995, chapter 6).

This withdrawal by conservative Protestants from public life came at a time when their "center of gravity" was moving south, as northern Protestantism "embraced modernity and expressed a willingness to apply scientific insight to religious belief" (Wald 2003, 203). The North-South Protestant divide harkened back to one of the earliest theological conflicts within Christianity: Was man saved by faith *and* works or by faith alone, as St. Paul suggested? Conservative Protestants concentrated in the South adopted the latter approach to salvation; northern Protestants adopted the former approach. Politically, this distinction is significant because it implies a theological imperative on the part of southern Protestants to withdraw from politics. If anything, engagement in the secular world got in the way of salvation. At the same time, northern Protestantism had a theological imperative to make the world better, to bring about social transformation in the secular world. This imperative requires active engagement in politics (Wald 2003, 203).

From 1925 until the 1970s engagement by evangelicals with the political world was sporadic. By the beginning of the Depression, existing evangelical groups were financially depleted. Some movement leaders became involved in extremist movements such as the Ku Klux Klan; others drifted toward fascism, anti-Semitism, segregation, and book censorship (Wilcox 2000, 33; Wald 1997, 220). The highest levels of evangelical political involvement in this era probably came in the fight against domestic communism. Indeed, evangelicals were the standard bearers for anticommunism in the 1950s and 1960s. Led by Senator Joseph McCarthy (R-WI), various political figures argued that communists had infiltrated all levels of the government. Wilcox (2000, 34) notes that entrepreneurial conservative Protestant leaders founded new political groups to fight this battle. One of these groups, the Christian Anti-Communist Crusade, arguably is the most direct ancestor of today's Christian Right groups. In retrospect, some scholars have identified the Christian Anti-Communist Crusade as nothing more than a radical fringe group. Even in its time the group was never as high profile and popular as the Moral Majority or Christian Coalition were in theirs. The group's existence, however, may have been "an early sign of the widespread, angry, conservative religious politics that came into prominence in the 1990s" (Fowler, Hertzke, and Olson 1999, 141).

By the 1970s conservative Protestants were reemerging as a political force to be reckoned with. Interestingly, they were reemerging with Republican allegiances. Historically they had tended to have strong Democratic leanings, probably as a function of class and regional considerations. Southern Baptists, the largest evangelical denomination, were firmly Democratic because the post–Civil War South was firmly Democratic. In the twentieth century, Democratic New Deal policies reinforced these Protestants' Democratic leanings. Ties to the Democratic Party began to weaken with the party's nomination of John F. Kennedy, a Roman Catholic, for president in 1960. It was the Democrats' position on civil rights, however, that drove Southern conservative Protestants en masse to the Republican Party (Benzel 1984; Wald 1997, 221–22). Thirty years earlier, northeastern labor Republicans had defected from the party to join southern Democrats in support of the New Deal. Three decades later, the partisan alignments shifted, with the Republican stronghold now in the South and the Democrats firmly in place in the Northeast.

In the 1970s these newly Republican conservative Protestants reengaged public life, focusing on an array of family issues. Wald (1987, 182) notes, "Of all the shifts and surprises in contemporary political life, perhaps none was so wholly unexpected as the political resurgence of Evangelical Protestantism in the 1970s." Attempting to explain the reemergence of the Christian Right confounds many scholars. Many assumed that in the twentieth century the forces of modernization would increasingly marginalize religion. With modernization, people were supposed to move to cities, be exposed to cultural pluralism, and leave behind the traditional influences on their lives.[5] That religious forces would remain individually and politically vital was entirely unexpected. In the 1950s and 1960s some scholars explained sympathy for religious conservatism and the political activism that followed as a function of extremist authoritarian personality disorders or feelings of alienation. In other words, psychological pathologies lead people to develop conservative orientations, religious or otherwise (Peterson, Doty, and Winter 1993; Adorno 1950).

The argument was that persons afflicted with this authoritarian personality disorder are likely to experience hatred for outsider groups such as feminists, gays and lesbians, and other minorities. They are attracted to the Christian Right because the Christian Right supposedly encourages hatred for such groups. Yet all movements attract extremists, and although there is evidence suggesting that many members of the Moral Majority displayed authoritarian personality traits, existing research does not compare members with the general public. Moreover, there is no definitive evidence that Christian Right activists have a disproportionate level of personality disorders (Wilcox 2000, 101–2). It also is worth noting that although Adorno's and others' work was hailed in its time as path breaking, Adorno's measure of authoritarianism, the California F scale, is somewhat tautological. The researchers found that conservatives tend to have authoritarian—that is, fascist—personalities. Arguably, however, some of the scale components tap conservative social values more than they tap cognitive rigidity.

The related alienation argument suggests that modernization has produced a society in which people no longer have strong social ties. This lack of connection leads to feelings of alienation on the part of rootless individuals. These individuals seek communities of fellow travelers and strong leadership. On this theory, community membership gives individuals a sense of belonging, but it also makes them "easy prey" for right-wing groups. "If this explanation is true, then the Christian Right may have attracted a core of activists who have few community ties to constrain their behavior" (Wilcox 2000, 104). There is little evidence, however, that evangelicals Christians are especially alienated. On the contrary, "[n]early all are deeply involved in their local churches, which can provide an all-encompassing social network replete with many close friends" (Wilcox 2000, 104). The alienation argument may explain why people join militias and domestic terror groups—which are hostile to the society from which they may feel alienated—but it does not explain participation in mainstream, albeit conservative, political activism.

No single argument explains the late twentieth-century mobilization (Wald 2003). This mobilization probably is a function of three "facets of religion": "social influences, institutional influences, and values" (Wald 2003, 217). First, certain objective and subjective social influences led to the political reemergence of conservative Protestantism. Evangelicals experienced dramatic increases in their socioeconomic status in the mid- to late twentieth century. They were more educated and had more money. "As evangelicals moved into the middle class, they gained resources that encourage political participation, such valuable assets as increased free time and energy, organizational skills, access to social and communication networks, contacts with government officials, and greater exposure to information" (Wald 2003, 218). These social structural changes also produced a "leadership class of clergy and secular activists," and as the affluence of the evangelical community increased, so did evangelicals' interest in the economic policies of the Republican Party (Wald 2003, 218). Moreover, as the socioeconomic status of evangelicals improved, they relocated from rural areas to cities and the suburbs. There they came into direct contact with challenges to their moral order. As a result, by the 1980s conservative Protestants emerged as a potent political force, loyal to the Republican Party.

As Wald (2003, 218) notes, however, attention to the changing objective status of evangelicals does little to explain why, once they were politically awakened, social rather than economic issues animated their activism. This focus on social rather than economic issues leads some observers to argue that the change in objective socioeconomic status did not mobilize evangelicals. Although that change might have enabled their activism, a change in perceived or "subjective social status" sparked their activism in the first place. Status-based arguments suggest that conservative Protestants perceived that traditional values were losing their hold on the cultural imagination of society. Therefore, they mobilized in an effort to retake the "means of production of lifestyles" (Page and Clelland 1978, 265). Wald, Owen, and Hill (1989, 12) find that "[p]eople who felt that society accorded too little respect to groups representing traditional values—churchgoers, ministers, people who worked hard and obeyed the law, people like themselves—were indeed more positively disposed to support the agenda, organizations and activities of the New Christian Right." Whether Christian Right adherents were or are actually accorded too little respect is irrelevant. The perception of a political threat, valid or not, is a critical influence on political behavior (Edelman 1971).

Three status-based controversies stand out as mobilizing events for the Christian Right, leading to national-level organization (Crawford 1980). In each event, adherents shared the perception that society was godless and experiencing moral degradation (Wald 2003, 207). Reversing their trend of disengagement from political life, conservative Protestants sought to defend Christian values. The first mobilizing event was a textbook controversy in Kanawha County, West Virginia. Page and Clelland (1978) use the social status discontent argument to explain this controversy. The wife of a local minister launched a campaign to have books that were approved by the school board removed from the curriculum. She and her followers argued that, among other things, the books were obscene, unpatriotic, and advocated secular humanism. Opponents of the textbooks constituted a status group, and they engaged the political system in a defensive effort.[6] The controversial textbooks were eventually approved, but the controversy led to school boycotts and the resignation of the school superintendent. Similar textbook challenges percolated all over the country in the wake of the West Virginia challenge (Wald 2003, 206).

A second local controversy was a battle over a 1977 Dade County, Florida, gay rights referendum. An aggressive petition campaign led by Anita Bryant and other religious leaders distorted the effects of the ordinance, claiming that it would require religious schools to hire gay teachers. The ordinance was soundly defeated, and similar ordinances were repealed in other parts of the country. Finally, evangelical groups resisted ratification of the Equal Rights Amendment (ERA) to the U.S. Constitution. Congress proposed the ERA in 1972 in an effort to prohibit sex discrimination, and the amendment was very quickly ratified by twenty-two state legislatures. A group called Stop-ERA formed in opposition to ratification. Led by Phyllis Schlafly, Stop-ERA aggressively lobbied against the amendment, and the rate of state ratification plummeted (Wald 2003, 206–7). Not surprisingly, Burris (1983) finds that opposition to the amendment was strong among fundamentalists and highly religious persons. Moreover, many participants regarded the battle over ratification as "less an issue of equal rights than a referendum on the legitimacy of different cultural and family arrangements" (Burris 1983, 315).

What these anecdotes share is a common concern among activists that their moral order was under attack and devalued. Ultimately, the objective and subjective status arguments are not mutually exclusive. The two may interact to bring about potent political activism. Evangelicals may have looked at the world and seen sin en masse. They may have perceived that society's dominant norms were moving away from their norms. There certainly is evidence of this perception in their rhetoric. At the same time, aggregate measures indicate improvement in the objective socioeconomic status of these same evangelicals, and that development encouraged and facilitated their political involvement. It allowed them to seek redress from the political system across an array of issues, both cultural and economic.

The development of a new public morality also may have encouraged conservative Protestants to "apply their religious values" to public life (Wald 2003, 222). For many years religious values seemed to keep evangelicals on the sidelines. By the 1970s these same religious values were providing them with a reason to join the political game. The application of religious principles to the policy process was a response to national trends that called into question the idea that morality is a private matter. "Wuthnow cited 'criticism of the Vietnam War as an act of public immorality, the various legislative actions taken in the aftermath of Watergate to institutionalize morality as a matter of public concern, and major Supreme Court decisions symbolically linking government with morality'" as evidence of public morality and the intersection of religion and politics (Wuthnow 1983, 176, quoted in Wald 2003, 223). In a more contemporary vein, George W. Bush campaigned for the presidency on a platform that focused on bringing honesty and integrity back to the Oval Office; government is trying to carve out a place for itself in regulating pornography; the Federal Communications Commission (FCC) is cracking down on obscenity on the public airwaves; and an array of policies dealt with in Congress are framed as cultural conflicts, representing the difference between good and evil, ethical and unethical. The point is that if government is a vehicle for spreading morality, it makes sense for conservative Protestants to apply their religious values to the political arena.

Finally, there also may be an institutional component to evangelical mobilization (Wald 2003, 220–21). Religious institutions provide the venue in which concerns for public morality and subjective and objective status interact. In the latter half of the twentieth century, churches became not only houses of worship but also providers of social services. From the largest megachurches to the smallest congregations, churches took up new tasks, such as offering day care and counseling. This evolution brought churches into contact and conflict with government. "The result was a series of classic confrontation between the state's interest in regulating the private provision of social services and the church's claim of immunity under the free exercise clause" (Wald 2003, 220). In addition, with the development of electronic, televised church services, evangelicals are on one hand in conflict with the FCC and, on the other hand, have greater access to potential supporters. Government has affected expanded church activities to such an extent that, practically speaking, churches have had no choice but to engage the political arena. It should come as no surprise, then, that in increasing numbers conservative Protestant ministers brought their political messages to the pulpit. In the 1960s conservative Protestant clergy gave fewer political cues than their mainline peers. Three decades later, evangelical parishioners "do not report receiving any less political direction than mainline Protestants or Catholics" (Wald 2003, 221).

In addition to the growth of megachurches, the 1970s and 1990s saw the emergence of religiously based interest groups, which—from a resource mobilization standpoint—facilitated the transformation of political grievances into political activism. The reentrance of the Christian Right into U.S. politics was marked by the formation of three major interest groups: the Moral Majority, Christian Voice, and the Religious Roundtable. Ed McAteer founded The Religious Roundtable hoping to make inroads into the single largest evangelical denomination—the Southern Baptist Convention (SBC). Organizationally, the Religious Roundtable allowed ministers to learn the skills needed to promote grassroots mobilization (Wald 2003, 209). Moen suggests that Roundtable "was formed primarily to recruit [SBC] ministers into politics, with the expectation that they would bring their congregations with them" (Moen 1992, 18). The Roundtable's reputation for anti-Semitism damaged the prestige of the organization, however, and it was eventually forced to close down its Washington, D.C., lobbying office. After its founder's unsuccessful Senate campaign in 1984, the Roundtable folded (Moen 1992, 18).

The Revs. Robert Grant and Richard Zone founded Christian Voice in 1978 as part of an effort to fight a California gay rights measure. Drawing its membership primarily from Assembly of God adherents in the West and Southwest (Wald 2003, 209), Christian Voice's agenda was broader than simply quashing gay rights in California. Its promotional literature railed against a variety of social pathologies, such as "legalized abortions, limitations on school prayer, rampant homosexuality," secular humanism, and the teaching of evolution (Liebman 1983, 52). Christian Voice was actively involved in electioneering and issued "moral approval ratings" for members of Congress (Wald 2003, 209; Wilcox 2000, 37). Moen (1992, 19) notes that in the 1980 presidential election campaign, Christian Voice attained considerable notoriety because its campaign materials suggested, among other things, that President Carter supported homosexuality. Following the 1980 election, Christian Voice scaled back its electioneering and turned its attention to lobbying Congress for a constitutional amendment to allow school prayer. Failing on that account, the group continued to issue legislator "report cards" into the late 1980s, when the organization essentially atrophied.

The Moral Majority, founded in 1979, was the most prominent and high profile of the new Christian Right groups. Leibman (1983) suggests that the group's endurance and success resulted from its ability to build on and coordinate a network of churches and church activists. "According to prominent theologian Richard John Neuhaus, the Moral Majority was 'the single most visible institutional expression' of the claims of religious conservatives" (Neuhaus 1984, quoted in Moen 1992, 19). Founder Jerry Falwell was and is the pastor of Thomas Road Baptist Church in Lynchburg, Virginia—the largest independent Baptist church in the country. Falwell also delivers a televised weekly service, "The Old Time Gospel Hour," that is broadcast on hundreds of stations. "Concentrated mostly in the southeastern states, the Moral Majority drew most of its membership and leadership from other independent Baptist churches" (Wald 2003, 209).

The Moral Majority experienced its greatest strength in the early 1980s, during President Reagan's first term. During that time, the Moral Majority expended considerable resources lobbying Congress on social issues. Falwell's organization achieved mixed results; it succeeded in getting its issues on the agenda, but it lost key roll calls. Moen (1992, 21) suggests that the Moral Majority's mixed success limited its future advocacy prospects. The Moral Majority's failure to secure victory on key policy objectives damaged its reputation, and its financial support dried up. Furthermore, Reagan's first-term emphasis on economic and defense policy could not have helped the Moral Majority advance its largely social moral agenda. By Reagan's second term, the organization was increasingly strapped for cash. Reagan's reelection campaign theme—"Morning in America"—undercut the Moral Majority's efforts to mobilize rank-and-file conservative Christians. After all, if it was "Morning in America," from what did America need to be saved (Wilcox 2000, 37)? Ultimately, the Moral Majority was not really as impressive as it looked on paper. In many ways the organization was a mailing list, and Wilcox (2000, 37) notes that the local arms of the Moral Majority often behaved in "divergent" and "embarrassing" ways. All of these factors contributed to the Moral Majority's collapse in the late 1980s.

The Religious Roundtable, Christian Voice, and the Moral Majority all lived relatively short lives. Seeing these organizations' declining stature on Capitol Hill, Moen (1989) projected a dim political future for the Christian Right. Rozell and Wilcox (1995) and Wilcox (2000) note, however, that from the 1970s to the 1990s, between 10 and 15 percent of Americans consistently supported Christian Right organizations. An even larger percentage supported portions of the Christian Right agenda. These writers make the argument that the political power of the Christian Right organizations diminished not because they lacked a following but because of institutional and political factors. The televangelist scandals of the 1980s and the saturation of the direct-mail market made their survival difficult.

As important as these groups were, by the 1980s they were not the only game in town. Whereas these organizations sought to affect policy through grassroots and professional lobbying efforts, Pat Robertson entered the political fray more directly. A Baptist minister, founder of the Christian Broadcasting Network, and host of *The 700 Club*, Robertson ran for president in 1988, campaigning on a platform of anticommunism and creationism (Wilcox 1988). "[Robertson's] charge that the feminist agenda called for killing children, practicing witchcraft, and becoming lesbians is merely the most often cited example of his extreme rhetoric" (Wilcox 1996, 62). Robertson gained additional notoriety for his agreement with Jerry Falwell's suggestion on an episode of *The 700 Club* that "abortionists" and "gays and lesbians" share some responsibility for the terrorist attacks of September 11, 2001. Robertson commented, "We have sinned against Almighty God, at the highest level of our government, we've stuck our finger in your eye. . . . The Supreme Court has insulted you over and over again, Lord. They've taken your Bible away from the schools. They've forbidden little children to pray. They've taken the knowledge of God as best they can, and organizations have come into court to take the knowledge of God out of the public square of America."[7]

After Robertson's electoral defeat and the folding of some of the original Christian Right interest groups, the Christian Right seemed rudderless. Although his presidential campaign itself was a disaster, it was part of "the birth of a new, more sophisticated Christian Right" (Wilcox 2000, 40). Participants in this movement became seasoned electioneers and gained a foothold in many state party organizations.

The 1990s saw a new generation of Christian Right political organizations. No longer a collection of direct-mail lists, these second-generation organizations were "well-established membership organizations" that used "mainstream language" (Moen 1995, 131). I highlight here four such organizations: the Christian Coalition, Focus on the Family, the Family Research Council, and Concerned Women for America. The Christian Coalition, founded by Robertson, is probably the most visible of these groups.

The Christian Coalition was founded in 1989 on the ashes of Robertson's 1988 presidential campaign, and it tried to craft a more inclusive religiously conservative organization. The Christian Coalition featured Jewish, African American, and Catholic speakers at its 1999 convention (Wilcox 2000, 61–62). Many observers credit Ralph Reed, former executive director of the Christian Coalition and an astute student of politics, with bringing potency and moderation to the organization. Certainly Reed was a more pragmatic figure than Robertson. Yet Reed did not moderate the Christian Coalition's vision as much as he moderated its rhetoric. Reed couched the organization's agenda in the language of rights and freedom, not Sodom and Gomorrah (Moen 1992; Wilcox 2000, 43, 62–63). Under Reed the organization encouraged activists to use secular, rights-based language and mainstream their message to listeners outside the evangelical family. The organization also encouraged "stealth candidates" who hid their Christian Coalition ties (Wilcox 2000, 42). In addition to Reed's efforts to mainstream the Christian Coalition message, many religious lobbyists in this era adopted incremental goals as they engaged in congressional advocacy (Hertzke 1988, 88). The Christian Coalition was a political powerhouse in U.S. politics for about a decade, and many observers credit the group with turning the electoral tide in favor of Republicans in the 1994 midterm elections. It still has a strong grassroots organization and lobbies Capitol Hill extensively on a broad range of issues. Today, however, it is a shell of its former self. It reached the zenith of its influence under Reed's stewardship, and after his departure in 1997 it reached its nadir. A series of gaffes by Robertson, including his implication that the September 11, 2001, terrorist attacks had been caused by American abandonment of God, caused a great deal of political controversy in the mainstream. In addition, Robertson's implicit approval of abortion policies in China rocked prolife Christian conservatives. In 1999 the organization experienced a mass exodus of leadership, and it entered the 2000 campaign $2 million in debt. In that election, an estimated 6 million Christian conservatives stayed home. In the mid-1990s, the Christian Coalition had chapters in all fifty states. By 2001 twelve state chapters were essentially defunct—including those in electorally important states such as Pennsylvania and Michigan. Also in 2001, the Christian Coalition faced a discrimination lawsuit by several African American employees from its Washington, D.C., office. Robertson resigned as Christian Coalition president in 2001 and was replaced by Roberta Combs, but the national organization continues to drift under her leadership.[8]

Focus on the Family also emerged as a force to be reckoned with in the 1990s. The Christian Coalition received more publicity, but many observers think that Focus on the Family was and remains more active. Essentially, Focus on the Family "is the radio ministry of James Dobson, broadcast on over 4,000 radio stations worldwide in fifteen languages" (Wilcox 2000, 64). The organization promotes conversion of homosexuals to heterosexuality and has a traditional profamily political agenda. Whereas the Christian Coalition has tried to build an inclusive ecumenical organization by mainstreaming its message, Focus on the Family makes no such effort. Lacking the pragmatism of the Christian Coalition, "Dobson's rhetoric is uncompromising and ideological" (Wilcox 2000, 64).

The Family Research Council originally was part of Focus on the Family. In 1992 it broke off from Focus on the Family and became an independent organization, with the complementary goal of promoting traditional family values. From 1988 to 1999 former Reagan administration official Gary Bauer headed the Family Research Council. Bauer left the organization in 1999 to launch a presidential campaign, and many observers regarded him as a rising star in conservative Christian circles. More than anyone else, Bauer seemed poised to pick up the mantle of Christian Right leadership in the wake of Reed's departure from the Christian Coalition. Bauer fell out of favor in many Christian Right circles, however, when his campaign appeared increasingly "heretical." Bauer met with union officials, advanced a patient's Bill of Rights, and rejected the idea of private retirement accounts. He sounded to many conservatives like a Democrat. His worst heresy, however, came when he dropped out of the race and committed the apostasy of endorsing Senator John McCain (R-AZ). The Christian Right "loathed" McCain because his "campaign finance bill would suffocate groups such as National Right to Life; he said he would respect his daughter's decision on a hypothetical abortion; he agreed to meet with gay Log Cabin Republicans; he admitted to cheating on his first wife."[9] When McCain made a famous speech in Virginia in which he called Falwell and Robertson "agents of intolerance," Bauer sat in the front row.

In recent years both Focus on the Family and the Family Research Council have focused their advocacy efforts squarely on opposition to gay marriage. Some observers even refer to gay marriage as "the new abortion" in view of the level of polarization and passion the issue evokes.[10] In the wake of the 2004 presidential election, Dobson urged Congress to again consider a constitutional amendment prohibiting gay marriage. This entreaty makes sense because many observers credit President Bush's reelection victory to conservative Protestants who came out in force to protect traditional marriage.[11] When Bush indicated after the election that he would not aggressively lobby Congress for the amendment, however, conservative Protestants were displeased. Tony Perkins of the Family Research Council and Tom Minnery of Focus on the Family both "called the White House to complain about Bush's position."[12] Perkins even suggested that a lack of presidential leadership on gay marriage might cost Bush the "support and trust of social conservatives on other issues, including Social Security reform."[13] No doubt conservative Protestants were buoyed by Bush's 2005 State of the Union address, in which he reiterated his support for a constitutional ban on gay marriage.

Concerned Women for America (CWA) cuts a smaller profile than the Christian Coalition, Focus on the Family, or the Family Research Council. Technically speaking, CWA is not really a second-generation organization, given that it was founded in 1979. I include it in this discussion, however, because it maintains a significant presence even today. Founded by grassroots Bible groups, Wilcox (2000, 65) notes, CWA may be more like the evangelical groups of the 1970s than like the second-generation organizations in the sense that its message is decidedly moral rather than political. Unlike the first-generation groups, however, CWA has always had a broader appeal, beyond evangelicals—particularly among Catholic women. CWA founder Beverly LaHaye did not feel that the National Organization for Women (NOW), Betty Friedan, and the feminist movement more generally spoke for her, so she organized accordingly in support of traditional families and gender roles. CWA engages in electioneering and lobbying, and it continues to lead Christian Right battles against left-leaning feminist groups (Wilcox 2000, 65–66). Although CWA's advocacy efforts tend to center on women's issues such as reproductive policy, CWA also has focused on gay issues in recent years.

## THE RIGHTEOUS AGENDA

There is no single Christian Right agenda. The movement is decentralized and comprises many independent groups. Several issues stand out, however, as particularly important to the Christian Right: education, pornography, traditional families, and building a Christian nation, to name a few examples. These issues continue to mobilize the Christian Right's rank and file. Opposition to abortion and gay rights and advocacy of prayer in schools are three issues that have pride of place among Christian Right activists. Many Christian Right adherents—like many nonadherents—believe that abortion at any stage of pregnancy is murder. Wilcox (2000) finds that consensus among the Christian Right regarding abortion is so high that he is unable to get dissent on the record. He notes, "One activist in Ohio made me turn off my tape recorder and promise never to reveal her responses to other Moral Majority members. Then she told me that she supported an exception for rape because she had been raped a few years before and had worried for weeks about a possibility pregnancy" (Wilcox 2000, 117).

Giving voice to a belief in exceptions for rape is controversial in many Christian Right circles. Some prolife advocates, such as former U.S. Attorney General John Ashcroft, even oppose the use of many standard forms of birth control, such as the pill and the intrauterine device.[14] It is no surprise, then, that abortion—particularly the *Roe v. Wade* decision—has been an important mobilizing issue for the Christian Right. Even though Catholics probably were the first religious organization to reject *Roe*, the opposition of the Christian Right was extraordinarily potent. Christian Right organizations were able to rhetorically connect the decision to an array of family-threatening issues, such as gay rights, school prayer, and education. "[C]onservative Republican anti-feminist" Phyllis Schlafly skillfully made a connection between *Roe* and the ERA, suggesting that both evidenced a pattern of moral decay (O'Connor 1996, 61). Thus, *Roe* was not just a single decision; it represented a challenge to traditional social relationships. Fundamentalist churches, including the Mormon church, also made the connection. Evangelicals were slower to mobilize against abortion. The first antiabortion evangelical group, the Christian Action Council, was not founded until 1975. Once evangelicals mobilized, however, their activism proved to be more significant than even Catholic activism. Like fundamentalists, evangelicals also tied abortion to an array of social issues. Collectively, evangelical groups, the Roman Catholic Church, and opponents of the ERA mobilized quickly and launched an aggressive lobbying campaign against abortion (O'Connor 1996, 61).

Opposition to gay rights comes from a variety of sources. Generally speaking, organized religion has tended to provide the most consistent and potent opposition to gay rights. "Simply put, most religious groups in the United States have long believed that homosexual behavior is morally wrong" (Green 2000, 122). The Christian Right has provided the most reliable opposition to gay rights. It may not speak in a single voice on the issue, but it is rooted in evangelical Protestantism, and, together with other doctrinally conservative denominations, such as the Mormons, the Christian Right has among its primary agenda items staunch opposition to policy that affirms gay rights (Rimmerman 2002, 122; Green 2000, 122). Button, Rienzo, and Wald (1997) found in their survey of 126 communities deciding on a gay rights ordinance that "[t]he most prominent opponents . . . were members of conservative religious groups who argued on doctrinal grounds against giving legal recognition to what they regard as sinful behavior" (177–78). Many religious traditionalists consider homosexuality a graver sin than adultery or fornication (Wilcox 2000, 121).

Christian Right opposition is rooted in scripture. However, scripture by itself would not necessarily lead to a belief in criminal prohibitions against homosexual behavior. "One seldom finds conservative Christians calling for similar penalties or legal restrictions on other forms of conduct, sexual or otherwise" (Button, Rienzo, and Wald 1997, 179). What makes homosexuality different—and worse than other sin—is that it assaults Western culture and civilization in a way that other behaviors do not. Individual marriages may fall apart because of the sin of adultery, but the larger institution of marriage remains intact. Allowing gays to marry would destroy an institution that is the bedrock of society. Unlike other sins, homosexuality—and, by extension, legal recognition of same-sex couples—challenges preferred social relationships and the status of longstanding values of dominant culture. Stated differently, legitimating homosexuality constitutes a challenge to "basic cultural norms" (Button, Rienzo, and Wald 1997, 179).

My argument in this chapter has been that the Christian Right, as a social movement, reemerged in the 1970s to repulse what adherents regarded as an assault on the larger culture of religious traditionalism. Evidence that this culture was under attack took the form of moral decay. The decline of the patriarchal family and the *Roe* decision, as well as "changes in social arrangements that once supported the traditional family, including schools, law enforcement, and popular culture," were all suggestive of this decay. Homosexuality was another aspect of this assault; it is so problematic for the Christian Right because it advances moral decay on all those fronts. It flies in the face of the traditional family; to the extent that gays and lesbians receive legal protections, social arrangements that once supported families are compromised (Green 2000, 124).

Thus, gay marriage "is not simply bad or inappropriate. It threatens virtually every social value cherished by religious traditionalists: role differences between men and women, the process of procreation, the raising of children, respect for authority," and so forth (Button, Rienzo, and Wald 1997, 179–80). To fight this assault, the Christian Right has framed the gay rights movement as a "radical gay agenda," implying that there is a nefarious conspiracy—and perhaps adherents believe there really is such a conspiracy (Herman 2000, 143–47). Adherents also have argued that gay rights protections would lead to infiltration of practicing homosexuals into schools and offices, where they could engage in recruitment activities. Many adherents resist any positive portrayals of homosexuality on television, in books, and in movies because they fear such portrayals would lead people to experiment with the homosexual lifestyle (Wilcox 2000, 121).

The effort of religious traditionalists to promote their culture involves more than just a "reactive opposition" (Green 2000) to gay rights and abortion rights. The conflict between cultures also appears in the issue of prayer in schools. As Jelen (1998, 152) notes, school prayer is a perennial favorite of members of Congress, who respond to public opinion and Supreme Court decision making. In a series of rulings, the Supreme Court has severely limited religious expression in public schools. In *Engel v. Vitale,* 370 U.S. 421 (1962), the Court struck down the practice of state-mandated, teacher-led prayer in public schools as a violation of the establishment clause of the First Amendment. A year later the Court expanded its decision in *Abington Township v. Schempp,* 374 U.S. 203 (1963), extending "the ban on state-mandated religious ceremonies. . . . By these two decisions, the Court seemed to say that 'establishment' included any celebration of religion conducted or promoted by an agency of the government" (Wald 2003, 91). The Court went so far as to strike down moments of silence in 1985, with its decision in *Wallace v. Jaffree*, 472 U.S. 38 (1985). As a guide for evaluating establishment claims during the period in which the Court took a strict separationist approach, the Court used what is commonly know as the Lemon Test, which is derived from the majority opinion of Chief Justice Warren Burger in *Lemon v. Kurtzman*, 403 U.S. 602 (1971). The Lemon Test requires that state actions have "a primarily secular purpose, primarily secular consequences, and no excessive entanglement of church and state" (Wald 2003, 94).

Religious traditionalists have been among the strongest supporters of school prayer (Moen 1984); they decry the school prayer rulings and reject the idea that schools should be totally secular. In fact, some Republicans in Congress have argued that the absence of religion in schools has led to a "very deep cultural problem" and that a remedy for the disorder that pervades public schools—the Columbine massacre is only the most tragic example—would be posting the Ten Commandments in schools.[15] Conservative Protestants see a role for government in promoting Christian values, which they believe will cure social ills. In an effort to challenge the Supreme Court's separationist stance, legal activists in the movement have developed a constitutional theory that "subordinates the establishment clause to the free exercise clause" (Wald 2003, 105). Thus, attacks on school prayer are considered attacks on the free exercise of religion. Without actually repudiating *Lemon*, in recent years the Court has allowed for an increasingly porous wall of separation.[16]

Congress did not have much to say regarding school prayer or religion in schools more generally from the founding until the 1960s. In the mid-1800s, the first conflicts concerning religion and schools took place not over prayer but Catholic school funding. Early public schools in the United States were unabashedly Protestant. To avoid Protestant instruction, Catholic parents were forced to establish a system of private parochial schools. A series of anti-Catholic riots in major metropolitan areas of the East Coast did little to convince Catholic parents that their children were welcome in the public educational system. Forced to establish alternative schools, Catholics pressed state governments for funding. Although they did not receive that funding, the public schools came under increased pressure to secularize in the early twentieth century with increased immigration by Catholics and Jews (Dierenfield 1997, 168–69; Marshall 2001, 12).

Religion in education did not emerge as a national conflict until well into the twentieth century, and Congress did not step into the fray until after 1962 *Engel* decision. After *Engel*, members of Congress directed a great deal of rhetorical vitriol at the Supreme Court. A constitutional amendment seemed to be the only remedy. "Within a year, 115 representatives . . . had introduced 152 bills to overturn [the Court]; 28 senators did likewise" (Dierenfield 1997, 172). Advocates of school prayer in and out of Congress continued to push for statutory and constitutional language that would enable school prayer in some form. Rep. Frank Becker (R-N.Y.) probably was the most outspoken school prayer advocate. He assembled a "bipartisan, geographically-balanced committee" to draft a constitutional amendment. Their end product was the most far-reaching amendment proposed—it included a clause in support of Bible readings—but Becker could not get it past the Judiciary Committee chaired by Rep. Emanuel Celler (D-N.Y.). Celler eventually agreed to hold hearings on the amendment but hoped to drag them out until the end of the Congress (Dierenfield 1997, 172–73).

Although religious organizations supported the amendment, including the National Association of Evangelicals, Celler had the support of many mainstream denominations, all of which had experience as religious minorities. Dierenfield (1997, 175) notes that the National Council of Churches, the American Jewish Committee, the United Presbyterian Church in the U.S.A., and even the Southern Baptist Convention opposed the amendment. Catholic groups also expressed reticence. As the hearings dragged on, support for Becker's amendment, or any of the prayer amendments offered in Congress, began to dissipate. The public also appeared to be divided on the issue. Lacking strong support from the chamber, the Judiciary Committee did not send a prayer amendment to the floor in 1964. Outside the South, most states began to comply with *Engel* and *Schempp*. With the exception of Louisiana—which incidentally has a large Catholic population—the former states of the Confederacy and some of the border states strongly resisted the Court's *Engel* decision (Dierenfield 1997, 176).

Congress had very little to say on the issue for the next two years. Then, in 1966, Sen. Everett Dirksen (R-IL) took up the charge for a school prayer amendment. Dirksen's concern was that the Supreme Court had eliminated even voluntary prayer, and he supported an amendment that would have provided for that (Dierenfield 1997, 176). Just as Becker faced opposition from the House Judiciary Committee chair, Dirksen faced opposition from Senate Judiciary subcommittee chair Birch Bayh (D-IN). Bayh agree to hold hearings, but the subcommittee ultimately failed to positively report the amendment. Nevertheless, Dirksen was able to get his amendment to the floor as a substitute for another bill. When the Senate voted on Dirksen's amendment in September 1966, a majority supported it—but the roll call fell short of the necessary two-thirds majority by nine votes.

Over the years legislators continued to offer school prayer amendments, but for the most part they went unconsidered. There was another House vote on the issue in 1971. Although a majority of representatives supported the bill, it too fell short of the required two-thirds (Dierenfield 1997, 183).

In 1979 school prayer supporters took a different tactic. Sen. Jesse Helms (R-N.C.) offered a rider that would have removed school prayer issues from the Supreme Court's jurisdiction, thereby giving states the ability to set policy on this question as they wished. Democratic leaders in the Senate opposed the rider, as did President Carter. Senate Democrats were confident, however, that the House would never pass this legislation. This confidence gave them the opportunity to bring the bill to floor, schedule a vote, and allow conservative Democrats the opportunity to cast a pro-prayer vote (Dierenfield 1997, 185). As expected, the Helms rider passed in the Senate by a wide margin but was buried in the House. By this time, newly formed Christian Right groups such as Christian Voice and the Moral Majority were prepared to advocate for a school prayer amendment; prayer was successfully coupled to their larger social agenda (Dierenfield 1997, 185–86).

With the election of Ronald Reagan as president in 1980, advocates of school prayer finally had an ally in the White House. Reagan aggressively courted Christian Right voters and secured them into the Republican fold. Yet by the end of Reagan's first term, some activists in the Christian Right expressed disappointment at the lack of progress on their social agenda. Reagan may have embraced the agenda of religious traditionalism, but the cold war and tax cuts were his top agenda items (Dierenfield 1997, 188). "By the time Congress and the administration got around to the New Right's agenda, Reagan's sway over Congress had subsided."[17] In 1982 Reagan did indicate his support for a constitutional amendment, but a prayer amendment never made it out of the Senate Judiciary Committee, in spite of having a sympathetic chair in Sen. Strom Thurmond (R-S.C.). Senator Helms again attached a rider that limited the Supreme Court's jurisdiction in this area—this time to a debt bill. When a filibuster ensued, long-time prayer supporter Sen. Howard Baker (R-TN) "convinced the Senate to send the debt bill back to the Finance Committee with the instruction to return a measure without any amendments" (Dierenfield 1997, 190).

In 1983 a school prayer amendment did make it to the floor of the Senate. Sponsored by Sen. Thurmond, at the request of President Reagan, S.J. Res. 73 fell eleven votes short of the required two-thirds majority. Needless to say, evangelicals were disappointed by the defeat, but other religious denominations were pleased with the outcome.[18] Prayer advocates did score a significant, albeit incremental, victory in 1984. Sen. Mark Hatfield (R-OR) submitted a bill known as the "Equal Access bill," which prohibited junior and senior high schools from restricting access to school facilities to religiously themed student groups and activities. The bill did not get a stand-alone vote; it was subsumed into a larger education bill and signed into law on August 11, 1984 (P.L. 98-377).

In the 1990s advocates of prayer had reason to be encouraged, although ultimately they did not win much. In 1994 the Senate passed an education bill that included a provision eliminating federal aid to state and local agencies that prohibit voluntary, constitutionally protected school prayer (Dierenfield 1997, 195). When Republicans won control of both chambers in the election of November 1994, a sympathetic leadership emerged. Although a school prayer amendment was not one of the Contract with America items, the presumptive Speaker, Rep. Newt Gingrich (R-GA), promised to bring such an amendment to a vote by July 1995; Gingrich made Rep. Ernest Istook (R-OK) the "point man" on this issue (Dierenfield 1997, 195).[19] In April 1995, however, Gingrich indicated that an amendment might not be necessary. He argued that a legislative remedy shielding children who wish to pray and employees who wish to display religious symbols was possible and that he opposed "official prayer."

Although some observers regarded the prayer issue as a plus for Republicans, a prayer amendment might have divided the new Republican majority just as it was gearing up to address budget-related matters (Dierenfield 1997, 196).[20] No fewer than ten prayer amendments were offered, some of which were hostile to school prayer. Istook's amendment accrued 115 cosponsors but never made it to the floor; neither did any of the other amendments.

By the end of the 105th Congress (1997–1998), Christian Right activists were expressing disappointment at the lack of progress on their agenda under the Republican leadership in Congress. There was a sense among some activists that the Republican Party took them for granted and that they might bolt the party. In April 1998 Gingrich promised to bring a prayer amendment to the floor by the end of the session.[21] As Gingrich promised, H.J. Res. 78 came to the floor in June 1998 but did not secure the necessary two-thirds majority. Rep. Istook resubmitted his prayer amendment in the 106th (1999–2000), 107th (2001–2002), and 108th (2003–2004) Congresses, but the amendment never made it to the floor. House prayer advocates in the 106th Congress (1999–2000) did achieve incremental successes, securing House agreement to an array of pro-prayer legislative amendments. After a decade of Republican control of the House, however, school prayer advocates have not been able to successfully offer a school prayer constitutional amendment.

The consistent inability of prayer advocates to secure a constitutional amendment comes against the backdrop of consistent public support for school prayer. Although the constituency that supports prayer tends to be the least efficacious (Elifson and Hadaway 1985), it also appears that legislators are most responsive to political activists, who tend to be the most extreme and ideological on this and other cultural issues. In the decades of Democratic control of Congress, majorities of the American people may have supported school prayer, but Democratic activists did not (Green and Guth 1989). In the current era, this same pattern does not hold. Instead, division among Republican activists, not unified extremism, appears to have precluded successful passage of a school prayer amendment. Religious conservatives may support an amendment, but other partisans prefer to focus on economic issues. Moreover, even if Republicans were squarely behind a prayer amendment, antimajoritarian Senate procedures would still stand in their way.

## THE CATHOLIC CHURCH

On May 1, 2004, Colorado Springs Bishop Michael Sheridan issued a pastoral letter in which he said that Catholic politicians who support abortion and same-sex marriage and Catholics who vote for these politicians place themselves "outside the full communion of the Church" and may not receive Eucharist until they receive the Sacrament of Reconciliation.[22] Bishop Sheridan's statement received considerable media attention because some of the country's most prominent Catholic politicians—such as Sens. John Kerry (D-MA) and Ted Kennedy (D-MA)—take positions that are contrary to church teaching on a variety of social issues. About six weeks later, the United States Conference of Catholic Bishops (USCCB) convened in Denver to discuss the issue of Catholics in public life (as well as the priest sex abuse scandal).[23] On June 18, 2004, the bishops issued a statement titled "Catholics and Political Life" that seemed to reflect a compromise between the Sheridan position and that of bishops who object to using the Eucharist as a "pawn of politics."[24] The USCCB ultimately left the question of the Eucharist to individual bishops, while reiterating its commitment to the church's teaching on abortion and encouraging individuals to examine their consciences on this issue.[25]

At the same time, President Bush—a Methodist and born-again Christian who, during a presidential campaign debate in 2000, named Jesus Christ as the political philosopher he most admires—aggressively campaigned for Catholic support in the 2004 election. In fact, Bush had courted (and tried to make amends with) Catholics since his 2000 visit to the anti-Catholic Bob Jones University.[26] Catholics constitute roughly one-quarter of the U.S. electorate and an even higher proportion of voters in key Midwestern battleground states. Although Catholics traditionally have constituted a reliably Democratic voting block, they narrowly split their vote between Democrat Al Gore and Bush in the 2000 election. Traditionalist Catholics, who align themselves with evangelical Protestants on issues such as gay marriage and

abortion, are particularly open to conservative Republican over-
tures. Thus, President Bush met with Vatican officials in June 2004,
asking them to push Catholic bishops in the United States to rally
American Catholics to support him on an array of moral issues.
Later that summer, Bush met with the Knights of Columbus, the
world's largest lay Catholic men's organization, and assured them
that they had an ally on moral issues in the White House.[27] Ultimately, President Bush's efforts paid off, and he won a narrow
majority of Catholic voters in 2004.

To this point in this chapter I have focused on conservative
Protestants as the standard-bearers of religious traditionalism. Yet
as Bishop Sheridan's pastoral letter and the USCCB statement
indicate, and as President Bush's Catholic outreach suggests, the
Catholic Church has been very actively promoting a social agenda
that is consistent with that of conservative Protestantism on issues
of reproductive policy and gay rights. For many years the Catholic
Church in the United States provided a consistently conservative
voice to the political landscape, probably as an outgrowth of
Catholics' "communal isolation and immigrant culture" (Wald
2003, 251). As Catholics became more upwardly mobile, particularly after World War II, the political tenor of the Catholic voice
in the United States began to change. The Second Vatican Council (Vatican II), called by Pope John XXIII in 1962, provided an
additional impetus for change. The Council called for Catholics
to "apply their Christian values to the problems of the world"
(Wald 2003, 252); in succeeding years Catholics worked on issues
such as poverty, nuclear proliferation, the status of the third
world, social justice, and civil rights. Gradually the Catholic voice
took a leftward turn, and the church took an active role in championing an array of progressive causes.

Meanwhile, the Catholic Church maintained a consistent
position on reproductive issues. The church has been a staunch
opponent of abortion rights. Well before the *Roe* decision, Pope
Paul VI articulated the Catholic Church's unequivocal opposition
to both abortion and artificial contraception in his 1968 encycli-
cal *Humanae Vitae*, which states that "each and every marital act
must of necessity retain its intrinsic relationship to the procreation
of human life."[28] Prior to 1973 the Catholic Church was active in
efforts to oppose liberalization of state-level abortion laws. The
leadership of the church in the United States focused their efforts

on lobbying elites, however. The bishops did not call for activism on the part of rank-and-file Catholics. This strategy changed after *Roe*. The activism of the church increased dramatically, and the bishops called on Catholics at the mass level to become engaged in the political conflicts surrounding this issue. "The bishops, in no uncertain terms, told Catholics that abortion was wrong and that they must organize to change the U.S. Constitution to make it illegal" (Fabrizio 2001, 86). In 1973 the Catholic bishops agreed that the church should engage in prolife activism in every state and that individual dioceses and the National Right to Life Committee should support these efforts. Two years later the bishops issued a statement titled "Pastoral Plan for Pro-Life Activities" that called for prolife activism in every congressional district (O'Connor 1996, 59; Wald 2003, 260).

Two things are worth noting. First, the post–Vatican II agenda is a prolife agenda, broadly construed. Thus, although the church opposes abortion, it also is an outspoken opponent of nuclear proliferation and the death penalty. Cardinal Bernardin was a singular advocate of balanced prolife advocacy, touching on all of these issues. In the 1980s, however, prominent church officials such as Cardinals Law of Boston and O'Connor of New York were joined by many other bishops in opposition to a balanced approach. They regarded abortion as the church's highest priority (Byrnes 1991, 1993).[29] Second, although the level of consensus within the church hierarchy on abortion is quite high, that level of consensus is not consistently reflected among American Catholics (Cook, Jelen, and Wilcox 1993). Lay Catholics do not like to be preached to on this issue; most lay Catholics support abortion rights under certain circumstances, and many Catholic voters vote Democrat (Wald 2003, 263).

In general, opposition to abortion provides an area of commonality with conservative Protestantism. On this issue, the Catholic Church and organizations of the Christian Right actively promote a public policy that is animated by religious traditionalism, even though the larger political agendas of the Catholic Church and the Christian Right are not necessarily consistent. There also is commonality on the issue of gay rights. In Massachusetts, the Catholic Church has been vocal and active in its opposition to gay marriage—even going so far as to encourage Catholics to communicate their "profound disappointment" to state legislators who did not oppose gay marriage.[30] The Catholic position on homosexuality is more nuanced, however, than the position of most conservative Protestant churches and organizations. *Persona Humana*, a church declaration on sexual ethics, states: "In the pastoral field, these homosexuals must certainly be treated with understanding and sustained in the hope of overcoming their personal difficulties and their inability to fit into society. Their culpability will be judged with prudence. But no pastoral method can be employed which would give moral justification to these acts on the grounds that they would be consonant with the condition of such people."[31]

As early as 1975 the Catholic Church made a distinction between homosexuals, who may or may not be responsible for what the church describes as their "affliction," and homosexual behavior, which the church regards as categorically improper and sinful. Thus, the Catholic position is to love the sinner but hate the sin. Since *Persona Humana* the church has reiterated its opposition to homosexual behavior, while teaching that gays and lesbians should be treated humanely. The church opposes gay marriage but does not consider homosexuals to be inherently evil and necessarily damned. Truth be told, not all evangelicals are "stridently" antigay either, but Catholics seem even more divided on this issue than Christian Right identifiers (Green 2000, 122)—perhaps because of nuanced Catholic teaching on homosexuality.

## CONCLUSION

Just as advocates of progressive sexuality have engaged in extensive political activism in support of their culturally imbued agenda, so have adherents of religious traditionalism. Because aspects of their cultures are inconsistent, the values of religious traditionalism and progressive sexuality often come into direct competition in the public square. In the 1970s and 1980s religious traditionalists framed their agenda as the work of God. This framework implies that one's opponents by definition are immoral and against God. It also has the effect of making compromise difficult. How can one compromise the will of God? These two factors made victory difficult to achieve (Wald 1997, 231–37). The rhetorical shifts of the Christian Coalition and the strategic shifts of the Christian Right as a whole in the 1990s probably helped put their issues on the agenda, however. The language of rights and freedoms and deemphasis of moral sectarian language articulated by Ralph Reed and others made the Christian Coalition and, by extension, its agenda mainstream and non-threatening.

In part because of these rhetorical and strategic shifts, there were small substantive and symbolic victories along the way. Abortions are legal, but they are restricted and not federally funded. Religious traditionalists have probably experienced important obstructionist victories, although they may be difficult to measure. For example, gays and lesbians have not been added to the 1964 Civil Rights Act as a protected class. Nevertheless, the movement has achieved few real victories. Long-time Republican Party loyalist Pat Buchanan was so disgusted by the lack of progress on social issues that he left the party and ran for president under the Reform Party banner in 2000. Even with unified Republican governance for most of 2001–2005, the culture of religious traditionalism has scored few real policy victories.

In a pluralist democratic system that provides minority rights, the legislative bias is on stasis. In this environment, one needs more than a majority to carry the day. As advocates of school prayer can attest, one needs a supermajority. Neither cultural group has accrued a supermajoritarian lock on Congress. Thus, Congress has become the institutional environment in which cultures compete, but do not win.

# 4

# Choosing Folkways

Stateways cannot change folkways.

—William Graham Sumner

Sumner's aphorism—often parsed as "You can't legislate morality"—endures as a common refrain in American politics. Yet even if stateways cannot change folkways, stateways certainly can institutionalize and legitimate folkways. The U.S. Congress does this every year—or, at least, it tries. Whereas in chapter 1 I provide a sense of how legislators perceive and cope with culturally significant moral issues (folkways), in this chapter I turn my attention to an analysis of legislator decision making on gay issues, reproductive policy, and school prayer, at two stages of the legislative process (stateways).

Legislators place these issues on the legislative agenda for a variety of reasons. For example, a legislator might submit legislation for symbolic purposes (Edelman 1964). Submission also may be simply an act of credit-claiming (Mayhew 1974), or it may be a combination of the two. A legislator may submit culturally significant legislation as a warning shot across the bow of the majority party or the administration to indicate that they care about a particular issue, or the legislator may regard introduction of such legislation, even when it appears futile, as an incremental step in advancing an important policy goal.[1] In short, submission of culturally significant legislation may be driven by the electoral connection or by an internal moral imperative. Its purpose may be symbolic—that is, to make a point; it also may be done in the expectation of changing policy.

On a more fundamental level, however, whatever the reason and purpose, submission of legislation on culturally significant issues is worthy of credit-claiming, symbolic posturing, and legislative advocacy because culture conflict at the structural level raises the salience of these issues. Reproductive policy, gay issues, and school prayer represent a larger cultural cleavage. Therefore, legislators care about them, and so do their constituents. One way or another, then, these issues make their way onto the legislative agenda. With that in mind, in this chapter I attempt to address two questions: How do legislators decide? And, with the understanding that these issues represent a cultural cleavage that draws on concerns about status (Tatalovich and Smith 2001), what sorts of considerations affect their decision making?

Scholars have tended to study cultural conflicts primarily at the state and local levels (Button, Rienzo, and Wald 1997; Fairbanks 1977; Haeberle 1996; Haider-Markel 1998; Meier 1994; Meier and Johnson 1990; Meier and McFarlane 1993; Mooney and Lee 1995, 1999, 2000; Morgan and Meier 1980; Schecter 2002; Sharpe 1999; Wald, Button, and Rienzo 1996, 2001)—and not without good reason. As a result of state police power, state legislatures often have been the hotbed of cultural and moral policymaking. In an analysis of midwestern state legislatures, Campbell (1980, 57) documents the state-level struggle over "cultural norms" and the "legitimization of values" going as far back as the mid-nineteenth century. As with contemporary moral issues, Campbell notes that legislative disagreement over social mores "was likely when no universal cultural standard existed to mold consensus" (Campbell 1980, 63).

The analysis in this chapter takes a different tack. I study decision making in the context of Congress—the national deliberative legislative body (for a few examples of national-level research, see Adams 1997; Haider-Markel 2001; Oldmixon 2002; Steiner 1983; Tatalovich and Schier 1993; Wattier and Tatalovich 1995). Given the increased national salience of issues such as abortion, gay marriage, and (to a lesser extent) school prayer, Congress has had to deliberate over these issues quite a bit in recent years, and this pattern is likely to continue well into the future (Huntington 1974).

## CULTURAL DECISION MAKING IN THE LEGISLATIVE ARENA

The collective wisdom of much of the aforementioned literature is that partisanship, ideology, and religion structure legislator decision making. This conclusion makes sense because these phenomena provide individuals with a cultural identity, behavioral norms, and group boundaries (see Wildavsky 1987). That is, party, religion, and ideology inform people about who they are, who they are not, and what behaviors are consistent with their identity and vision of society. These phenomena also inform individuals' perspectives toward cultural groups that are competing for legitimacy in the public space. Therefore, the importance of these phenomena is precisely what one should expect in assessing the politics of cultural conflict, and it is consistent with Jelen's (1997, 55) argument that "the economically based New Deal party system is giving way to a new alignment based primarily on cultural issues." Party, religion, and ideology all swing on the axis of that alignment.

My expectation in this analysis is that with cultural issues, legislators are motivated primarily by a desire to legitimate, through policy, a set of preferred social relationships. In decision making, legislators must be responsive to the cultural contours of their districts, given that these policies relate to high-salience, easy issues. Therefore, increasing levels of Democratic partisanship within a district should produce higher levels of support for progressive sexuality, whereas increasing levels of conservative Christianity should produce lower levels of support for progressive sexuality. At the same time, legislators have their own policy preferences and act in ways that promote them (Fenno 1973; Meier 1994). It is reasonable to expect, then, that on these issues they will try to legitimate their own personal moral order in law. Thus, Democratic Party legislator identification should produce higher levels of support for progressive sexuality, and religious and ideological conservatism among legislators should produce lower levels of support for progressive sexuality.

## QUANTIFYING CULTURE

The dependent variables are additive indices that tap the level of individual legislator support for progressive reproductive policies, progressive gay-related policies, and traditional prayer policies in each Congress from the 103rd through the 107th.[2] I used logit or ordered logit to measure support for religious traditionalism and progressive sexuality. I ran separate models for roll call votes and sponsorship/cosponsorship decisions, to assess decision making at different stages of the legislative process. High scores on the reproductive policy and gay indices models indicate high levels of support for progressive sexuality. High scores on the prayer indices indicate high levels of support for religious traditionalism. See Appendix B for a thorough explanation of how the dependent variables were generated.

## INDEPENDENT VARIABLES

I use partisanship, ideology, and religion to approximate culture because, conceptually, all three provide individuals with a set of norms and a vision of what social relationships are compatible with those norms. (Appendix B provides specification information.) Over the years, Democrats and Republicans have moved farther and farther apart on cultural issues, with Democrats embracing progressive sexuality and Republicans embracing religious traditionalism (Abramowitz 1995; Adams 1997; Campbell and Davidson 2000; Haider-Markel 1999a, 1999b, 2001; Haider-Markel and Meier 1996; Wald, Button, and Rienzo 1996; Norrander and Wilcox 2001). Consequently, legislator Democratic partisanship and higher levels of district Democratic partisanship are expected to produce higher levels of support for progressive sexuality. Poole and Rosenthal's (1991) DW-NOMINATE scores measure ideology. Because conservatism is associated with traditionalism and the stability of social norms, it is expected to depress support for progressive sexuality (Haider-Markel 1999b, 2001; Meier and McFarlane 1993; Peltzman 1984; Tatalovich and Schier 1993; Vinovskis 1980).

To a certain extent, I give religion pride of place in this analysis, with the assumption that religious values profoundly influence the crystallization and pursuit of goals. After all, "the religious motivation is one of the most compelling" reasons to violate self-interest as it traditionally is understood (Hertzke 1988, 10). Although partisanship, ideology, and religion all inform cultural norms, religion is particularly relevant to the cultural cleavage under consideration here. Religion is a specific kind of culture that is oriented toward the sacred, and its effect on social life tends to "give it an initially and primarily conservative thrust" (Smith 1996).[3] The culture of religious traditionalism is a good example of this dynamic. Supporters or adherents of religious traditionalism embrace a moral vision guided by what they perceive to be God's ordination of traditional families and sexual relations as correct, preferred, and worthy of honor.

It is no surprise, then, that religion appears to structure attitudes across an array of issues, including issues of sexual morality (Jelen 1997). Opponents of gay rights, for example, often are affiliated with conservative religious denominations that regard this issue as a threat to moral traditionalism and "proper" social values (Wilcox 2000). At the mass level, the relationship between public attitudes and religion and the relationship between community-level religious conservatism and support for religious traditionalism have been well documented. So has the relationship between religious identification and elite behavior (for examples, see Benson and Williams 1982; Duke and Johnson 1992; Fairbanks 1977; Fastnow, Grant, and Rudolf 1999; Green and Guth 1991; Guth et al. 1993; Haeberle 1996; Haider-Markel 1999a, 1999b, 2001; Haider-Markel, Joslyn, and Kniss 2000; Haider-Markel and Meier 1996; Meier and McFarlane 1993; Mooney and Lee 1995; Morgan and Meier 1980; Oldmixon 2002; Oldmixon, Rosenson, and Wald 2005; Smidt 2001; Tatalovich and Schier 1993; Wattier and Tatalovich 1995).

Legislator identification with a religiously conservative denomination and the presence of religiously conservative identifiers at the district level are expected to produce higher levels of support for religious traditionalism on the part of legislators across all three policy areas. This relationship is expected to hold for Roman Catholics with regard to reproductive policies. Because Catholic teaching on homosexuality tends to be more nuanced than fundamentalist and evangelical teaching, the relationship between Catholic identification and the proportion of Catholic identifiers in the district and opposition to gay rights is expected to be weak. School prayer is not a high-salience issue among Catholics, so the relationship between Catholic identification and support for school prayer should be negligible.

A few things are worth acknowledging about the specification of religion. First, I operationalize the religious contours of congressional districts with data from the Glenmary Research Center (Bradley et al. 1992). These data are widely used by religion and politics scholars, but in using them in this analysis I am reminded of Putnam, Leonardi, and Nanetti's (1994) characterization of their own data as "fragile." Reliable data that aggregates religious denominations geographically are difficult to come by. Although the Glenmary data arguably are the best available, they include a certain amount of error, "[g]iven that only established religious bodies are contacted, and given that different organizations have different criteria for counting members (Baptist churches, for example, only count baptized adults as members)" (Calfano, Oldmixon, and VonDoepp 2005). Nevertheless, they do provide a useful perspective on the distribution and strength of religious communities.

Second, the analysis uses categorical denominational classifications to measure legislator religion. I operationalize mass-level religion as the proportion of denominational adherents in each congressional district. Ideal measures of religion at either level would move beyond discrete denominational categories and ascertain the level of religious commitment on the part of individual adherents. There can be little doubt that one's level of commitment to those categorical groups surely affects the internalization of group norms, but such measures are profoundly difficult to quantify (Benson and Williams 1982). Guth and Kellstedt (2001) have made important initial strides in this area at the elite level, however, as have Yamane and Oldmixon (in press). It also is worth noting that in the legislative arena, Fastnow, Grant, and Rudolf (1999) have demonstrated the usefulness of categorical religious measures.

Denominational identification is a central component of an individual's religious identity, and it "remains a strong source of political attitudes and orientations" (Wilcox, Jelen, and Leege 1993, 89). Kellstedt and Green (1993) concede that measures of religious commitment are a crucial factor in fully understanding one's religious identity and its effect on politics, but they note that denominational identification encapsulates "differences in belief, practice, and commitment, even for individuals with minimal religiosity. Thus, we would expect denominational preference to influence political attitudes and behavior" (Kellstedt and Green 1993, 55). Denominational identification provides individuals with a group identity that is attached to "broader cultural traditions," and it is politically important for that reason (Kellstedt and Green, 65).

For analytical purposes, I collapse denominations into major religious traditions, or families, on the basis of religious beliefs, in a manner that is closely consistent with Kellstedt and Green (1993), Green and Guth (1991), and Roof and McKinney (1987). The groupings are as follows: (1) religious conservatives, which include evangelicals, fundamentalists, Mormons, and other non-traditional conservative denominations; (2) Roman Catholics; (3) mainline Protestants; (4) black Protestants; (5) liberal Protestants; (6) Jews; and (7) others. Table 4.1 provides a breakdown of the denominational families used in the analysis. As figure 4.1 demonstrates, the patterns of religious affiliation in the U.S. House of Representatives were fairly stable in the decade under consideration. Mainline Protestants constituted the largest family, followed by Catholics and then religious conservatives.

Because of the difficulty of deriving an accurate count of black Protestants from the Glenmary data, I use the percentage of African Americans in each district as a proxy.[4] The models also include a legislator race dummy, to isolate African American elites from white Catholics and Protestants. It is worth noting that Mormons and traditional conservative Protestants have different sources of scripture and make different eschatological assumptions. Indeed, there are "massive doctrinal differences" between Mormons and Assemblies of God, for example. I group them together in this instance, however, on the basis of each denomination's support for traditional norms on issues of sexual morality (Wald, Button, and Rienzo 1996, 1162). Nevertheless, it may not always be appropriate to group traditional and nontraditional conservatives together.

I include a variety of district-level socioeconomic and demographic variables in the analysis: per capita income, level of education, percentage of urban dwellers, and percentage of African Americans. These variables are generally employed when studying economic policies because they are indicators of policy demand (Wald, Button, and Rienzo 2001). They may affect the politics of cultural issues, however. For example, Cook, Jelen, and

**Table 4.1.** Classification of Religious Denominations

| Fundamentalists and Nontraditional Conservatives | | Mainline Protestants | Roman Catholics |
|---|---|---|---|
| | | | *Jewish* |
| American Baptist Convention | Adventists | American Lutheran Church | |
| Assemblies of God | Christian Scientist | Christian | *Liberal Protestants* |
| Baptist | Evangelical wings of | Disciples of Christ | Congregationalist |
| Baptist Missionary Association | mainline denominations | Lutheran Church in America | (United Church of |
| Brethren in Christ | (such as Missouri Synod | Episcopal Church | Christ) |
| Christian Missionary Alliance | Lutherans and Free | Presbyterian Church U.S.A. | Society of Friends |
| Christian Reformed Church | Methodists) | Protestant | (Quakers) |
| Church of God | Church of Jesus Christ | Reformed Church in America | Unitarian- |
| Church of Christ | of Latter-Day Saints | United Methodist Church | Universalist |
| Conservative Baptist Association | (Mormons) | | |
| Evangelical | Nazarene | *Black Protestants* | *Other small groups* |
| Independent Baptist | | Black Baptists | |
| Southern Baptist | | Black Pentecostals | |
| | | African Methodist Episcopal | |

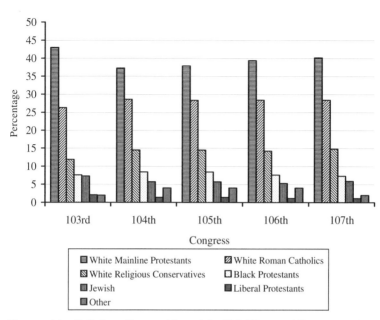

**Figure 4.1.** Religious Composition of the U.S. House of Representatives

Wilcox (1992) find that higher levels of socioeconomic status are associated with support for legalized abortions. In this analysis, higher levels of socioeconomic status at the district level are expected to produce higher levels of legislator support for progressive sexuality across all three policy areas.

I include the percentages of district residents classified as Latino and African American (black Protestants) to control for attitudinal and behavioral racial patterns that have been documented by various scholars (for an overview, see Conway 2000; Glynn et al. 1999; Erikson and Tedin 1995). Scholarship assessing the relationship between race and support for abortion rights provides mixed results. At the mass level, African Americans tend to be less supportive of abortion than whites (Cook, Jelen, and Wilcox 1992), but Combs and Welch (1982) and Wilcox (1990) suggest that the racial difference in abortion attitudes is diminishing. Hall and Ferree (1986) argue that the attitudinal gap endures. More generally, African Americans tend to have more left-leaning ideological tendencies than whites, although African Americans in the electorate tend to be more conservative on an array of moral issues. On gay issues, for example, African Americans tend to support equal opportunities but not necessarily civil rights protections (Button, Rienzo, and Wald 1997, ch. 3). In an analysis of elite behavior, Tatalovich and Schier (1993) find that legislators representing districts with high percentages of nonwhite populations are more supportive of prochoice policies. The same result is expected here. Higher levels of education usually are associated with higher levels of tolerance and liberalism (Cook 1997, 139). Thus, higher levels of education are expected to produce higher levels of support for progressive sexuality (Button, Rienzo, and Wald 1997, ch. 3; Cook, Jelen, and Wilcox 1992; Guth et al. 1993; Haider-Markel and Meier 1996; Haider-Markel, Joslyn, and Kniss 2000; Wald, Button, and Rienzo 1996; Wilcox and Wolpert 2000). Research suggests that the urban/rural variable will be particularly important with regard to cultural issues. Levels of urbanism are positively associated with support for gay rights at the state and local levels (Haeberle 1996; Wald, Button, and Rienzo 1996), and early gay communities in this country developed in urban areas after World War II (Button, Rienzo, and Wald 1997). Moreover, most abortion clinics are located, and therefore most abortions are performed, in urban areas (Henshaw and Van Vort 1994). Therefore, urban constituencies may be more supportive of permissive or progressive (depending on one's point of view) reproductive policies. District-level urbanism therefore is expected to produce higher levels of legislator support for progressive sexuality.

The models control for representative sex; representative sexual orientation is included in the analyses of gay issues. Scholars have documented systematic attitudinal differences between men and women on a variety of issues. Men and women do not differ with regard to all policy issues, but women have tended to express more liberal opinions about the role of government, the use of violence, and affirmative action (Conway, Steuernagel, and Ahern 1997; Erikson and Tedin 1995). In the aggregate, men tend to be less supportive than women of gay rights and marginally more supportive of abortion rights, although this relationship varies with age and employment status (Cook 1997; Cook, Jelen, and Wilcox 1992; Erikson and Tedin 1995). In the legislative arena, scholars find that women are generally more liberal than men, although this pattern may be narrowing (Vega and Firestone 1995; Welch 1985). Female legislators also tend to embrace policy priorities directed toward feminist issues (Bratton and Haynie 1999; Dodson and Carroll 1991; Swers 1998; Thomas 1994; Thomas and Welch 1991; Vega and Firestone 1995; but see also Reingold 2000). With regard to abortion, female legislators generally are more prochoice than their male colleagues (Oldmixon 2002; Schecter 2002).

In the same way, although sympathetic heterosexual legislators can provide good representation for gays and lesbians, gays and lesbians tend to make better representatives of their community's interests (Haider-Markel, Joslyn, and Kniss 2000). Because an accurate count of gays in Congress cannot be made, this research identifies gays who were "out" at the time or subsequently came out.[5] "Since the emergence of feminism (coupled with the politicization of orthodox Protestantism) drives the cultural cleavage examined" here, women legislators are expected to be more supportive of progressive sexuality than their male peers—though this observation is not meant to suggest that men cannot be supportive of feminist causes (Oldmixon 2002, 781).

One might assume that interest groups should not have much influence over legislator behavior with regard to high-profile moral issues, given the "easiness" of these issues and the constituent pressures that go along with it. Nevertheless, Haider-Markel (1999a, 1999b, 2001) demonstrates that interest group activity affects legislative voting even under the "suboptimal" conditions present with moral policymaking. Although the effect of interest group activity may be slight—and not necessarily causal—high levels of financial support from groups promoting progressive sexuality, such as the Human Rights Campaign and the National Abortion Rights Action League (NARAL), should be associated with higher levels of support for progressive sexuality. Similarly, high levels of financial support from groups promoting religious traditionalism, such as the Eagle Forum, should be associated with higher levels of support for religious traditionalism.

## REPRODUCTIVE POLITICS

Table 4.2 reports the results of the reproductive policy vote analysis, and table 4.3 reports the results for the reproductive policy sponsorship/cosponsorship analysis. The statistically significant chi-square statistic for each model in each Congress indicates that the models perform robustly and that the independent variables

**Table 4.2.** Analysis of Support for Progressive Reproductive Policy on Vote Indices

| Characteristics | Congress | | | | |
|---|---|---|---|---|---|
| | 103rd | 104th | 105th | 106th | 107th |
| **District** | | | | | |
| % College educated | .104 / (.000) | .161 / (.000) | .169 / (.000) | .106 / (.000) | .116 / (.000) |
| % Urban | -.007 / (.233) | -.010 / (.123) | -.018 / (.014) | -.011 / (.078) | -.006 / (.489) |
| % Democrats | .027 / (.198) | .051 / (.057) | .074 / (.012) | .072 / (.006) | .066 / (.027) |
| % African American | -.010 / (.506) | .007 / (.730) | -.009 / (.608) | -.001 / (.962) | -.020 / (.401) |
| % Latino | .019 / (.080) | .038 / (.003) | .055 / (.000) | .047 / (.000) | .045 / (.001) |
| % Religious conservative | -.015 / (.274) | -.068 / (.000) | -.074 / (.000) | -.058 / (.002) | -.029 / (.170) |
| % Roman Catholic | -.020 / (.123) | -.039 / (.012) | -.064 / (.000) | -.030 / (.040) | -.032 / (.069) |
| **Legislator** | | | | | |
| NARAL support | .001 / (.000) | .001 / (.000) | .001 / (.006) | .001 / (.001) | .002 / (.001) |
| Sex (Male = 1) | -1.170 / (.008) | -1.021 / (.032) | -1.015 / (.044) | -1.295 / (.004) | -1.313 / (.029) |
| Party (Democrat = 1) | 5.549 / (.000) | 5.884 / (.000) | 6.737 / (.000) | 4.563 / (.000) | 7.432 / (.000) |
| Ideology | -7.174 / (.000) | -6.580 / (.000) | -10.424 / (.000) | -6.387 / (.000) | -11.956 / (.000) |
| African American Protestants | -.034 / (.972) | -1.237 / (.390) | 1.226 / (.593) | -1.408 / (.201) | 1.2196 / (.426) |
| White religious conservative | -.502 / (.191) | -.197 / (.681) | -.631 / (.282) | -.491 / (.327) | -.045 / (.935) |
| White Roman Catholic | -.954 / (.002) | -1.436 / (.000) | -1.757 / (.000) | -1.742 / (.000) | -2.726 / (.000) |
| $N$ | 419 | 414 | 416 | 420 | 413 |
| Pseudo $R$ square | .4099 | .4579 | .5168 | .4776 | .6426 |
| Log likelihood | -330.92424 | -248.56779 | -230.13919 | -265.96494 | -140.41608 |
| LR chi² (14) | .4099 | 419.84 | 492.37 | 486.34 | 504.88 |

*Notes:* Chi² significant across all models. Entries are ordered logit coefficients; $p$ values in parentheses.

**Table 4.3.** Analysis of Support for Progressive Reproductive Policies on Sponsorship/Cosponsorship Indices

| Characteristics | 103rd | 104th | 105th | 106th[a] | 107th |
|---|---|---|---|---|---|
| | | | Congress | | |
| **District** | | | | | |
| % College educated | .099 / (.000) | .059 / (.014) | .098 / (.000) | | .038 / (.033) |
| % Urban | .003 / (.631) | .002 / (.765) | −.017 / (.049) | | .002 / (.788) |
| % Democrats | .012 / (.594) | .004 / (.873) | .048 / (.097) | | .027 / (.258) |
| % African American | −.004 / (.807) | .002 / (.936) | .009 / (.651) | | −.037 / (.045) |
| % Latino | .037 / (.001) | .013 / (.296) | .026 / (.069) | | .009 / (.459) |
| % Religious conservative | −.035 / (.084) | −.028 / (.174) | −.033 / (.246) | | −.031 / (.186) |
| % Roman Catholic | −.013 / (.376) | .010 / (.523) | −.024 / (.164) | | −.013 / (.359) |
| **Legislator** | | | | | |
| NARAL support | .001 / (.000) | .0004 / (.000) | .0003 / (.016) | | .00001 / (.815) |
| Sex (Male = 1) | −.501 / (.202) | −1.299 / (.001) | −1.017 / (.011) | | −.825 / (.024) |
| Party (Democrat = 1) | 4.481 / (.000) | 4.888 / (.000) | 4.427 / (.000) | | 4.601 / (.000) |
| Ideology | −4.909 / (.000) | −6.666 / (.000) | −5.351 / (.000) | | −5.452 / (.000) |
| African American Protestant | −.799 / (.301) | −1.571 / (.074) | −1.924 / (.022) | | −.387 / (.654) |
| White religious conservative | −.964 / (.104) | −.607 / (.407) | .009 / (.992) | | −.965 / (.199) |
| White Roman Catholic | −1.143 / (.001) | −1.350 / (.000) | −1.213 / (.005) | | −1.532 / (.000) |
| N | 423 | 428 | 430 | | 430 |
| Pseudo R square | .4314 | .4204 | .4059 | | .4101 |
| Log likelihood | −214.20977 | −172.90152 | −146.83237 | | −178.1995 |
| LR chi² (14) | 325.10 | 250.82 | 200.64 | | 247.82 |

*Notes:* Chi² significant across all models. Entries are ordered logit coefficients; *p* values in parentheses.
[a]No relevant items for analysis.

significantly increase one's ability to explain both voting and sponsorship/cosponsorship decision making on the issue. The coefficients indicate the direction of the relationship between each independent variable and dependent variable. The $p$ values in parentheses indicate the level of statistical significance each relationship achieves.

Note that across the voting and sponsorship/cosponsorship models, legislator partisanship emerges as a strong and significant predictor of legislator decision making. As expected, the direction of the coefficients indicates that legislator Democratic partisanship produces higher levels of support for progressive reproductive policies. The effect of district-level partisanship is highly significant in four of the five vote models, and the direction of the effect again is as expected. Higher levels of constituency Democratic identification produce higher levels of support for progressive reproductive policy. The direction of the effect is the same in the sponsorship/cosponsorship models, but the relationship achieves significance only in the 105th Congress.

Legislator ideology, district level of education, and NARAL support also emerge as strong and significant predictors in all of the reproductive policy models. Conservative ideology produces lower levels of support for progressive policy. Higher levels of constituent educational attainment produce higher levels of legislator support for progressive reproductive policy, and legislators receiving higher levels of support from NARAL support progressive reproductive policy at higher levels than their peers. Finally, it is important to note that as expected, legislator gender produces a significant and negative effect on the dependent variable in all but one of the models. In other words, controlling for the "usual suspects" (party, ideology, etc.), female legislators support progressive reproductive policies at higher levels than their male colleagues.

Very little can be said about the effect of African American constituencies on legislator behavior. The direction of the relationship appears to vary, and it is significant in only one of the models. Given the scholarly contention that the attitudinal gap between African Americans and whites on abortion is diminishing, perhaps the lack of significance makes sense. In contrast, the proportion of Latino constituents produces a strongly significant effect on legislator behavior. Larger Latino constituencies produce higher levels of support for progressive reproductive policy. This relationship is significant in all of the vote models and two of the four sponsorship/cosponsorship models. The dynamics of this relationship are particularly interesting, given that Latinos are such a devoutly Catholic ethnic group. They have tended to be loyal Democratic voters. In the 2004 presidential election, however, the Bush campaign aggressively (and smartly) courted Latino voters and captured about 44 percent of their vote. Postelection analysis credits the strong Republican showing to President Bush's ability to connect with the strong family values sentiment that is prevalent in the Latino community.[6] The issues of gay marriage and abortion, in particular, are thought to have brought Latinos to Bush. Nevertheless, this analysis indicates that strongly Latino constituencies tend to have strongly prochoice representatives.

The effect of religion in these models presents interesting results. When the Republicans took control of the legislative branch in the 104th Congress, the number of abortion-related roll calls increased dramatically, and over the succeeding eight years the House voted on a battery of high-salience abortion issues—the partial-birth abortion ban among them. Reproductive policy moved to the forefront of the legislative agenda. As a result, district levels of religious conservatism and Catholicism emerged as strong and significant predictors of legislator decision making in the voting models. The direction of the coefficients indicates that legislators with large religiously conservative or Catholic constituencies supported progressive reproductive policy at lower levels than their peers. These results are as expected. Again, reproductive policy often is identified as one element of the issues triune for conservative Christians (homosexuality and prayer in school being the other two issues), and the Catholic Church has been among the most outspoken opponents of abortion in the post-*Roe* era.

In that context, the effect of legislator religious identification comes as a bit of a surprise. In both the voting and the sponsorship/cosponsorship models, the results indicate that at significant levels Catholic legislators support progressive reproductive policy at lower levels than their non-Catholic colleagues. In all models there appears to be a consistent Catholic effect. Legislator identification as a religious conservative, however, does not seem to have a significant impact on abortion-related decision making.

Although legislators appear to be responsive to religiously conservative constituencies, personal identification as a religious conservative does not produce a significant effect on either voting or sponsorship/cosponsorship decisions. Also, district-level religion does not appear to have a pronounced effect on reproductive policy sponsorship/cosponsorship decisions. Because these decisions are lower profile than roll calls, it is not entirely surprising that district-level forces fail to pack a significant analytical punch.

## GAY ISSUES

Table 4.4 reports the results of the gay issues vote analysis, and table 4.5 reports the results for the gay issues sponsorship/ cosponsorship analysis. Again, the statistically significant chi-square statistic for each model in each Congress indicates that the models perform robustly and that the independent variables significantly increase one's ability to explain both voting and sponsorship cosponsorship decision making on the issue. The coefficients indicate the direction of the relationship between each independent variable and dependent variable. The $p$ values in parentheses indicate the level of statistical significance each relationship achieves.

Note that across all models, ideology, legislator partisanship, and level of Human Rights Campaign (HRC) contributions emerge as strong and significant predictors of legislator decision making. The negative coefficients indicate that ideological conservatism produces lowers levels of support for gay issues, regardless of whether legislators are voting or making sponsorship/ cosponsorship decisions. The effect of legislator partisanship on support for gay issues is positive and statistically significant across all models, indicating that legislator Democratic partisanship produces higher levels of support for progressive gay policies. In the sponsorship/cosponsorship models, district-level partisanship is highly significant in four Congresses and approaches significance in a fifth, again indicating that higher levels of district-level Democratic partisanship produce legislator support for progressive gay policies. The coefficients for HRC contributions indicate that there is a positive and statistically significant relationship between interest group electoral support and support for gay rights. Higher contribution levels are associated with higher levels of legislator support for gay issues. As in

**Table 4.4.** Analysis of Support for Progressive Gay Policies on Vote Indices

| Characteristics | Congress | | | | |
|---|---|---|---|---|---|
| | 103rd | 104th | 105th | 106th | 107th |
| **District** | | | | | |
| % College educated | .090 / (.001) | .028 / (.245) | -.014 / (.620) | .035 / (.134) | .037 / (.063) |
| % Urban | .001 / (.898) | .019 / (.004) | .020 / (.005) | .003 / (.612) | .005 / (.427) |
| % Democrats | .032 / (.215) | .085 / (.001) | .033 / (.150) | -.016 / (.534) | .010 / (.669) |
| % African American | -.039 / (.044) | -.047 / (.023) | -.027 / (.162) | -.001 / (.941) | -.021 / (.248) |
| % Latino | .017 / (.159) | .006 / (.604) | .028 / (.032) | .016 / (.221) | .020 / (.076) |
| % Religious conservative | -.069 / (.000) | -.068 / (.001) | -.079 / (.000) | -.057 / (.015) | -.067 / (.000) |
| % Roman Catholic | -.029 / (.054) | -.007 / (.641) | -.043 / (.010) | -.002 / (.888) | -.028 / (.057) |
| **Legislator** | | | | | |
| HRC support | .001 / (.000) | .0002 / (.005) | .001 / (.003) | .0002 / (.003) | .0003 / (.000) |
| Sex (Male = 1) | -.079 / (.873) | -.785 / (.051) | -.491 / (.347) | -.246 / (.641) | -.123 / (.786) |
| Gay/Lesbian (Out = 1) | 3.293 / (.002) | 5.523 / (.000) | 29.907 / (1.000) | .207 / (.919) | -.039 / (.984) |
| Party (Democrat = 1) | 5.718 / (.000) | 5.005 / (.000) | 6.061 / (.000) | 9.065 / (.000) | 7.389 / (.000) |
| Ideology | -7.423 / (.000) | -5.639 / (.000) | -8.678 / (.000) | -15.033 / (.000) | -7.986 / (.000) |
| African American Protestant | .789 / (.435) | .5136 / (.607) | -1.013 / (.442) | -.5175 / (.670) | -.669 / (.491) |
| White religious conservative | -1.248 / (.043) | -.658 / (.271) | -.203 / (.678) | -.075 / (.895) | .475 / (.327) |
| White Roman Catholic | -.590 / (.092) | -.844 / (.013) | -.707 / (.053) | -.266 / (.492) | -.573 / (.113) |
| $N$ | 421 | 417 | 424 | 421 | 420 |
| Pseudo $R$ square | .5314 | .5491 | .5973 | .6463 | .6017 |
| Log likelihood | -195.45771 | -181.33508 | -178.17451 | -153.88051 | -178.43265 |
| LR chi$^2$ (15) | 443.29 | 441.60 | 528.63 | 562.32 | 538.99 |

*Notes:* Chi$^2$ significant across all models. Entries are ordered logit coefficients; $p$ values in parentheses.

**Table 4.5.** Analysis of Support for Progressive Gay Policies on Sponsorship/Cosponsorship Indices

| Characteristics | 103rd | 104th | 105th | 106th | 107th |
|---|---|---|---|---|---|
| | | | Congress | | |
| **District** | | | | | |
| % College educated | .074 / (.003) | .140 / (.002) | .052 / (.103) | .078 / (.000) | .069 / (.001) |
| % Urban | .008 / (.229) | .010 / (.304) | .012 / (.147) | .010 / (.153) | .005 / (.502) |
| % Democrats | .076 / (.004) | .065 / (.140) | .112 / (.003) | .128 / (.000) | .093 / (.000) |
| % African American | -.038 / (.052) | -.035 / (.228) | -.037 / (.125) | -.062 / (.004) | -.027 / (.194) |
| % Latino | -.010 / (.417) | .030 / (.098) | -.013 / (.362) | -.005 / (.688) | .017 / (.157) |
| % Religious conservative | -.046 / (.036) | -.134 / (.000) | -.046 / (.111) | -.077 / (.009) | -.053 / (.014) |
| % Roman Catholic | .013 / (.382) | -.035 / (.123) | .008 / (.642) | -.020 / (.216) | -.017 / (.243) |
| **Legislator** | | | | | |
| HRC support | .0002 / (.000) | .0002 / (.068) | .001 / (.000) | .0002 / (.000) | .0002 / (.000) |
| Sex (Male = 1) | -.259 / (.549) | -.922 / (.156) | -1.168 / (.047) | -.2672 / (.523) | -.331 / (.437) |
| Gay/Lesbian (Out = 1) | 2.100 / (.097) | —a | 35.496 / (.000) | 3.495 / (.162) | 36.322 / (1.000) |
| Party (Democrat = 1) | 4.519 / (.000) | 6.872 / (.000) | 5.031 / (.000) | 4.641 / (.000) | 7.314 / (.000) |
| Ideology | -4.984 / (.000) | -7.927 / (.000) | 7.111 / (.000) | -5.374 / (.000) | -9.459 / (.000) |
| African American Protestant | -.977 / (.259) | -.005 / (.998) | 1.528 / (.285) | -.154 / (.877) | -1.229 / (.254) |
| White religious conservative | -1.595 / (.056) | -.772 / (.425) | .532 / (.466) | -.635 / (.419) | -.500 / (.428) |
| White Roman Catholic | -.610 / (.093) | -.395 / (.433) | -.570 / (.187) | -.415 / (.277) | -.175 / (.632) |
| Constant | — | -8.340 / (.000) | — | — | — |
| N | 423 | 424 | 425 | 423 | 430 |
| Pseudo R square | .04730 | .6998 | .6612 | .6211 | .6550 |
| Log likelihood | -187.64824 | -78.930066 | -125.03655 | -139.44644 | -152.07559 |
| LR chi² (15) | 336.81 | 368.03 | 488.14 | 457.19 | 577.32 |

*Notes:* Chi² significant across all models. Entries are ordered logit coefficients; logit is used in 104th Congress; *p* values in parentheses.
aThis variable was dropped from the model because it perfectly predicted variation in the dependent variable.

the reproductive policy models, this finding does not suggest that campaign donations *cause* higher levels of support for gay issues. Perhaps lobbyists do buy votes and access with their donations. Even if that is the case sometimes or generally, it probably is not the case with a high-salience, nontechnical, easy issue such as gay rights. What these findings do suggest is that the HRC (like NARAL, with respect to progressive reproductive policy) works very hard to identify and elect representatives whose stated preference is for gay rights.

As in the reproductive policy models, district-level religious conservatism and support for progressive gay policies are negatively related. This relationship achieves significance in all of the vote models and four of the sponsorship/cosponsorship models. The proportion of Catholics at the district level also is negatively related to support for progressive gay policies, but the relationship is significant in only three of the five vote models. There is no statistically significant relationship between district Catholicism and decision making in the sponsorship/cosponsorship models. As noted in chapter 3, the Catholic Church speaks loudly in opposition to gay marriage but the church articulates a more nuanced position on gay issues than many religiously conservative churches. Having Catholics in one's district does not necessarily produce lower levels of legislator support for gay issues because Catholics may not be receiving clear messages from their priests and bishops (Calfano and Oldmixon 2005). Therefore, they may not be sending clear messages to their legislators. Even if the church sends clear messages to the flock, the Catholic effect is likely to wax and wane depending on the political opportunity structure presented by the larger terms of the political debate (Byrnes 1991, 1993). In any case, the church is unequivocal in its opposition to abortion, birth control, and progressive reproductive policy. The church's position on gay issues is not so clear, and the inconsistent Catholic effect may speak to that lack of consistency.

As in the reproductive policy models, legislator identification as a religious conservative does not seem to have a robust impact on legislator decision making. In both the voting and the sponsorship/cosponsorship models, the relationship is significant only in the 103rd Congress. The anomalous result for the 103rd Congress suggests that the salience of this issue may have been ginned up among congressional religious conservatives in the first Congress of the Clinton administration. Candidate Clinton had sent progressive signals on gay issues. After his inauguration, Congress quickly held hearings on the possibility of lifting the ban on gays in the military. Religious conservatives were up on their haunches, and progressives were back on their heels. After that initial skirmish, the relationship lost significance. Again, legislators appear to be responsive to religious conservatives in their districts, but individual identification as a religious conservative does not have a measurable effect on decision making pertaining to gay issues. Legislator identification as Catholic, however, has a significant and negative impact on decision making in three of the five vote models.

The effect of religion presents an interesting puzzle. As in the reproductive policy models, there is a consistent Catholic effect. Personal religiosity and grassroots Catholicism act in concert on this issue, for the most part. That is, legislator identification as Catholic and the presence of Catholic communities produce independent negative effects on support for progressive sexuality, although the level of statistical significance of these relationships varies. At the same time, legislator identification as a religious conservative has little measurable effect on decision making, but district-level religious conservatism does have an effect. Opposition to gay rights has been a major agenda item for many Christian Right groups for about thirty years (Wilcox 2000). It has been their rallying cry. Therefore it comes as no surprise that as the salience of this issue increased in the 1990s with the battles over gays in the military and same-sex marriage, risk-adverse legislators responded to grassroots religious conservatism. What is surprising is that legislator religious conservatism is so muted in its effect when the other variables are controlled for. To the extent that there is an imperative rooted in religious conservatism to legitimate a particular moral order, it comes from the district—not from within.

The attempt to test for the effect of gay/lesbian identification on support for gay issues produced mixed results. The relationship between gay identification and support for progressive gay policies is positive, for the most part. It is significant in the 103rd and 104th Congress vote models. In the sponsorship/cosponsorship models, the relationship is highly significant in the 105th Congress. The variable was dropped from the 104th Congress model because it was a perfect predictor of decision making. Although this finding suggests that for gays and lesbians there is some value to "descriptive" representation beyond the symbolic element, this argument could not be tested as such. The effect of gay identification in the early models comes as no surprise, given the issues on the table—employment nondiscrimination and hate crimes, for example. The loss of significance in the later models may be a measurement artifact. The number of openly gay legislators in the House diminished during the decade this research explores. The number was never very high, but it went from five in the 103rd Congress to four in the 104th Congress, two in the 105th Congress, and then back to three in the 106th and 107th Congresses (Reps. Baldwin, Frank, and Kolbe). With Reps. Studds, Gunderson, and Huffington gone, however, a meaningful test of gay/lesbian identification became impossible.

## SCHOOL PRAYER

Table 4.6 reports the results of the prayer vote analysis, and table 4.7 reports the results for the school prayer sponsorship/cosponsorship analysis. Again, the statistically significant chi-square statistic for each model in each Congress indicates that the models perform robustly and that the independent variables significantly increase one's ability to explain both voting and sponsorship/cosponsorship decision making on this issue. The coefficients indicate the direction of the relationship between each independent variable and dependent variable. The $p$ values in parentheses indicate the level of statistical significance each relationship achieves.

The results reported in tables 4.6 and 4.7 suggest that decision making on school prayer issues is structured by party and ideology. As one would expect, Democratic legislators are less supportive of expanding school prayer than their Republican colleagues, and ideological conservatism produces support for religious traditionalism. District level of education is negatively associated with support for religious traditionalism, although the relationship is only intermittently significant. The effect of religion at either elite or district level is muted. Religiously conservative constituencies promote legislator support for school prayer. The relationship is significant in three of the four sponsorship/cosponsorship models. In the vote models, however, it is significant only in the 105th Congress. In the vote models, large Catholic

**Table 4.6.** Analysis of Support for School/Public Prayer on Vote Indices

| Characteristics | Congress | | | | |
| --- | --- | --- | --- | --- | --- |
| | 103rd | 104th[a] | 105th | 106th | 107th[a] |
| **District** | | | | | |
| % College educated | -.043 / (.054) | | -.008 / (.809) | -.051 / (.007) | |
| % Urban | .0004 / (.947) | | -.010 / (.228) | -.0002 / (.978) | |
| % Democrats | -.023 / (.270) | | -.049 / (.120) | -.025 / (.290) | |
| % African American | .036 / (.029) | | .005 / (.843) | -.019 / (.287) | |
| % Latino | .001 / (.932) | | .015 / (.350) | -.008 / (.454) | |
| % Religious conservative | .017 / (.289) | | .064 / (.016) | -.003 / (.901) | |
| % Roman Catholic | -.010 / (.460) | | -.005 / (.798) | -.027 / (.067) | |
| **Legislator** | | | | | |
| Eagle Forum support | .001 / (.073) | | -.001 / (.003) | .149 / (1.000) | |
| Sex (Male = 1) | .322 / (.389) | | .706 / (.230) | .295 / (.465) | |
| Party (Democrat = 1) | -6.505 / (.000) | | -6.542 / (.000) | -7.618 / (.000) | |
| Ideology | 8.196 / (.000) | | 8.643 / (.000) | 10.024 / (.000) | |
| African American Protestant | -.108 / (.888) | | 3.912 / (.006) | -.191 / (.847) | |
| White religious conservative | .514 / (.331) | | .415 / (.529) | -.126 / (.821) | |
| White Roman Catholic | .554 / (.083) | | 1.242 / (.008) | .210 / (.542) | |
| $N$ | 420 | | 423 | 422 | |
| Pseudo $R$ square | .4561 | | .5968 | .5990 | |
| Log likelihood | -222.16544 | | -130.49381 | -174.20212 | |
| LR chi² (14) | 372.61 | | 386.24 | 520.38 | |

*Notes:* Chi² significant across all models. Entries are ordered logit coefficients; $p$ values in parentheses.
[a] There were no relevant votes in the 104th and 107th Congresses.

**Table 4.7.** Analysis of Support for School/Public Prayer on Sponsorship/Cosponsorship Indices

| Characteristics | Congress | | | | |
|---|---|---|---|---|---|
| | 103rd | 104th | 105th[a] | 106th | 107th |
| **District** | | | | | |
| % College educated | -.033 / (.362) | -.027 / (.361) | | -.048 / (.106) | -.017 / (.495) |
| % Urban | -.002 / (.835) | -.014 / (.039) | | -.010 / (.188) | -.002 / (.801) |
| % Democrats | -.043 / (.177) | -.029 / (.261) | | -.012 / (.654) | -.067 / (.007) |
| % African American | .033 / (.175) | .050 / (.009) | | .024 / (.151) | .041 / (.020) |
| % Latino | -.005 / (.772) | .010 / (.493) | | -.016 / (.524) | -.085 / (.010) |
| % Religious conservative | .038 / (.045) | .034 / (.025) | | .010 / (.540) | .032 / (.052) |
| % Roman Catholic | .030 / (.138) | .010 / (.544) | | -.027 / (.219) | .013 / (.506) |
| **Legislator** | | | | | |
| Eagle Forum support | .0002 / (.471) | .0001 / (.521) | | -.0001 / (.731) | .0001 / (.514) |
| Sex (Male = 1) | .197 / (.806) | .930 / (.172) | | .490 / (.563) | .588 / (.478) |
| Party (Democrat = 1) | -3.420 / (.000) | -4.305 / (.000) | | -3.034 / (.000) | -3.246 / (.000) |
| Ideology | 3.249 / (.012) | 4.767 / (.000) | | 4.289 / (.000) | 3.557 / (.001) |
| African American Protestant | 1.878 / (.248) | .101 / (.930) | | .596 / (.585) | 1.150 / (.350) |
| White religious conservative | .189 / (.687) | .231 / (.541) | | .645 / (.100) | .317 / (.416) |
| White Roman Catholic | .214 / (.635) | .444 / (.229) | | .397 / (.373) | .184 / (.663) |
| Constant | -.317 / (.854) | .440 / (.765) | | .552 / (.727) | 1.205 / (.416) |
| N | 423 | 428 | | 425 | 430 |
| Pseudo R square | .2573 | .3598 | | .3169 | .3759 |
| Log likelihood | -112.64023 | -157.49863 | | -127.64638 | -133.41706 |
| LR chi2(14) | 78.05 | 177.04 | | 118.43 | 160.72 |

*Notes*: Chi$^2$ significant across all models. Entries are logit coefficients; $p$ values in parentheses.
[a]No relevant items for analysis.

137

populations produce the opposite result, but this relationship is only significant in the 106th Congress. In both the vote and sponsorship/cosponsorship analyses, legislator identification as a religious conservative is positively associated with support for school prayer in all but one model. The relationship is insignificant in all but one model, however, and even then the relationship is barely significant.

The relationship between Catholic identification and support for school prayer was expected to be negligible because school prayer has never been high on the Catholic policy agenda; if anything, the issue has produced antagonism between Catholics and Protestants. To the extent that a Catholic effect emerged, it was expected to be negative. The effect of district-level Catholic constituencies in the vote analyses lends cautious support to that expectation. Legislator Catholic identification runs against expectation, however. Indeed, Catholic identification produces higher levels of support for school prayer. This relationship achieves significance in two of the three vote models. Although these results are unexpected, they are consistent with the reproductive policy and gay issues analyses. Again, Catholic identification enhances support for religious traditionalism, whereas religious conservative identification fails to pack an analytical punch.

Many observers consider school prayer to be among the conservative Christian triune of important issues. The importance of district religious conservatism in the sponsorship/cosponsorship models speaks to the importance Christian conservatives place on religion in schools. A more thorough analysis of school prayer and Christian conservative activism, however, probably should focus on state and local government or perhaps the courts. Given the role that state and local governments play in education policy, Congress is less likely to be the proper arena for conflict in this area than it is for reproductive policy or homosexuality. This study confines itself to congressional policymaking, but the action on prayer may be happening somewhere else, which may explain why there seems to be less analytical fodder.

## ASSESSING CULTURAL DECISION MAKING

Whatever else the preceding analyses demonstrate, reproductive policy, gay issues, and school prayer are partisan and ideological conflicts. The coalitions of support and opposition surrounding these issues clearly overlap partisan and ideological coalitions in the House of Representatives. Nevertheless, religious phenomena clearly and demonstrably inform legislator decision making, although the effect is more nuanced. A few observations in particular are worth noting. First, there appears to be a consistent Catholic effect on decision making. Legislator identification as Catholic and the presence of Catholic constituencies produce higher levels of support for religious traditionalism on the part of elites. This finding suggests several possibilities.

The Catholic Church seems to do an excellent job of instilling in the faithful the social teachings of the church. Perhaps congregational life allows for a contagion effect, or perhaps Catholic congregations are self-selecting communities that share a common vision. Perhaps the hierarchical Catholic infrastructure facilitates mobilization and communication of group preferences to the faithful. Of course, in this study the legislator is the unit of analysis. It would be inappropriate to draw conclusions about mass-level Catholic behavior on the basis of these findings. Nevertheless, these possibilities warrant further attention. What can be said, however, is that district and elite Catholicism work in concert. Moreover, as far as elite behavior is concerned, Catholic identification provides individuals with a consistent and powerful set of norms. Are Catholic legislators monolithically prolife, anti–gay rights, and pro–school prayer? Of course not. Even controlling for party and ideology, however, there does seem to be a consistent and unmistakable Catholic effect on legislator decision making, and it runs in the direction of traditionalism.

Second, although religious conservatism also produces support for religious traditionalism, the sole locus of the effect appears to be at the district level. Legislators are indeed responsive to large religiously conservative constituencies. The relationship achieves significance in all of the gay rights roll call models, three of the reproductive policy roll call models, and one of the school prayer roll call models. As with district-level Catholicism, religious conservatives appear to have a good ground game. The various churches and denominations presumably do a good job of socializing members in social teachings that are consistent with conservative Christianity. Even absent an official hierarchy, these churches and denominations are ripe for culturally motivated mobilization.[7] This is conjecture, but these possibilities are notable. The point is that conservative Christians are a potent political force, and their numbers, aggregated by congressional district, appear to influence what legislators do. In contrast, legislator identification as a religious conservative does not seem to have a measurable effect. The relationship between legislator religious conservatism and religious traditionalism is positive but not statistically significant. Having noted the significance of legislator Catholic identification and the nonsignificance of legislator religious conservative identification, it is worth noting that the analyses may be comparing unlike things. The Catholic Church is a single, highly institutionalized denomination. The term *religious conservative* refers to a family of Protestant denominations that may or may not be institutionalized and do not necessarily adhere to the same religious doctrines across the board. Although collapsing Protestant denominations makes analytical sense, this approach may explain the lack of a significant result at the elite level. The alternative interpretation is that individual Catholics are guided by the principles of their faith, whereas conservative Protestants are not. This conclusion seems absurd on its face.

Third, the performance of the religion variables in the roll call models versus the sponsorship/cosponsorship models merits comment. In the reproductive policy vote analyses, district-level religious conservatism and Catholicism produce significant effects on the dependent variable. Even in models where the effects are not significant, the $p$ values are reasonably low—under .200, in two instances. In the sponsorship/cosponsorship models, both district religious indicators lose significance—with the exception of religious conservatism in the 103rd Congress. There is a similar pattern in the gay rights analyses, although the effect is not as dramatic and seems to be contained to the import of Catholic constituencies. The performance of Catholic elite identification also varies. In the school prayer and gay rights vote analyses it tends to produce significant effects on the dependent variable, but in the sponsorship/cosponsorship models it tends not to. Taken as a whole, these findings suggest that sponsorship and cosponsorship decisions may not be as culturally charged or culturally informed as roll call votes.

Voting and sponsorship/cosponsorship decisions are qualitatively different from one another. In both cases, legislators have the opportunity to express preferences. The stakes are higher with voting, however. The consequences for preference expression in this context may be very real. That is, votes may result in substantive policy formation. When the issue at hand draws on cultural considerations, and when the stakes are at their highest, legislators are attentive to phenomena that reflect cultural values—party, ideology, and religion. The stakes for sponsoring and cosponsoring legislation are lower. There is less *there* there. Legislators therefore do not need to make sponsorship/cosponsorship decisions with an eye toward cultural aggrandizement.

This observation is especially true if culturally significant legislation makes it to the House floor. Assuming that the majority party allows access to the floor—that is, allows votes—on these issues, legislators have ample opportunities to claim credit, signal key constituency groups, or simply pursue their own agendas. They do not need to make an effort to use different aspects of the legislative process, such as sponsoring and cosponsoring, in this regard. The results of the reproductive policy analysis are consistent with this argument. Under Republican control of the House of Representatives in the 104th Congress, the number of reproductive rights bills and amendments increased dramatically from the number in the 103rd Congress. This increase gave legislators multiple opportunities to demonstrate their prolife or prochoice stripes. If opportunities for voting are limited, however, or if cultural bills are denied access to the floor, we might expect vulnerable members to demonstrate aggressive legislative activity and minority members to advocate for their preferred policy outcomes by using the sponsorship/cosponsorship process (Kroger 2003).

The disparate influence of interest group support also merits attention. At a general level, the analyses support the argument that attentive interest groups play a role in the policy process. The relationship between campaign giving and legislator decision making is significant, though one hesitates to say that it is directly causal. The effect of political action committee giving probably takes place before a single vote is cast or bill introduced. The Eagle Forum, the HRC, and NARAL are organizations that advocate for particular cultural visions. They have political committee arms that attempt to elect legislators whose views are consistent with theirs. In electing sympathetic legislators, they attempt to create a legislative environment in which their vision can be affirmed by statute. At the very least, they can hope to create a bulwark against competing cultural groups. Nevertheless, the effect of campaign giving by the Eagle Forum, the HRC, and NARAL varies. The influence of NARAL support is highly significant in eight of nine reproductive policy models. HRC support is significant in all of the gay issues models. Eagle Forum support is significant in none of the prayer sponsorship/cosponsorship models and two of the three vote models. Bizarrely, Eagle Forum support produced *lower* levels of support for religious traditionalism in the 105th Congress vote model. Two possible explanations stand out. First, as table 4.8 suggests, the Eagle Forum distributed fewer resources to winning candidates at the congressional level. In each Congress, they are outstripped by the HRC and NARAL. In the 107th Congress, for example, the HRC gave more than ten times as much to winning congressional candidates as the Eagle Forum. With fewer and smaller checks to write, perhaps the Eagle Forum bought itself less influence.

**Table 4.8.**  Mean Campaign Contributions to Winning Congressional Candidates

| Election Cycle | Donation Source | | |
|---|---|---|---|
| | **HRC** | **NARAL** | **Eagle Forum** |
| 103rd Congress | $816.10 | $470.71 | $133.95 |
| | *$356,637* | *$205,537* | *$58,537* |
| 104th Congress | $678.41 | $422.25 | $247.40 |
| | *$298,500* | *$185,788* | *$108,857* |
| 105th Congress | $981.63 | $311.64 | $152.27 |
| | *$432,900* | *$146,255* | *$67,150* |
| 106th Congress | $1,342.66 | $509.89 | $63.06 |
| | *$585,400* | *$222,312* | *$27,496* |
| 107th Congress | $1,483.90 | $648.89 | $105.68 |
| | *$652,915* | *$285,513* | *$46,500* |

*Note:* Total donations to winning congressional candidates in italics.
*Source:* The Center for Responsive Politics.

Second, the HRC and NARAL are single-issue interest groups. They have a laser-like focus on gay issues and reproductive policy, respectively, and base their giving on those issues alone. The Eagle Forum is more generally a "profamily" group. In that sense, its influence may be more diluted. The gay and reproductive policy models were rerun substituting Eagle Forum support for NARAL and HRC support. In theory, Eagle Forum support should be significant, but the effect should run in the opposite direction. Eagle Forum support performed inconsistently in these models. The direction of the relationship was negative, as we would expect, but the relationship achieved significance only some of the time. Again, this finding suggests that as a group with an expansive agenda and perhaps more limited resources to expend at the national level, the Eagle Forum's effect on decision making is less potent.

## CONCLUSION

Theories of cultural conflict suggest that such conflict represents a style of argumentation in which policy issues take on symbolic significance and therefore are framed as nonnegotiable by legislators and activists. As chapter 1 demonstrates, legislators perceive culturally based cleavages surrounding certain policy issues, and they further concede that the presence of culture framing complicates legislative decision making. In this chapter I analyze legislator decision making on issues that are commonly considered exemplars of the conflict between religious traditionalism and progressive sexuality. The expectation around which the analyses were designed and conducted is that decision making should be influenced by phenomena that tap cultural identify— party, ideology, and religion. The findings comport with this expectation. Phenomena that approximate cultural progressivity produce higher levels of support for progressive reproductive policy and gay rights and diminish support for traditionalistic school prayer policy. Obviously, indicators of religious traditionalism produce the opposite result.

Elite partisanship and ideology, in particular, perform robustly. Party and ideology are the proverbial usual suspects of congressional scholarship, however. Time and again they are the single best predictors of legislative behavior regardless of policy domain—which speaks to the utility of cartel theory (Cox and McCubbins 1993). The real test of the cultural lens is the performance of religion in these models. Ultimately, the religion indicators do not disappoint. Controlling for party, ideology, and other factors, district and elite religion contribute to scholarly understanding of legislator decision making on these issues. When legislators cast votes on abortion, gay rights, and school prayer, they reference the values of their own denominational affiliation, the denominational contours of their constituencies, or both. Religion does not produce consistent effects across the board, however. The effect varies by policy issue and by stage in the legislative process, yet there is an unmistakable religious dimension to legislative politics of these issues.

# 5

# Managing Morality

You can't outlaw sin. You're always going to have sin. So, you
know, it's just difficult to deal with. And I guess you could go
through the state and on the federal level, we try to.
                                    —Democratic legislator

I now turn my attention to *how* the House of Representatives
tries to "outlaw sin," focusing in particular on the role
leaders play in managing the politics of cultural issues. Individual legislators are free to pursue their own goals in the foreground, but leaders must concern themselves with larger issues
of governance. Their goals are collective. Moreover, although legislators are continually forced to choose between dyadic alternatives, leadership shapes these alternatives (Arnold 1990, 7). Yet the
U.S. Constitution charges House leaders with no specific tasks.
Indeed, the Speaker of the House is the only House officer mentioned in Article I, section 2, and even the role of Speaker is given
little description. Over time the Speaker and the House leadership
more generally have taken on the responsibility of building winning coalitions around their party's agenda. In meeting their partisan responsibilities, leaders enact their preferred policies and
establish a reputation for governing ability among colleagues and
the public. Although leaders have a variety of strategies for advancing their party's agenda, good leaders bring legislators together. They are—to paraphrase George W. Bush—uniters, not
dividers.

When legislator preferences are flexible, leaders may persuade partisans and nonpartisans alike to support their agenda. Persuasion could come in the form of a rhetorical argument. That is, leaders might simply make a compelling case for a new policy and change the minds of uncommitted or previously committed legislators. Persuasion also could be characterized as either coercion or charm. For example, leaders can keep legislators off or, conversely, put legislators on preferred committees; they can quash or facilitate legislation; and they can make it difficult or easy for legislators to bring federal "goodies" to their districts. Because cultural issues are easy, legislator preferences are likely—though not necessarily—fixed in this policy domain. When preferences are fixed, leaders must try to bargain with legislators. This bargaining often involves compromise and modification of existing legislation (Arnold 1990, ch. 5; March and Simon 1958, 129). With bargaining, leaders may not be able to get legislators to agree, but they may be able to tinker with legislation and procedures enough to garner the necessary votes for passage. No individual will get everything; most legislators in the winning coalition will get something. Compromise, then, is the key to legislating.

Yet cultural issues are the very issues on which compromise is theoretically difficult to secure. In this context, the job of leaders is made more difficult. How are they supposed to manage the chamber and their respective parties under these circumstances? With that dilemma in mind, in this chapter I explore how leaders build winning coalitions around issues that take on cultural significance. I begin with a description of leadership ebbs and flows in the contemporary era and proceed to a discussion of leadership strategies that may be useful in garnering culturally significant legislative victories. The argument I pursue in this chapter is that constructive approaches to party governance are more likely to produce the compromises required to pass culturally significant legislation.

## THE 1990S AND THEN SOME

In 1987 Jim Wright (D-TX) succeeded Tip O'Neill (D-MA) as Speaker of the House. As speaker, O'Neill had presided over the beginning of a "revitalization" of that position (Schickler 2001, 238–42). In the late 1970s a series of congressional reforms centralized power in the House by giving the Speaker more power in making committee assignments and by permitting multiple referrals. The Speaker also regained the right to appoint majority-party members to the Rules Committee. Thus, the Speaker gained greater control over committees and the flow of legislation, which made the speaker more powerful vis-à-vis committee chairs. For their part, committee chairs faced challenges to their once-preeminent positions of power from above and below. In the postreform Congress, the hands of subcommittee chairs were strengthened and the Democratic caucus started to elect committee chairs by secret ballot (Wright 2000).

Speaker O'Neill did not have many of the formal powers enjoyed by his nineteenth-century predecessors, but he exerted power by transforming the position. He made the Democratic leadership more service oriented, he used what formal powers he had to influence outcomes, and he made caucus decision making more inclusive (Sinclair 1989). He enhanced party loyalty by expanding the whip system and bringing many Democrats, including junior members, into the leadership fold. Junior legislators also were placed on leadership task forces (Sinclair 1983).

The 1970s reforms and the contentious political climate of the 1980s made legislating more difficult, however. Democrats looked to their leadership to respond. Democratic leaders, in turn, became involved in postcommittee adjustments and helped develop special rules to facilitate the legislative process and thwart the Republicans (Sinclair 1997). Moreover, because O'Neill led the only elective branch of government controlled by Democrats, he became a well-known party spokesman, and the general stature of the speakership increased (Davidson and Oleszek 2000, 157).

Wright, on the other hand, was an aggressive and unilateral leader who unabashedly pushed a Democratic agenda in the face of divided government. One of the more egregious examples of his "procedural authoritarianism" (Koopman 1996, 42) occurred in October 1987, when a "Wright-written" rule pertaining to a welfare reform/budget deficit reduction bill failed after some of his own partisans revolted against the measure. Wright adjourned and then reconvened the House, thereby starting a new legislative day and allowing for a new rule to be considered. Wright also kept the vote on final passage open after time had expired so that freshman Democrat Jim Chapman (D-TX) could be convinced to change his vote, thereby producing a narrow Democratic victory.[1] Wright's major exercise of power was over the rules process. In using the rules as leadership tools, Wright raised the level of partisanship in the House—a trend that is reflected in roll call votes (Koopman 1996, 43).

Wright's aggressive partisanship earned him the ire of many Republicans and even the disaffection of some fellow Democrats (Schickler 2001, 240–41). Rep. Newt Gingrich (R-GA) was among Wright's most outspoken critics. Gingrich had famously cut his teeth on challenges to the Democratic leadership in 1984, when his tactic of using special order speeches to attack the Democrats—and the House, more generally—so inflamed O'Neill that the Speaker said in an outburst from the floor, "My personal opinion is that you deliberately stood in that well before an empty House and challenged these people, and you challenged their Americanism, and it is the lowest thing that I have ever seen in my 32 years in the House." In a stunning embarrassment, O'Neill's words were ruled out of order by the chair.[2]

Gingrich, who at the time was presciently characterized as the Robespierre to Wright's Louis XVI,[3] turned his sights on Wright and pushed for an investigation by the House Committee on Standards of Official Conduct into an array of alleged ethical violations. The committee eventually accused Wright of violating sixty-nine House rules, and he was forced to resign.[4] When Rep. Tom Foley (D-WA) took the reigns as Speaker in 1989, he did so at a highly partisan and poisonous time in the House. In the wake of the Wright departure, Foley's primary goal was to restore civility in the House, and he chose his leadership style accordingly. Although he used procedural tactics to frustrate the Republican minority, he generally acted as a consensus builder within his own caucus (Davidson and Oleszek 2000, 157). Foley retained the speakership through the 103rd Congress (1993–1994), but in a remarkable turn of events the sitting Speaker was defeated in his bid for reelection in 1994. Of course, it did not help Foley's cause that he had essentially sued his constituents, filing a lawsuit challenging Washington state's term limits law.[5]

In the 1994 midterm elections, the Republicans regained control of the House after having spent four decades as the minority party, and they went into the 104th Congress with a healthy twenty-six-seat majority. They were led by Gingrich, who by this time had worked his way up through the Republican conference leadership structure. Gingrich successfully changed the culture within the conference, convincing Republicans that the chamber could be theirs. He was an aggressive minority partisan. He had challenged House Democrats on procedural and ethical matters, and he pushed a conservative agenda that comprised issues such as the line-item veto, a balanced budget amendment to the U.S. Constitution, and an array of social issues (Connelly and Pitney 1994; Dodd and Oppenheimer 2001a, 23–24; Koopman 1996).

In 1988 Gingrich had taken the reigns at GOPAC, a political action committee that assists Republican candidates for office at the state and local levels. Using GOPAC to recruit and assist candidates, Gingrich developed a highly competitive Republican "farm team." In 1994 the large number of open seats and freshmen Democrats up for reelection for the first time made the Democratic majority vulnerable, and the Republicans were ready with a slate of strong candidates. Under Gingrich's leadership, the Republicans ran on a common national agenda, the "Contract with America," which advanced several important conservative issues and principles. This combination of strong Republican candidates, open seats, vulnerable Democrats, and an agenda around which to rally carried the Republicans to a historic victory (Dodd and Oppenheimer 2001a, 24–25).

In the wake of the Republicans' stunning victory, Gingrich was elected Speaker of the House with the unanimous support of his conference. The powers invested in him were unrivaled since the days of Czar Joe Cannon. Many Republicans felt they owed their newly won majority status to Gingrich's careful stewardship and aggressiveness. Moreover, having run on a common agenda, the conference needed a strong speaker who would be able to see the Contract items through to the floor, as promised. With the centralization of power in the hands of the leadership, the power of committees in this new era continued to deteriorate, although this process had been under way for many years (Deering and Smith 1997; Evans 2001; Evans and Oleszek 1997; Smith and Lawrence 1997). Gingrich appointed committee chairs, sometimes bypassing seniority to reward loyalists, and he was influential in making committee assignments. Of course, sometimes committees were bypassed altogether. When the Republicans took control of the House, they made use of task forces to bring many items to the floor (Evans and Oleszek 1997; Smith and Lawrence 1997). Task forces are composed only of majority-party members. They keep no records, and they work behind closed doors. According to Gingrich, the goal was efficiency. Gingrich bypassed committees to such an extent that he angered senior Republicans, who regarded his tactics as encroaching on their turf. When Rep. Dennis Hastert (R-IL) became Speaker in 1999, he vowed to respect committee autonomy.

Dodd and Oppenheimer (2001a, 25) note that although Gingrich did not chair the Rules Committee, he stacked it with partisan allies and thereby had de facto control over the flow of legislation. One journalist characterized the Rules Committee as similar to "the Central Committee of the Communist Party in the old Soviet Union": "Meetings are public. Speeches are made. Debates are vigorous. Votes are cast. But all that is really irrelevant. The final decision is always made by one person behind the scenes—in this case, the Speaker of the House. 'How much is the Rules Committee the handmaiden of the Speaker?' said Representative Porter J. Goss of Florida, a senior Republican on the panel. 'The answer is, totally.'"[6]

Because Rules Committee members are handpicked lieutenants of both parties, and because the Rules Committee structures the legislative process, it should come as no surprise that the committee can become rife with partisan acrimony. Former committee chair Gerald Solomon (R-N.Y.) is even reported to have challenged Rep. Patrick Kennedy (D-R.I.) "to step outside and put up his dukes during the furious debate on a bill repealing the ban on assault-style weapons."[7] For many years, the Republicans decried the Democratically controlled Rules Committee as unfair. When the Republicans had the opportunity, they turned the tables.

The beginning of the first session of the 104th Congress marked the height of Gingrich's success as speaker. The party acted on all of the major components of the Contract with America, and the leadership crafted legislation on the budget, welfare, and the environment that challenged the liberal legacy of the New Deal (Dodd and Oppenheimer 2001a, 26). The leadership circumvented committee deliberation and, in particular, used the House Appropriations Committee to advance their party's agenda (Aldrich and Rohde 2000; Gordon 2004). This is not to suggest, however, that the Republican majority always met with legislative success. Some Contract measures, such as term limits and the requirement of a three-fifths majority to raise taxes, died in the House. Other measures, such as the balanced budget amendment, were scuttled by the Senate.[8] The more moderate Republican-controlled Senate often was unwilling to go along with House measures. According to a Republican legislative director, "The reality is that . . . the Republican conservatives represent a majority of the Republicans in the House, but they don't represent a majority of Congress. And so while they can win battles in the House, they end up losing either because their position never gets voted on that way in the Senate or when you end up conferencing something and factor in what the White House position is, they always end up losing."[9]

Nevertheless, Gingrich was able to command the discipline of his conference, use the tools of the legislative process to their utmost, and produce Republican victories within the chamber. Because Gingrich had "acted on the major promises of the Contract with America," Dodd and Oppenheimer (2001a, 26) suggest that his stature as a national policymaking figure rivaled the president's.

That first session of the 104th Congress, which started with so much promise for the Republicans, ended in two government shutdowns—one in 1995 and another in 1996—for which the American people held the Republican majority responsible. Years later, Gingrich acknowledged how badly the majority party had misjudged its mandate: "'The idea of a grand showdown over spending had long been a staple of conservative analysis,' Gingrich wrote. 'I was to learn something about the American people that too many conservatives don't appreciate. They want their leaders to have principled disagreements, but they want these disagreements settled in constructive ways. This is not, of course, what our activists were telling us. They were all gung ho for a brutal fight over spending and taxes. We mistook their enthusiasm for the views of the American people.'"[10]

Ardent House conservatives objected to Gingrich's eventual compromise with President Clinton that reopened the government. Later in the Congress, Gingrich was able to work with Clinton on landmark welfare reform legislation, but internal divisions were emerging within the Republican conference and the Republicans never regained their preshutdown momentum

(Dodd and Oppenheimer 2001a, 27). In the 1996 elections, the Republicans maintained their majority but lost seats. This outcome was not altogether surprising because Republicans had won some traditionally Democratic seats in 1994. As a result, many Republican incumbents were highly vulnerable in 1996. Lacking a legislative agenda for the 105th Congress—after all, the economy was booming, welfare had been reformed, and the Contract had been dispensed with—the Republican majority depended on the Monica Lewinsky scandal and impeachment proceedings against Clinton to unite their party, cow the president, and strengthen their hand in Congress—in the same way Watergate had solidified the Democratic majority two decades earlier. But the public objected to the Republican pursuit of impeachment. By the end of the 105th Congress, a lack of legislative accomplishments coupled with a dearth of open seats and Democratic retirements left the Republican majority vulnerable. In the 1998 midterm elections the Republicans lost five more seats (Dodd and Oppenheimer 2001a, 28–31).[11]

After the honeymoon in early 1995, Gingrich faced problems not unlike Foley had. That is, he took over a highly partisan House. Gingrich and his friends in the Conservative Opportunity Society had successfully taken the House by rhetorically tearing it down (Schickler 2001, 243). They then faced the challenge of governing an institution that was internally divided and held in contempt by the American people (Hibbing and Smith 2001). This was no easy task, and the difficulty Gingrich faced in the second session of the 104th Congress and in the 105th Congress is testament to that. The 1998 electoral losses were almost as historic as the Republican victory in 1994 because the president's party generally loses seats in midterm elections. In this case, however, the Democrats had picked up seats. After the 1998 election, Gingrich lost the support of even his most loyal Republicans, and representatives such as Bill Archer, Mary Bono, and J. D. Hayworth encouraged him to step down.[12] Gingrich resigned the speakership and his seat in the House, having lost the support of his party. (This is where the Robespierre comparison seems apt.)

In the 106th Congress (1999–2000), the Republican conference replaced Gingrich as Speaker with Dennis Hastert—a mild mannered, little-known conservative from Illinois—after their first choice, Bob Livingston, resigned from Congress in the wake of infidelity allegations. Even though Hastert was (and remains) solidly conservative, his deliberative, "anti-Gingrich" persona suggested a more moderate approach to governance. Facing a factionalized House and a razor-thin majority, Hastert regarded his main challenge as laying the groundwork to elect more Republicans in the 2000 elections.[13] Among other things, such electoral gains would require regaining the confidence of the American people by establishing a record of legislative accomplishments and avoiding political disasters (Dodd and Oppenheimer 2001a, 36–37). Again, this was no easy task, given that the beginning of the 106th Congress was dominated by impeachment proceedings in the Senate against Clinton.

In the 106th Congress Hastert embraced a more "constructive" form of partisanship that sought to build shifting coalitions, drawing on majority and minority partisans, in an effort to construct policy victories that the public would embrace. Thus, the Republicans worked more closely with Clinton and congressional Democrats. They "gave up on across-the-board tax cuts as their central legislative agenda and focused instead on targeted tax cuts [and] . . . on popular social programs dealing with health and education that were supported by Democrats" (Dodd and Oppenheimer 2001a, 39). This strategy paid off. In the 2000 elections, the Republicans lost two seats, but they retained control of the House and managed to avoid the leadership instability that ensued after the 1998 election. It is worth noting that in 2000 the Democrat at the top of the ticket received more votes than the Republican. It is possible that Democratic congressional candidates benefited from an ironic form of coattails.

With the election of George W. Bush as president in 2000, the Republican party won unified control of Congress and the presidency. Although Bush's victory was contentious, he embarked on an ambitious agenda. Speaker Hastert's style of leadership changed in the 107th Congress. Because he no longer had to concern himself with outmaneuvering a Democratic president, Hastert worked closely with Bush to advance the president's agenda. The Speaker characterized his role in the following manner: "It's my job to make sure that we can pass bills the president can sign . . . and if we [pass] bills the president can't support, then I'm derelict in my duty" (quoted in Davidson and Oleszek 2000, 162). Even after the Senate briefly returned to Democratic control with the defection of Senator James Jeffords (Vt.) from the Republican party, Dodd and Oppenheimer (2005, 30–31) note, House Republicans pursued a very conservative agenda, frustrating the moderates in their own party. This pattern continued even after the terrorist attacks of September 11, 2001. Although it seems profane to discuss how September 11 shifted the game of electoral and congressional politics, the events of that day did recast politics in ways that benefited President Bush and his fellow Republicans on Capitol Hill, at least in the short run.[14] Republicans continued to pursue a partisan agenda, as was their prerogative as the majority party. Constructive partisanship seemed to be eroding; the parties rarely collaborated on legislation. Education reform and homeland security legislation stand out as notable exceptions (Dodd and Oppenheimer 2005, 33, 35).

The 2002 midterm congressional elections were the first since September 11, 2001, and they were thematically dominated by the war on terror. Analysts changed their focus from "soccer moms" to "security moms." The nation was engaged in armed conflict in Afghanistan and on the cusp of armed conflict in Iraq, and many Americans wanted to support President Bush and his party in Congress. For their part, the Democrats tried to run as a loyal opposition, without actually opposing Bush.[15] Some Democratic congressional candidates ran as explicit Bush supporters. Not surprisingly, the Republicans achieved significant victories in 2002, regaining many of the seats they had lost in the two preceding elections. *Washington Post* columnist David Broder characterized the 2002 elections as a "powerful boost" to President Bush, resulting from his "sterling" leadership after September 11. Bush could finally shake the "accidental president" label.[16]

In the 108th Congress, House leaders continued to craft conservative legislation that, among other things, reformed Medicare (and added a prescription drug benefit), banned partial-birth abortions, and provided tax cuts. This legislation was passed in the face of moderate Republican wavering and Democratic hostility. Medicare reform, for example, had few Democratic supporters. The House leadership had to keep the vote on final passage open for hours to garner sufficient Republican support (Dodd and Oppenheimer 2005, 43–47). Meanwhile, Speaker Hastert and Democratic Leader Nancy Pelosi (D-CA) failed even to speak to each other on a regular basis. One journalist noted, "There is, in fact, a dearth of meaningful cross-party dialogue in the House, from the leaders on down. And that, longtime and former members say, is one big reason for the mounting incivility they say undermines the legislative process, erodes public faith in Congress as an institution, and makes the House more difficult than ever to govern."[17]

Nevertheless, House Republicans could claim an impressive record of legislative accomplishments by the end of the 108th Congress, and the partisan acrimony did not seem to hurt them. In the 2004 elections they expanded what was already a working majority. (Senate Republicans also expanded their majority, although they still lacked a filibuster-proof majority of sixty seats.) In securing legislative victories in the 108th Congress, Republican leaders balanced the preferences of competing Republican factions: House conservatives and Senate moderates. House conservatives often had to make difficult concessions (Dodd and Oppenheimer 2005, 46).[18]

As the House Republicans moved into their second decade as the majority party and President Bush moved into his second term in January 2005, there was every reason to believe that Speaker Hastert and the Republican leaders would provide strong support for the president's legislative agenda and that the trend of strong partisanship would continue. After all, in 2004 House Republicans had picked up seats for the second consecutive election. A highly partisan style of governance may have backfired during the Gingrich years, but in the 1990s Republicans faced a skilled Democratic rival in President Clinton. They were engaged in a continuous policy conflict with a damaged but popular president—and they lost. Now the Republican majority has regained its lost seats and is operating with (or under the guidance of) a Republican president.

For his part, President Bush entered his second term with an ambitious domestic agenda that included Social Security, tax, tort, and bankruptcy reform and a gay marriage constitutional amendment, as well as an international agenda that continues to project U.S. power abroad in an effort to prevent terror attacks in the homeland. The problem Bush and congressional Republicans seem to confront is that their party remains internally divided.[19] There are obvious cleavages over cultural issues such as gay marriage. There also are significant cleavages over Social Security reform.[20]

As of this writing, Congress has passed bankruptcy and class action reform, and it continues to fund the war in Iraq. Along with Social Security reform, however, medical liability and major tax reform have languished thus far, having been set aside while the Senate coped with the fight over judicial nominations and President Bush's nomination of John Bolton to be U.S. Ambassador to the United Nations. When Congress comes back into session after the summer 2005 recess, legislators may turn their attention to these reform issues. The conservative House faction may be less inclined to make concessions to Senate moderates, however—which will make the leadership's job more difficult.[21]

After the 2004 election *New York Times* columnist William Safire quoted Sam Rayburn's (D-TX) reaction to the Democratic victories in 1936: "When you get too big a majority, you're immediately in trouble."[22] The Democratic majority did not truly unravel for another fifty-eight years, although in that time Republicans wielded considerable power as part of the conservative coalition. Rayburn's comment makes a good cautionary mantra for House Republicans. Of course, if the moderate faction of the party is quiescent, Republicans will not need the Democrats to secure legislative victories. If Republicans enact Social Security reform, they may be rewarded for their aggressive partisanship with three generations of dominance, as Democrats were in a different era.

Cultural issues are a component of the president's agenda, though it is unclear how unrelenting he will be in his advocacy. Shortly after Bush's reelection, presidential advisor Karl Rove announced that the president would push for a constitutional amendment defining marriage as a union between a man and a woman.[23] The president reiterated this position in his 2005 State of the Union address. Many House conservatives strongly support such an amendment, and there is little doubt that conservative Christians expect Congress and the president to act on it.[24] The issue divides congressional Republicans, however; as a result, conservatives probably cannot successfully pass such an amendment (at least in the 109th Congress). Moreover, after his State of the Union address, President Bush traveled all over the country holding "town hall meetings" on Social Security reform, not gay marriage. The president even seemed to suggest in a *Washington Post* interview that he would not lobby the Senate on a gay marriage amendment.[25] Early in his second term, the president's rhetorical efforts were not focused on cultural issues.

## THE CONTEXT FOR STRENGTH AND STRATEGY

The story of leadership strength in the House of Representatives comprises gradual accrual of formal powers in the nineteenth century, dispersion of powers in the early twentieth century, accrual of informal powers in the mid-twentieth century, and reintroduction of formal powers in the late twentieth century. The current era is at the tail end of this progression. As observers of congressional politics have seen, the 1990s were marked by interparty and intraparty leadership instability and accrual of formal leadership powers. These powers had to be exercised, however, in an environment characterized by intense partisanship and resentment. They still do. The questions remain: In that kind of environment, how do leaders lead? How do they build winning coalitions? To what extent can they act decisively?

In a classic essay on this topic, Froman and Ripley (1965) suggest that strong party leadership emerges when leaders are active, the issues and actions under consideration are low visibility and procedural, constituency pressure is low, and state delegations are not engaged in collective bargaining. If these criteria were met, however, strong leadership would be largely irrelevant because it would emerge only over nonsalient issues of consensus. Yet strong leadership may emerge even when all of these conditions are not met (Dodd 1983). In some instances, leaders have a hand in producing outcomes that are not foregone conclusions.

Cooper and Brady (1981) argue that at a fundamental level, leadership strength depends on the electoral context. Heterogeneity at the social-structural level gives way to heterogeneity within the institution. That is, when districts are social-structurally diverse, legislators are politically diverse. The opposite also is true, and when the social-structural context for elections produces a more homogenous set of legislators, party leaders will be stronger. Formal and informal powers will tend to be concentrated in their hands as they work toward achieving party policy goals.

Aldrich and Rohde's model of conditional party government, which they articulate in at least two places (Aldrich and Rohde 2001; Rohde 1991), builds on Cooper and Brady (1981), among others. The conditional party government model suggests that when the electoral bases of the parties in the House and the parties themselves are internally homogenous and externally polarized, rank-and-file members cede substantial powers to their leadership to pursue the policy interests of the party across an array of issues characterized by party consensus, though not all issues across the board. Members cede these powers for both re-election and policy reasons. In theory, conditional party government "builds a base for reelection by enacting policies desired by majorities in members' constituencies and enables members to achieve their personal policy goals" (Dodd and Oppenheimer 2001b, 369). Aldrich and Rohde (2001) suggest that Republicans have governed and, barring any cross-cutting issues, will continue to govern on this model. Indeed, they propose that the "theoretical account" offered by their model "is as applicable in 2004 as it was in 1995" (Aldrich and Rohde 2004, 267).

One can hardly argue with success. Notably, however, since 1994 a variety of circumstances have challenged conditional party governance (Dodd and Oppenheimer 2001b, 376–82; Dodd and Oppenheimer 2005, 48–50). Seat losses in 1996, 1998, and 2000 produced close seat distributions between the parties. To win on the floor, Republicans needed near-unanimity on the part of their conference, which sometimes was difficult to garner. With a shrinking majority cushion, the party could ill afford defections. Coupled with the emergence of postindustrial issues, this situation presented a problem for party leaders. The cultural issues under consideration in this volume are a subset of the larger postindustrial agenda, which is marked by a concern for quality of life. These issues tend to produce cross-cutting party cleavages. Thus, although these issues are profoundly important to conservative Republicans, they are precisely the issues on which party moderates are likely to defect. This reality has the effect of either scuttling or diluting the conservative cultural agenda.

This concern has been mitigated by the 2002 and 2004 Republican gains. Yet even with an expanded majority and a shrinking moderate faction in the 107th and 108th Congresses, conservative House Republicans' actions were moderated by Senate Republicans. Therefore, resolving interchamber differences required difficult concessions on the part of conservatives. This pattern is likely to continue into the foreseeable future. The point is not to challenge Aldrich and Rohde's characterization of party governance in the Republican era. With the possible exception of the 106th Congress, the conditional party government model superbly captures the current era. Models of strong party governance are unlikely to resolve cultural conflicts, however. Parties that want to develop a record of legislative accomplishment on cultural issues may want to consider a more constructive approach to governance.

## CONSTRUCTIVE STRATEGIES

Instead of a centralized leadership that aggressively pursues partisan outcomes, constructive partisanship promotes compromise, subdued ideological factions, and majority party cooperation with the president and the Senate. On cultural issues, the strategy of majority leadership should be to assemble shifting coalitions of majority and minority legislators. These issues are framed in a manner that undermines traditional norms of bargaining and compromise. Unfortunately, "[w]ithout a spirit of compromise among legislators, party leaders cannot build majority coalitions and pass controversial policy" (Dodd 1983, 148). Constructive strategies may provide a way to overcome the intractable nature of cultural conflicts by mitigating partisanship and facilitating compromise. This model may lack stability, but it is likely to produce policy outcomes that the American public will favor (Dodd and Oppenheimer 1997, 2001b).

Cultural issues seem to defy constructive partisanship because their nonnegotiable framing belies compromise. As one Democratic staff member remarked, "Prayer in school: Can you half pray? It's either no or yes."[26] The parties seem to be polarized on these issues. Yet these issues also divide Republicans and Democrats internally, to a certain extent. Cultural issues cause division "within the Republican Caucus, but they also divide within the Democrat Caucus, so you get these coalition bills."[27] Progressive Republicans are likely to defect on cultural legislation; so will conservative Democrats. Thus, rather than building strictly partisan coalitions, leaders can build centrist, shifting, bipartisan coalitions on these issues. This sort of compromise often will produce incremental policy outcomes that the most committed religious traditionalists and sexual progressives probably will resist. However, "unless you're an incrementalist, you really don't have any business [on Capitol Hill]. . . . [P]eople that don't accept the moral legitimacy of an incremental approach on a moral issue such as abortion probably aren't going to be in Congress."[28] The problem for leaders is that incrementalism, compromise, coalition building, and constructive partisanship almost certainly require the sacrifice of ideological extremists. According to one Democratic legislative director, "the party has to be very careful not to let extreme issues take over."[29] A Republican legislative director concurs: "Leadership has one of the toughest roles in both the Republican and Democratic leadership because for moral issues compromise almost isn't an option for some guys."[30] Compromise and moderation are necessary but difficult to fashion. Therefore, I now turn my attention to coalition-building strategies.

## COLLABORATION AND FLOOR ACCESS

Parties that use a constructive partisan approach offer their leaders a variety of strategies. First, leaders must act collaboratively. They do not have the formal resources necessary to act in a centralized or unilateral matter. Therefore, policy goals must be set by a consensus of the conference, not a small leadership cadre. This point was particularly important in the 1990s, given the distinctly Southern, conservative flavor of the House leadership at the time. A collaborative strategy that includes many legislators—and many different kinds of legislators—may have the effect of generating policy that is acceptable to larger numbers of representatives and might even appeal to moderates in both parties. Even if this kind of collaborative approach generates a policy that a portion of the conference dislikes—as it almost certainly will—at least dissident legislators will have had a voice in the process. The benefit of this approach for the conference is that the leadership maintains a sense of legitimacy, and dissidents do not become frustrated.

A Republican legislative director suggests that the spirit of collaboration is alive and well among majority partisans: "We have conferences every Wednesday, at least. If there's a tough issue, we'll have them more than that, and that will be on the agenda. And that's members only, and leadership, staff sometimes, but they just sit there and hash out the differences. And they get to debate, and they try to come out with a unified position. That doesn't work that easily with moral issues, because they all tie into religion, and they all tie into convictions of your faith. . . . [T]he fiscal and the budgetary things, policy issues are a lot easier to compromise on than your moral and ethical bills."[31] The Republican leadership makes an effort to develop intraparty consensus, and as a group House Republicans communicate effectively and regularly. Nevertheless, compromise on cultural issues is difficult to attain even within the party.

Beyond consensus building, collaboration can take a variety of forms. For example, developing an extensive whip system that brings an array of legislators from different regional and ideological bents into a position of leadership—as Speaker O'Neill did—is one aspect of collaborative leadership in action. More than just creating an inclusive leadership structure, an extensive whip system can provide leaders with valuable information about conference or caucus support for legislation. Leaders also should consider strengthening the lines of communication with caucuses and other informal chamber groups. Because these groups form in reaction to external policy demands made on the House (Hammond 1997, 1998), their initial development threatened party leaders. Leaders have come to see caucuses, however, as groups around which winning coalitions can be built (Hammond 1991). The Republican majority therefore has made an effort to attend to the formal and informal conference and chamber groups. "[O]n every leadership staff is the coalition member, a member that is in charge of working with the outside groups and working with the coalitions. And those staff members will go to the Values Action Team meetings, and they will find out what the groups mean. And they will explain, if the groups want this done and the leadership knows that it doesn't have the votes, that they won't take it up. . . . And so the leadership is really engaged in everything that is going on."[32]

This sort of collaboration ensures that disparate groups within the conference are at least represented in the inner circle. In a House with such a narrow margin, this kind of inclusion is particularly important because leaders cannot afford to write off any group of legislators. Moreover, caucuses and informal groups sometimes are bipartisan. Therefore, reaching out to these groups has the added benefit of providing leaders with a way to reach out to minority legislators and include them in their shifting coalitions.

Under Speaker Gingrich, decision making tended to be centralized, whereas under Hastert the leadership has made more of an effort to establish a collaborative decision-making process. According to one Republican legislative director, "I'll make a comparison between leadership under Newt Gingrich and leadership under Denny Hastert. [With] Newt Gingrich, to a certain degree the approach and the decision and the policymaking were top-down. Decisions were made by the leadership, whether . . . Gingrich or Delay. . . . Decisions were made about . . . the manner in which a bill would move, when a bill would move, what the conference position was going to be, and the whip was cracked. . . . The whip was cracked, and you were supposed to fall in line." On the other hand, "Under Denny Hastert as Speaker, there has been much more of a negotiative kind of, if not consensus-building approach, then attempts to at least give each kind of segment of the conference—and even in certain degrees segment of the Congress, Republican and Democrat—the right and the opportunity to make their views known, and to be involved in the process of developing a bill, amendment, or policy. . . . One example is most if not all appropriations bills in the last couple of years—this year and last especially—have been brought to the floor under essentially open rules: Anybody at any time can offer an amendment to the bill if they don't like it or they want to improve it. They will at least have the opportunity."[33]

Centralized partisanship may have emerged under Gingrich because Republicans appeared so unified. Yet in spite of this centralized, aggressive stance on the part of Gingrich and his allies, the Republican House majority attained few significant policy victories on abortion, gay rights, or school prayer in the 104th and 105th Congresses. Passage of the Defense of Marriage Act stands out as the Republican majority's only major cultural legislative victory under Speaker Gingrich, and that legislation awaits inevitable court challenges now that Massachusetts is permitting same-sex marriages. With regard to abortion, the Partial-Birth Abortion

Ban Act was signed into law only after Gingrich left the House. Under his leadership, access may have been limited by funding restrictions, but the procedure remained legal. The original partial-birth legislation, which was considered in the 104th Congress, very likely would have been enacted into law but for the Republican leadership's ability to keep a compromise amendment off the floor. According to a Democratic administrative assistant, "Republicans, since they're in control of Congress right now, brought it up specifically because they wanted members to take that vote, and they wanted Clinton to veto it—because there was a compromise that could have passed, which would have dealt with the vast majority of these late-term abortions, which would just have expanded the exception slightly to allow [late-term abortions when there were] severe adverse health consequences to the mother. . . . But with that exception, Clinton would have signed it and it would have passed. And the Republican leadership—not only would they say no, we don't want that particular amendment to be added, they wouldn't even allow that amendment to be offered on the floor of the House."[34]

The foregoing assessment of Republican leadership motives may or may not be correct, but the larger point is that the leaders would not allow a vote on an amendment they perceived to be unfriendly because the amendment in all likelihood would have been agreed to—and that would have produced an unacceptable compromise. When the 108th Congress revisited this issue, House Republicans did not have to choose between a compromise bill or nothing at all because there was a Republican in the White House. House leaders also did not have to worry about losing moderates because support for banning the procedure was so strong. Passing a more sweeping abortion restriction probably would have caused intraparty divisions, but only four House Republicans defected on the vote for final passage, and sixty-three Democrats joined the Republican majority. The bill also attracted enough Democratic support in the Senate to break a filibuster, had that been necessary.

Under Speaker Hastert, the leadership is still conservative and still pursues a conservative agenda. Republican leaders have shown an occasional willingness, however, to give "minority factions" access to the floor.[35] Does this general pattern hold true for cultural issues? Yes and no. Table 5.1 breaks down congressional votes analyzed in chapter 4 as either "friendly" or "unfriendly" to progressive policy on gay issues and reproduction and traditionalistic policies on prayer in school. There are not enough prayer-related votes to detect a pattern: five votes in the entire decade. On support for gay rights, Democrats actually allowed more unfriendly votes than friendly votes in the 103rd Congress (1993–1994). Republicans continued that pattern in the 104th Congress (1995–1996), and in the 105th Congress (1997–1998) they did not allow votes on *any* gay-friendly measures. In the 106th and 107th Congresses, however, the Republican majority took a balanced approach, allowing as many friendly as unfriendly gay measures access to the floor. On support for progressive reproductive policies, the Democratic majority allowed twice as many unfriendly as friendly votes. In the 104th Congress, the Republicans reversed that pattern, allowing thirteen friendly votes and only six unfriendly (i.e., prolife) votes. The approach in the 105th, 106th, and 107th Congresses was more balanced.

What is remarkable about the transition from Democratic to Republican control is the spike in the number of reproductive policy votes overall—up from six in the 103rd Congress to nineteen in the 104th Congress, twenty-two in the 105th Congress, seventeen in the 106th, and ten in the 107th. The spike in the number of votes, and the decline that followed, reflects a shift in strategy on the part of the Republican leadership. On one hand, open access to the floor demonstrates inclusiveness, or a willingness to collaborate *on the floor*. It allows many different factions to at least offer their alternative. "[T]here has been at least an opportunity for most of the tax bills, campaign finance bills, for there to be at least one alternative that the Democrats or some group in opposition can rally around and say that this is our bill."[36] On the other hand, scheduling many votes on an issue also can be characterized as saber rattling. According to one Democratic legislative director, "the Republican leadership, because they control 100 percent what comes to the floor, they pull one or two [bills] out of the pack to give their members specific issues that they want their members to have a few votes to bolster their record on abortion or to bolster their record on being against 'special rights for gays,' or something like that. They'll put them out there, and then usually they'll do that with the understanding—implicit if not explicit—that the Senate will not take up those measures because

**Table 5.1.** Friendly and Unfriendly Votes on Gay Issues, Reproductive Policy, and School Prayer, by Congress

| Congress | Gay Issues | | Reproductive Policy | | School Prayer | |
|---|---|---|---|---|---|---|
| | Friendly | Unfriendly | Friendly | Unfriendly | Friendly | Unfriendly |
| 103rd | 2 | 4 | 2 | 4 | 1 | 1 |
| 104th | 1 | 2 | 13 | 6 | 0 | 0 |
| 105th | 0 | 3 | 10 | 12 | 1 | 0 |
| 106th | 3 | 3 | 9 | 8 | 1 | 1 |
| 107th | 2 | 2 | 4 | 6 | 0 | 0 |

*Note:* These figures include only votes referenced in Appendix B and analyzed in chapter 4. Some votes, such as motions to recommit legislation on which the final vote is included in the analysis, are omitted.

they are purely political. . . . Sometimes they will also do the same thing, not so much to give their members a vote in favor of something but to make Democrats take a difficult vote."[37]

Hence, Republican leadership management of cultural issues sometimes reflects a desire to bolster their conference's record on cultural issues, while forcing Democrats into the unenviable position of "standing up for sin." Republican leaders use culturally significant legislation instrumentally and strategically. Some of these votes are simple resolutions and do not even have the force of law.[38] Thus, rather than resolving issues, the legislative process is used to highlight and inflame cultural differences.

Prolife Republican leaders also may schedule some abortion-related votes in hopes that a restrictive statute will be enacted and reviewed by the Supreme Court, where *Roe* might be overturned.[39] Congress certainly has considered many abortion-related bills in the past decade that made—or tried to make—significant policy changes, such as the Partial Birth Abortion Ban Act and the Freedom of Access to Clinics Act. Many of the votes from the 103rd to the 107th Congresses (1993–2002), however, reflect a decision on the part of congressional Republicans to set their sights lower than complete elimination of abortion. One Democratic legislative director notes, "There are a lot of these things that [the prochoice community] will never win, or haven't in a decade or more. You know, the Hyde Amendment and things like that. . . . But there's some of these new bills that come up that are much closer. You know, the antichoice community is very, very clever and have more or less, for practical purposes at least, abandoned the tactic of a constitutional amendment on abortion. They are now going at death by a thousand cuts."[40]

Many of these "cuts" came in the form of amendments to appropriations bills. Notes one Republican staffer, "most of the prolife stuff we have, we've seen more . . . amendments to appropriations bills than anything else, just because those are the one thing that we have to do every year."[41] That is, riders make for a potent weapon because, ultimately, appropriations bills must pass or the government shuts down. The use of riders puts appropriators in the position of substantive policymakers. One Democratic chief of staff notes that "appropriations members are supposed to be funding programs that already exist. They're not supposed to be deciding abortion policy. But I guess actually they do, because in some ways the funding is the decision." Contrast this issue with school prayer: It also is a cultural issue, but it is not tied to the appropriations process. If the House ignores it, no structural harm is done—that is, the government continues to operate.[42]

Using riders to appropriations bills raises the level of partisanship in what traditionally has been a bipartisan committee (Fenno 1966). It injects partisanship into a place where it usually does not reside. Moreover, it weakens the committee to a certain extent. Appropriations subcommittees lose their independence and ability to move policy in their area of expertise. "We've had our bills held up between subcommittee and committee markup for weeks and months, with a totally prolife chairman—we now have a prochoice chairman—because of [international family planning]," notes one Republican Appropriations Committee staffer. "So we have no independence on this issue and frankly at this stage don't want it because we can deal with issues that are resolvable or that have substance to them. You cannot deal with hallucinations."[43] Ultimately, the committee is left to write language that forges a compromise that is acceptable to the leadership because "there is no one right now . . . capable of making legislative compromises and substantive decisions in the leadership." The same staffer notes that compromise often takes the form of a "face-saving scheme to give each side reason to believe they've won something. . . . We have a desk drawer full of various proposals." Of course, none of this transpires until after the committee's business has been delayed by political manipulation.

As figure 5.1 illustrates, the strategy of using the House Appropriations Committee as a policy vehicle on abortion peaked in the 105th Congress.[44] The number of abortion-related votes overall and the number of abortion-related appropriations votes dropped off after that. In fact, in the 107th Congress the number of abortion-related appropriations votes fell almost to 103rd Congress levels. Again, this dropoff may reflect a shift in strategy. Aggressive use of the Appropriations Committee occurred during Gingrich's tenure as Speaker, when Republican governance was highly consistent with conditional party government. As Republicans moved toward constructive governance, the use of riders diminished. As one Republican legislative director notes, "[Y]ou have some conservative members that are just zealots.

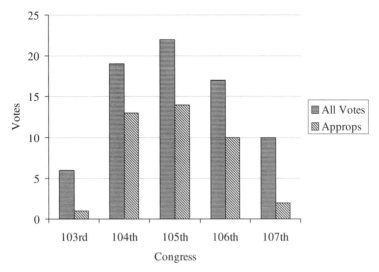

**Figure 5.1.**   Abortion-Related Votes

They just yell and scream, and it's oftentimes easier for DeLay . . . to just schedule a vote and do whatever rather than to have to continuously put up with that kind of behavior. Frankly, I think with Speaker Hastert's leadership you haven't seen the House have to vote as frequently on those kinds of issues."[45]

The leadership must be responsive to the members of the conference for whom life issues are paramount and who wholeheartedly embrace traditionalism. Nevertheless, the leadership cannot cater to this segment exclusively. Again, a Republican legislator makes the point that effective leadership demands that the number of symbolic abortion votes be limited. "We used to have umpteen votes on abortion. If you probably went back and documented in '95, '96, abortion-related—when I say abortion . . . I include everything, family planning issues, Mexico City policy— you name all [and it was] there. And I think what the leadership has been trying to do over the last couple of years is to limit the number of votes. Let's decide these are the critical abortion issues that we'll address . . . this year. . . . [T]hey try to keep riders off of appropriations bills. This year we've really done a good job on that."[46]

It is not surprising that an exuberant new majority would aggressively use the floor to advance its agenda—which is precisely what the Republicans did. Of course, they could use the floor effectively because of the leadership's control over the Rules Committee. "[W]e try to stack the outcome with the rule," notes one Republican staffer.[47] These issues are inflammatory, however, and they paint moderate Republicans as well as Democrats into a corner. Inclusiveness and open rules may be productive generally speaking, but the blowback of that strategy when it is applied to the appropriations process creates an environment in which compromise is difficult to foster.

Forcing extraneous cultural votes is a strategy one might expect to see under conditional party government if the majority party is united on a cultural issue, but it does not necessarily produce a strong reputation for governance, and it is not clear that such a strategy truly reflects the wishes of the conference. Many members wish abortion, for example, would not surface to such an extent. A Republican Appropriations Committee staffer notes, "I know almost half the members of the House personally, and they know me by name, and most of the people dealing with this, and know it is being driven by basically two individuals. . . . A monomaniac can go a long way in a place that he has a narrow majority." The Republican conference as a whole might be prolife, but the desire to consider life issues on a regular basis probably reflects the preferences of a vocal minority within the party. For example, on the issue of population control and international family planning, the same Appropriations Committee staffer suggests, "I don't think there are 200 people in the United States who think much about it, other than paid lobbyists. But the right-to-life movement is understandably very important, and they subcontracted the international aspect of this issue to Congressman Smith and his staff."

To the extent that multiple cultural votes produce acrimony and division, such a strategy undermines constructive partisanship and the possibilities for compromise. Although cultural votes may manufacture symbolic victories, there is a sense among some Republicans that they should be limited. One Republican legislator notes, "I think the things they attempt to keep off the docket or off the calendar are those things that are believed to be or perceived to be great moral issues, but in fact are political efforts to get folks on the record of no consequence to the real issue, if you understand what I mean. . . . And I think leadership should [keep these issues off the docket] because I think that's just playing with the minds and hearts of people when you put something up there that for all intents and purposes does nothing but establish a voting record that paints somebody in some kind of position.[48]

This point is echoed elsewhere.[49] Since Hastert has taken over as Speaker, the Republican majority has pursued a cultural agenda with a more constructive style. Indeed, the House has voted on many important cultural issues—on abortion, in particular—since 1997, but the majority leadership has scheduled fewer purely symbolic votes and fewer abortion appropriations riders.

As a Democratic representative suggests, even when leaders know they can push an aspect of their cultural agenda and win, it is best to proceed with caution because consideration of this kind of legislation generates polarization not just between the parties but also within the party.

> I think there are other issues where the leadership may realize that these are issues that divide their party and that they're not really amenable to compromise, and so therefore they don't want to put them out there. . . . I remember there was an attempt, a straightforward attempt on the surface anyway, to codify *Roe v. Wade*, back when we were in charge. I think our leadership was reluctant to bring that out, simply because they knew it would split our caucus. Even though it would have won easily, it still was seen as a down side to it because you put that kind of wedge in your own caucus. . . . I'm not sure how much the Republicans operate that way, but I think they have to some extent. I think in the Reagan years there was a kind of understanding, and the White House wouldn't push the social and cultural agenda as their first priority. And something may be going on like that with the leadership here now.[50]

Thus, in many instances leaders and legislators would prefer that these issues not come to the floor because they are divisive and do not lend themselves to compromise—the staple of the legislative process. The compromise, then, is that some votes are scheduled—"they offer a few votes that they pretty much have to do because the caucus demands it, but there may be lots of other stuff that's kept off of the floor"[51]—and policy is advanced on those votes, but the floor is not used to raise partisan cultural stakes, ideally.

An obvious question is this: How does the leadership determine which votes it will cherry-pick to represent the cultural banner of their party? Generally speaking, support from the leadership and widespread chamber support—in that order—are the most important factors in getting bills to the floor. "Whether or not a bill gets to the floor depends on who's in charge and whether they're sympathetic," a Democratic legislator says.[52] A Republican legislative director echoes the point: "Leadership decides what moves."[53] For example, a Republican legislative director notes "if [Hate Crimes legislation] would get to the floor, I think it would pass, but the leadership won't let that get to the floor because they oppose it."[54] A Democratic representative suggests that, "The Non-Discrimination Act, I think under Democratic leadership, with that issue having come as far as it has, I think under Democratic leadership that bill would probably come to the floor. It depends on who's in charge and whether they're sympathetic."[55] A Democratic administrative assistant notes that the Employment Non-Discrimination Act has "quite a few cosponsors, over 100 I think in the House. If the Democrats were in the majority now, that bill would be voted on the floor of the House. Would it pass? We'd have to see. It's a very simple reason why it won't come up. Because the Republicans are against it, and they won't let it come up."[56]

One Republican legislative director echoes this point about the importance of leadership support: "One is clear support among a majority of the House. Whether it's Republican or Democrat, whether it's just Republicans or just Democrats, there has to be clear, widespread support, enough so that you can win the votes to pass the bill. That being said, the leadership has got to be willing to bring it to the floor. If it's a campaign refinance bill that the leadership, and the majority of the Republican conference, hate or a bill . . . that had a clear majority of members of the House, but the leadership didn't want to bring it up for a vote, it will not come to the vote on the floor."[57]

Leadership decides what gets to the floor, and if leaders are not sympathetic to legislation, it probably will not get a vote. Furthermore, without a winning coalition, leaders—no matter how sympathetic they may be—will tend not to allow losing votes.

In some cases, it is possible to envision a situation in which an unsympathetic leadership will let a bill get to the floor. This possibility generally requires grassroots pressure. Many issues, such as abortion and gay politics, have devout supporters and opponents that can be mobilized to such an extent that leaders are forced to move an issue when they might otherwise let it die.[58] When support in the chamber grows for a piece of legislation, leaders can resist for only so long. "[T]he important thing to remember obviously, is 218 wins. . . . I mean, there's no way to keep stuff off the floor if you have that. There are ways to keep it off, but not on [morally controversial] issues."[59] When a petition starts to accrue close to the necessary number of signatures, the leadership generally will move the bill.[60]

## DEFECTION

On June 27, 2002, an interview with a Republican legislator was disrupted when the buzzer went off, signaling a vote. The legislator proceeded to the basement of the House office building and hopped the train that connects the office buildings to the Capitol.[61] The interview proceeded as the legislator went in and out to cast a series of votes. Questions were asked in between the votes. The legislator was making the argument that Republican leaders in no way pressure their rank and file to vote one way or another on moral issues, when a Democratic leader hurriedly walked by on his way to the floor. The interviewee yelled after him, "Hey, you guys don't whip on abortion, do you?" "Oh, no. No we don't," said the Democrat, vigorously shaking his head. Then he headed into the chamber to vote.

Because legislators are electorally independent of their party, leaders must allow defections, as Speaker Rayburn famously did (Cooper and Brady 1981). The party provides legislators with money and services, but the party cannot prevent a candidate's name from appearing on the ballot. Under conditions favorable to conditional party government, this situation might not create a problem for leaders in managing their caucus or conference because party districts presumably would be relatively homogenous and representatives would not feel a district pull to vote against their party. However, representatives represent diverse districts and depend on the continued good will of their districts to remain in Congress. To the extent that party positions and district positions diverge, it will be in a legislator's best electoral interest to vote against the party and with the district. Leaders who seek to punish dissident representatives risk losing their support in the future. Moreover, leaders who take a constructive approach will attempt to form shifting, rather than consistently partisan, coalitions. This strategy makes defection more tolerable.

None of this is to say that leaders cannot cajole and coerce legislators to vote one way or another. Good leaders will do both of those things in an effort to build winning coalitions. Moreover, ambitious leaders will use the election resources they have at their disposal to win support (Currinder 2003). They will do so, however, in the context of persuasion and bargaining.

The leadership's power to influence committee assignments is a valuable source of leverage. The rise of the seniority system diminishes leadership's ability to completely control committee assignments because once legislators are on committees, they cannot be removed. Leaders can manufacture committee positions for loyal legislators, however, by increasing committee sizes (Westfield 1974), and they can overlook seniority in making committee chair appointments. Leaders also delegate whipping of wayward partisans to friends and associates. For example, Rep. Tom DeLay (R-TX) might say to a stalwart Republican, "I know that you're friends with so and so; can you please talk to so and so for me and help me bring them around. See what they need to be with us on this vote."[62]

More generally, many legislators desire career success and power within the chamber, and leaders are in a position to affect both of these goals (Dodd 1977, 1983). Thus, legislators may be willing to support leaders on controversial or difficult issues as a sign of loyalty and reliability. "Leaders, anxious to reward and nurture party loyalty, can help members with committee assignments, party appointments, electoral assistance, and the passage of personal legislation" (Dodd 1983, 158). Again, an extensive whip system is important because whips provide leaders with support in trying to persuade dissident or fence-sitting legislators. Whips also provide information that allows leaders to know when and with whom to bargain (Dodd 1983).

Again and again, legislators and staff indicate that Republican and Democratic leaders do not apply pressure to legislators to vote a certain way when the House is considering morally controversial legislation. They are loathe to do so. "Leaders may say, 'It's the right thing to do,' but not, 'You must.'"[63] Leaders "are careful not to trample on people's strongly held moral and religious beliefs."[64] A staff member to a prochoice Democrat notes, "Our caucus does not go out and tell members to vote one way or the other on abortion."[65] Republicans and Democrats alike make this point.[66]

> Well, really, leadership is pretty good about not pressuring on these things, because moral issues are issues of principle, and so when it comes to issues of principle, the leadership usually backs off, and people just have to vote their conscience.[67]

> [T]he Democratic Party simply has a very clear position, like on hate crimes, gay rights or affirmative action. . . . And while certain Democrats leave the fold and wander away, I think that . . . leadership tells them that we would like you to vote this way, but of course you must vote your conscience and your district—but if you're going to vote against the Democratic position, will you at least inform us?[68]

Indeed, as I demonstrate in chapters 1 and 4, representatives draw heavily on ideology and religion in voting on these issues. Thus, representatives are not likely to be responsive to leadership pressure because these issues are so fundamental. One Democratic legislative director notes, "I think leadership knows that on particularly high-profile moral questions they don't have a lot of control. Votes are going to be votes of conscience, no matter what."[69]

Republican and Democratic leaders alike are permissive of dissent, perhaps because they have no choice. Republicans who express high levels of support for gay rights and prochoice policies do not have a great deal of influence with leadership on these kinds of issues, however. One Republican staffer makes this point in reference to Rep. Christopher Shays (R-CT), who consistently supports gay rights. "Chris Shays . . . is on the more moderate end of Republican policies, and I think he is probably doing it, he may very well have a personal belief this ought to happen. But he doesn't have a lot of, I guess, pull with the leadership on social policy stuff."[70] The party might even allow dissidents to offer amendments. "Jim Greenwood and a lot of the other prochoice people have, on occasion, gone to the leadership saying, 'What are you doing? We're taking up too many abortion [votes]. . . .' [A]nd he will have an opportunity to offer an amendment basically to replace or substitute" prolife measures.[71] Procedurally, however, these amendments can be stricken at a later stage in the legislative process. For example, a staff member to a Republican on the Rules Committee points out that on the fiscal year 2000 foreign operations appropriations bill, the Republican majority allowed Rep. Jim Greenwood (R-PA), a prochoice member of the conference, to offer a prochoice amendment. They also allowed contradictory amendments, however: "There was Mexico City policy language in the bill. And we allowed a prochoice type amendment, and we also allowed a prolife type of amendment, so that both sides of the issue could be voted on. . . . Chris Smith got [a prolife] amendment on the floor. . . . But then I think it was Greenwood that . . . had an amendment on the other side of the issue which also passed. And then the details were just kind of worked out in conference. . . . Mysteriously, the Greenwood stuff disappeared, so what we came out with was a prolife position."[72]

Opposing camps within the party received an outlet, although it was on an appropriations bill and procedurally the deck was stacked against the prochoice Republican. Furthermore, although the leadership allows Greenwood to get votes on abortion, they do not allow Shays to get votes on the Employment Non-Discrimination Act that he traditionally sponsors. Moreover, the Republican majority allows their dissidents a legislative outlet but no real influence over policy. The leadership and much of the conference are largely supportive of a culturally traditional agenda, and that is what they pursue. Yet Republicans understand that to win in the era of narrow margins they must avoid alienating culturally dissident Republicans who are with the party on an array of noncultural issues. Allowances must be made for Republican moderates.[73] Ultimately, Republican leaders cannot punish Republican moderates (any more than Democratic leaders can punish the so-called Blue Dog Democrats) because the leaders will need moderates' votes on future noncultural measures.[74]

Democrats, on the other hand, allow cultural dissidents to hold positions of authority but limit their influence on cultural bills. Former Rep. David Bonior (D-MI), for example, was the Democratic whip although he expressed low levels of support for prochoice policies during his time in the House. Yet as one Democratic representative points out, "Leadership has to balance, come to a balance in terms of how the majority or a simple minority or whatever of the caucus is favoring an issue. Leadership cannot afford to take his or her own point of view and be the Democratic caucus."[75] According to one Democratic legislative director, "[Rep. Richard] Gephardt is a fence-sitter [on abortion]. He has voted both ways in the past. And Mr. Bonior, his second-in-command, is not prochoice. He does not believe his district, his district he believes requires him to vote against most abortion bills. . . . [T]hese two individuals' personal and district-related views have enormous implications for the caucus because they run the whipping operations. So what has happened is because they will not whip those issues, the prochoice caucus and Congresswoman DeLauro, as assistant to the whip, take over the whipping operation."[76]

The Democratic caucus deals with the disjunction between the leadership and the caucus by agreeing to disagree with the leadership and turning over the whipping operation to a prochoice Democrat. Prolife Democrats are given positions of power, but the dominant preferences of the caucus are still pursued. Admittedly, the Democratic leadership has changed since the foregoing interview was conducted. The current dynamic might be different. Nevertheless, a Democrat reiterates the importance of putting the whipping operation outside the "official apparatus" of the caucus on the "choice issue." Using the official whipping operation on abortion-related votes could divide the party and alienate prolife Democrats. The caucus may be overwhelmingly prochoice, but it cannot afford to lose the loyalty of its prolife members.[77]

This analysis applies to both Republican and Democratic use of whipping operations. Both parties may allow dissent in voting, but they nonetheless make use of their whipping operations. They do not use the whips to apply pressure on cultural issues; they use the whips to get a feel for conference and caucus support for controversial legislation so they can design bills that will achieve support. They also use whip counts to pinpoint members with whom the leaders need to bargain on legislative language. A Republican representative notes, "There's not whip counts in the sense of finding out who to lean on to vote a certain way. There are whip counts, though, because they try to design bills that Republicans can pass. . . . Now one example is writing funding for foreign countries, the equivalent of Planned Parenthood–type organizations, which end up using the money for abortions. . . . And they sometimes whip that because sometimes that's a bill breaker on getting enough votes to pass the bill, if it goes too far one way or the other." Thus, the whipping operation is informational, rather that coercive. One Republican legislative director notes, "They'll whip check us and just get a feel for where we're at."[78]

There is no indication, as far as this research has determined, that leaders explicitly "career-bargain" regarding committee assignments or positions of power in the party. Such bargaining may happen, but it simply has not been measured. Nevertheless, leaders do consider dissident behavior in making committee assignments. According to one Republican legislative director who is a former staffer to a former member of the Republican leadership, "In the Speaker's office, because my old boss was in charge of the Steering Committee, which assigns members to committees, . . . we requested members' right-to-life scores, and that way we could make sure that if we put them on committees that had jurisdiction over abortion, we knew that we could keep a prolife majority on that committee. Because the last thing you want to do is put a prochoice majority on the Armed Services Committee and have them pass an amendment overturning current law, thus allowing abortions on military installations overseas."[79]

By the same token, leaders make an effort to appoint loyalists to committees that consider salient policy issues. One Democratic legislative director points out that his boss is on the Judiciary Committee "for a reason. The Judiciary Committee is the battleground for the morals of America." The membership on the committee has a left-right ideological split, and the Democrat in question is a standard bearer of the left.[80] Before a bill even gets to the floor, then, leaders indirectly shape legislative language by forming committees so that legislation will be crafted, quashed, or reported by representatives who are sympathetic to the leadership. Thus, leadership stacks the deck for and against certain legislation. In taking ratings and policy views into consideration, leaders ensure that legislation will be marked up in a way that is consistent with the leadership's agenda.

## CONCLUSION

Cultural conflicts present a distinct challenge to leaders because their nonnegotiable framing can render certain aspects of the legislative process, such as compromise, unavailable. Although the conditional party government model accurately characterizes much of the past decade, that style of governance may or may not secure legislative victories on cultural issues. If parties are internally unified on cultural issues, conditional party government probably is an effective way to secure legislative victories. Yet even though Republicans have solidified their majority, cultural issues divide both parties and certainly represent an axis of conflict (or at least distance) between House and Senate Republicans. This assessment suggests that application of strong party models to cultural policymaking probably remains imprudent. Effective policymaking under these circumstances most likely requires constructive strategies that permit collaboration and toleration of dissent. This approach to party government is directed toward building moderated consensual policies that are likely to receive the support of the American people.

How have Republican leaders managed cultural issues? Their approach is a decidedly mixed bag. Although the Republicans pursue a conservative cultural agenda, they appear willing to tolerate dissent among their ranks. There even is some evidence that leaders provide legislative outlets for dissent. Generally speaking, however, dissenters are unlikely to be rewarded with positions of power in the conference,[81] and they lack influence on cultural issues. Moreover, although the Republican leadership has allowed moderates to put forward several culturally significant amendments, it also has used floor access for entirely symbolic and partisan ends. Over the past decade Republican leaders in the House have scheduled many abortion-related votes—often as amendments to appropriations bills. These measures have served to gin up cultural conflict and forced moderates in both parties to cast difficult votes. They did little to foster consensus policymaking on this especially difficult issue. Starting in the 106th Congress, however, House Republicans have appeared more restrained in their use of the floor with regard to abortion measures.

The interview data suggest that Republican leaders coordinate with their own partisans. It is difficult to say, however, how much they really have sacrificed their ideologues over the past decade in an effort to construct shifting coalitions. A certain amount of sacrifice was inevitable, given the ideological contours of the Senate, but there is every indication that the House still has passed strongly conservative bills, and the leadership throughout this era has been strongly conservative. It also is difficult to determine the extent to which House Republicans coordinated with President Clinton, other Democrats, and the Senate, as constructive approaches suggest. Of course, with George W. Bush's election as president in 2000, there was less need to coordinate with anybody. This new situation allowed them to turn to a more robust style of partisanship. As a result, Republicans have been far from constructive in their governance. Nevertheless, cultural policymaking since the 106th Congress has included some constructive elements, if for no other reason than that underlying cultural cleavages rule out anything else. Republican management, then, has alternated between constructive and partisan tactics.

Ultimately, the quality of leadership management is a question of policy outputs. Over the past decade, House Republicans have secured incremental (but important) cultural victories on reproductive policy and gay issues. In passing the Partial-Birth Abortion Ban Act and the Defense of Marriage Act,[82] the party secured two widely popular, high-profile legislative victories. Nevertheless, Congress still confronts the same cultural conflicts as when the Republicans took over, and there is little anticipation of impending consensus politics. None of these conflicts have been transformed into instrumental conflicts, and neither traditionalists nor progressives could reasonably look back on the past decade with complete satisfaction. The use of strongly partisan tactics does little to induce transformation—although, in all fairness, issue transformation may be predicated on societal transformation.

In the era of unified Republican governance after the 2002 midterm elections and fortified by the 2004 elections, there is some indication that the Republicans have recentralized control over policymaking, even going so far as to move and quash legislation *against* the wishes of the conference but in support of the president.[83] If this trend extends to cultural issues, House Republicans may produce strongly conservative bills only to face stalemate with the Senate. More generally, if Republicans continue down the path of strong partisanship in the 109th Congress, then, to paraphrase The Who, "Meet the new Republican majority—same as the old Republican majority."

# 6

# Cultural Scuffles
# and Capitol Hill

[A] case needs to be made for cooperative work on a committee and in a party setting. . . . I think there's an ethical burden of proof on the person who will not cooperate in doing what needs to be done to bring policies to fruition.

—Rep. David Price (D-N.C.)

The original working title of this manuscript was "Culture Wars and Capitol Hill." That title, however, mischaracterizes the argument I pursue. As a national deliberative body, the U.S. Congress is an arena for punctuated cultural conflict (or scuffling) but probably not continuous culture war. Consider, for example, the spring 2005 conflict over judicial nominations. Democrats threatened to filibuster five of the president's nominees, and Senate Majority Leader Bill Frist (R-TN) threatened to invoke the "nuclear" option (also known as the "constitutional" option), which would have eliminated the filibuster for judicial nominations with a ruling from the chair and would have set a Senate precedent.

The cultural stakes were high. After all, courts ultimately decide what constitutes establishment of religion and what is and is not protected by the right to privacy. Prayer, abortion, and homosexuality: the Supreme Court has ruled on all of these issues, and religious traditionalists have suffered several major defeats (*Roe v. Wade, Engel v. Vitale, Lawrence et al. v. Texas*, to name a few). Thus, Christian conservatives support confirmation of judges who reflect their values. Of course, progressives also support nomination of fellow travelers to the federal bench. The matter is especially pressing for traditionalists, however, in that they hope that the Supreme Court will overturn a string of precedents. Ultimately, a bipartisan group of fourteen senators forged a compromise: The Republicans agreed to oppose the nuclear option, and Democrats agreed not to filibuster three of the five contested nominations and not to filibuster future nominees except under "extraordinary" circumstances. To be sure, some political observers repudiated this arrangement.[1] If nothing else, however, this episode illustrates that compromise is possible on seemly nonnegotiable cultural issues.

Religious traditionalists and sexual progressives embrace different values and, accordingly, different policy agendas. For many culturally animated activists, their policy agendas are truly incompatible. Yet many Americans are moderate in their cultural preferences and are likely to support moderate policymaking. The challenge for congressional leaders, then, is to govern constructively, in a way that builds policy from the center outward. In this way, culture war will be avoided though cultural scuffles will endure—which probably is inevitable in a pluralistic society. With this context in mind, in this chapter I revisit the argument and findings of the preceding chapters and suggest implications and directions for future research.

## COMPETING CULTURES

Implicit in this analysis is the assumption that congressional politics unfolds as the foreground and background interact. In the foreground, goal-oriented legislators pursue reelection and policy outcomes on a continuous basis. In the background, the modern era of American politics has seen the development of two sociocultural groups that have nursed conflicting visions of the good life.[2] The culture of religious traditionalism embraces a vision of society in which individual decisions are made with an eye toward divinely ordained social relationships. The culture of progressive sexuality embraces a vision of society in which individual decisions are made autonomously, and traditional sex and gender relationships are not taken for granted as preferred. As this cultural conflict relates to Congress, legislators operating in the

**Table 6.1.** Vote for President in 2004, by Religion and Attendance

| Religion | President Bush | Senator Kerry | Other |
|---|---|---|---|
| | | % | |
| Protestant | 59 | 40 | 0 |
| Born-again/evangelical | 78 | 21 | 0 |
| Attend weekly | 70 | 29 | 0 |
| Attend less often | 56 | 43 | 0 |
| Catholic | 52 | 47 | 0 |
| Attend weekly | 56 | 43 | 0 |
| Attend less often | 49 | 50 | 1 |
| Jewish | 25 | 74 | 0 |
| Other | 23 | 74 | 1 |
| None | 31 | 67 | 1 |

*Note:* Figures may not total 100 percent because of rounding.

institutional foreground will find themselves in a position to aggrandize their values in law. Again, however, this is not to suggest that there is a continuous culture war raging at either the mass or institutional level of American politics. The exit polls of the 2004 election seem to belie that possibility.[3]

Certainly there are cultural undercurrents that have the potential to produce political conflict. For example, the data in table 6.1 point to a pronounced electoral cleavage centering on religion. In the 2004 election, a majority of Catholics, mainline Protestants, and born-again and evangelical Protestants voted for President Bush. Moreover, among Protestants and (to a lesser extent) Catholics there appears to be an attendance gap. Overall, 59 percent of Protestants voted for President Bush; among Protestants who attend church weekly, however, 70 percent voted for Bush. Among Catholics, 52 percent voted for Bush. Among Catholics who indicate weekly church attendance, 56 percent voted for Bush. By themselves, these data do not allow for assessment of the causal relationship between vote choice and religion, but the 2004 election was marked by unmistakable religious voting patterns. The most observant and conservative Christians voted for Bush, and a majority of the rest voted for John Kerry.

This observed religious cleavage may have been more pronounced in 2004 because of the opportunity structure provided

by the gay marriage debate. The presence of that issue on the
national agenda and on state-level ballots may have raised the
significance of the 2004 election among religious voters. Regardless, elections—and American politics, more generally—are rife
with religious undercurrents. Therefore, it comes as no surprise
that when Americans make their choices in the political market-
place, they sometimes reference cultural themes. Yet the same exit
poll data that point to religious cleavage also point to moderated
consensus. (Figures 6.1, 6.2, and 6.3 provide these results.)

When voters were asked about their preferred policy toward
same-sex couples, 25 percent of respondents supported legal
marriage, 35 percent supported civil unions, and 37 percent supported no legal recognition of same-sex couples. Moreover, 52
percent of those who supported civil unions voted for President
Bush. With fully one-third of the public supporting civil unions,
and with that third divided between the two major political parties in the United States, there seems to be room in the middle
for compromise. The exit poll data on abortion suggest similar
possibilities for compromise. Twenty-one percent responded that
abortion should always be legal, and 16 percent indicated that
abortion should always be illegal. However, 60 percent staked
out a position in the middle: 34 percent indicated that abortion
should be mostly legal, and 26 percent indicated that it should

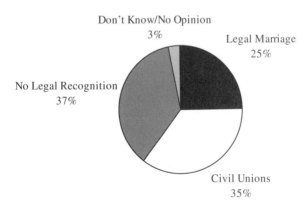

**Figure 6.1.**   Preferred Policy toward Same-Sex Couples, 2004 Exit Polls

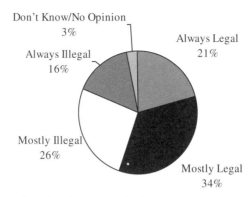

**Figure 6.2.** Preferred Policy toward Abortion, 2004 Exit Polls

be mostly illegal. Finally, when voters were asked about what they regarded as the most important issue in the election, "moral values" was the modal category (22 percent of respondents); 80 percent of those respondents who selected Moral Values voted for President Bush. Pundits and analysts made much of this figure, and it *is* remarkable, given that the United States, by President Bush's own account, is entrenched in a war on terrorism.

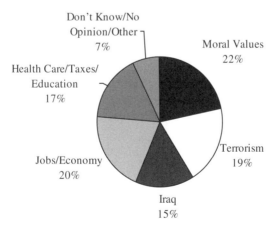

**Figure 6.3.** Most Important Issue, 2004 Exit Polls

It is worth noting, however, that 78 percent of respondents said something else: 34 percent said either terrorism or the war in Iraq was the most important issue, 20 percent named jobs and the economy, and the rest indicated taxes, education, and health care.

In spite of the religious undercurrents, the exit poll data on abortion and gay issues demonstrate that many Americans do not view cultural policymaking as a choice between dyadic alternatives representing good and evil. Rather, sociocultural groups at the mass level develop shared values, and attitudes on abortion, gay issues, and prayer are informed by those values. To the extent that different sociocultural groups embrace incompatible values and develop incompatible policy preferences, there is potential for political conflict. Cultures do not necessarily exist at extreme ends of a left–right continuum, however. They probably look more like a Venn diagram, imposed on a left-right continuum. Thus, there is room in the middle for compromise. The distribution of policy preferences at the mass level seems to bear out this conclusion.

To this point, one is left with a picture of cultural groups whose values seem to be influenced by religion and whose voting choices seem to follow accordingly. Yet the aggregate policy preferences of most Americans show a streak of moderation, which probably is evident among advocates of both religious traditionalism and progressive sexuality. Under these circumstances, where does the conflict in "cultural conflict" come from? This question brings the discussion full circle. Cultural conflict is a style of argumentation, not an ontological fact. It is an artifact of elite manipulation in which elites frame policy issues as nonnegotiable, and cultural groups align themselves accordingly. Why? Such framing may be strategic—intended to win votes—or it may be a reflection of true preferences. In either case, representation is a byproduct of elite behavior (Carmines and Stimson 1986), and cultural conflict is a byproduct of elite cue-giving.

## MAKING MORAL DECISIONS

Because cultural conflict is the stuff of electioneering, cultural issues make their way onto the congressional agenda once the polls have closed. Legislators then find themselves in a position to make moral decisions. Tatalovich and Smith (2001) make the point that moral or cultural conflicts arise out of competing concerns for social status. One group, typically on the left, fights for equalization and recognition of their social status. Another group, typically on the right, perceives the status claims of this new group as a threat to its status and joins the battle to fight for preservationist policies. These issues, therefore, do not draw on traditional class-based economic considerations. Hence, my expectation for this analysis was that economic predictors would have minimal influence on elite decision making. Cultural theory predicts that phenomena that are representative of sociocultural values should structure decision making. In particular, Republican partisanship, ideological conservatism, and legislator identification as Roman Catholic or a religious conservative were expected to produce support for religious traditionalism.

In personal interviews, legislators and staff repeatedly indicated that certain issues are different. Certain issues tap fundamental ethical considerations—and reproductive policy, homosexuality, and (to a lesser extent) school prayer are among those issues. Interview respondents indicated that when they consider these issues, their decision making is guided by internal values rather than economic or electoral considerations. Many respondents specifically referenced the importance of religious faith in decision making. Because cultural issues are easy issues, however, there tends to be correspondence between legislator attitudes and modal district preferences—at least, that is how legislators perceive the dynamic. As a result, basing decision making on personal ethical principles lacks significant electoral risk. The results of the decision-making analysis I discuss in chapter 4 comport with the narrative account of decision making I develop in chapter 1. To varying degrees, religion, party, and ideology all inform moral decision making, as expected.

The Catholic effect is particularly significant. Both elite Catholic identification and district-level Catholicism are associated with higher levels of legislator support for religious traditionalism. The presence of religious conservative constituencies also is associated with higher levels of legislator support for religious traditionalism, although elite identification as a religious conservative is not significant, for the most part. One might have expected the opposite result because whereas religious conservatives thematically have a singular policy focus and can concentrate their efforts on traditional relationships, Catholics do not. The Catholic agenda comprises traditional moral issues, on one hand, and social justice issues on the other. Even the Catholics bishops are divided with regard to which set of issues deserves a pride place (Byrnes 1993). Thus, in theory the linkage between Catholicism and elite decision making could be muddled—but it is not. The seamless effect of Catholic identification may be attributable to the work of the Catholic hierarchy in establishing social teaching and the work of congregations in socializing members. This question warrants further investigation.

## MANAGING MORAL DECISIONS

Legislators and staff indicated in interviews that a significant impediment to policymaking is that cultural issues may defy the normal legislative process, which inevitably requires compromise, give and take. The ideological extremes in both congressional parties are the locus of this problem. They do not want to compromise because the normative stakes are too high. Legislators may differ in opinion on energy policy, but at least compromise in this area does not damn anyone to hell, constitute an assault on western civilization, or indicate misogyny. With culturally significant issues, the bias is slanted toward standing one's ground. As Rep. (and political scientist) David Price (D-N.C.) notes, "[T]here's bias that being ethical means standing alone, and your individual integrity takes precedence over everything else. Of course I'm not about to minimize the importance of individual integrity, but what I'm saying is that often individual integrity might direct us to the kind of role we need to play in the institution as opposed to a kind of contrarian view which suggests that we think we're the only righteous person here in Sodom on the Potomac. You know, that kind of a case needs to be made for cooperative work on a committee and in a party setting. . . . I think there's an ethical burden of proof on the person who will not cooperate in doing what needs to be done to bring policies to fruition."[4]

Rep. Price's point is well made. Standing on principle may garner electoral points; it may reduce an individual legislator's internal dissonance; it may even be regarded as heroic. It probably is not a good way to govern, however, if legislators want to accomplish anything.

Obvious compromise positions are available on cultural issues that would be widely popular among the American people. Legislatively, it is difficult to produce those compromise policies because issues take on a nonnegotiable framing that is embraced by the elites and the base constituencies of both parties. This framing creates a partisan incentive within the House of Representatives to sacrifice moderated consensus for absolutist partisanship. As a result, for the most part policymaking is either incremental or nonexistent, although there are a handful of notable exceptions. Yet in the U.S. constitutional system, legislators have the responsibility to, well, legislate. This responsibility often entails resolving regional, economic, and ideological differences, thereby overcoming factious tendencies.[5] Perhaps, then, the most laudable legislators are those who sacrifice their fundamental principles in the name of consensual policy development. The alternative is legislators who stand their ground—at the expense of fulfilling their responsibilities to the public.

The strength of democratic governance in the United States is based on the ability of Congress—the national deliberative institution—to identify issues of common concern and manage them effectively (Dodd 1993). Congress has done this very well in the face of national traumas, such as war and economic depression. It has overcome wedge issues in the past. Therefore, the student of Congress has reason to be optimistic about the ability of the institution to address cultural wedge issues in the current context. Doing so will require skilled leaders who build winning coalitions across party and coalition lines, while sacrificing ideological extremists. To be clear: The onus is on the leadership of *both* congressional parties.

Over the past decade, the Republican majority in the House has embraced a style of strong party governance. Although this style left the party wobbly after the 105th Congress, House Republicans have reclaimed their lost seats and are reasonably skilled at passing partisan legislation. With a working majority and less need to accommodate the minority party, the 109th Congress might be characterized by conditional party government. Given the political context, this approach clearly makes sense. If any party since the end of the New Deal/Roosevelt Congresses could legitimately claim a mandate—and I use that term with some skepticism—it almost is certainly the current Republican Party.[6] Not only are the Republicans operating under unified government, President Bush garnered a majority of the vote in 2004 and the Republicans picked up seats in both legislative chambers. When Speaker Hastert was asked about the possibility of major tax reform in Bush's second term, Hastert responded, "I think this is the only time in generations that you might have a chance to be able to do it."[7]

Hastert senses the opportunity. Republicans have the votes, so observers of politics should expect Republicans to pursue ambitious goals. The problem for House Republicans is that they still confront a more moderate Senate. So they may not win, and they may have to moderate their reform agenda. Nevertheless, their best opportunity to rack up significant legislative victories is in the 109th Congress (2005–2006). Developing a record of legislative accomplishment on cultural issues, however, probably requires a more constructive approach to party governance. Since the Republicans took over as the majority party, their management of these issues has included constructive elements and produced important incremental results, but cultural issues also have been a vehicle for partisan confrontation. Thus, efforts to seriously bridge cultural cleavages to build shifting coalitions have been few. Moreover, even when the Republicans made such efforts, Democrats have not always been amenable to coordination. They appear no more willing to sacrifice their ideological extremes than Republicans.

The distribution of preferences on abortion and gay relationships—as captured by the exit poll data—suggests, however, that the public supports a middle-ground approach to cultural policymaking. Developing a record of accomplishment on these issues, then, requires that Congress craft policy around that middle ground. Again, this strategy will require sacrificing the ideological extremes in both parties, which may be unrealistic. Nevertheless, policy that reflects the moderate preferences of the American people requires legislative compromise. Alternatively, both parties can continue to engage in polemics, ratcheting up the tenor of cultural conflict as an homage to their bases. That strategy will win votes in the short run, but it will produce a dearth of real legislative accomplishment in this area.

## CONCLUSION

In the interest of candor, it is worth acknowledging that this volume provides a snapshot of cultural politics. This volume assesses cultural decision making in one legislative chamber over the course of a single decade. Therefore, the results are suggestive, but incomplete. Religion and the other cultural phenomena, party and ideology, inform decision making. Legislators and staff support this assessment, and the analysis bears it out. Moving the analysis backward and forward would allow for better analytical appreciation of the mechanism of the cultural effect. Cultural identity provides individuals with preferences, but it also creates grievances for which they seek redress in the political process. How and when those grievances are politicized, however, is less clear. Is this process punctuated? If it is, is it tied to opportunity structure or available resources? In short, the connection between elite cultural markers and the presence of culturally significant communities and legislator decision making matters, but I treat the connection as implicit. A more rigorous assessment of cultural politics should move forward and backward in time, and it should turn its attention to the background factors I discuss in chapters 2 and 3. This analysis certainly would help in understanding the foreground findings discussed in chapters 1, 4, and 5.

I have discussed the implications of the findings throughout. The implications are written in the future and conditional tenses, however. The truth is that the political context can change quickly. Cultural cleavages that define one era are relegated to irrelevance in the next. Before September 11, 2001, President Bush's defining moment was his decision on stem cell research. Now, by his own account, he is a wartime president. Assuming continued peace in the homeland, the cleavage between religious traditionalism and progressive sexuality will endure, and it is reasonable to expect that elites and activists will continue to frame policy issues in a culturally charged and "uncompromising" way. If that is the case, Congress will continue to be a venue for cultural conflict.

One should concede that Congress has learned to deal with this conflict in a routine manner, at least as far as reproductive policy is concerned. Subsuming reproductive policy into the appropriations process has allowed legislators to skip over the fundamental questions of "Should abortion be legal? How will we teach our children about sexuality? Does the pill facilitate normal sexual behavior, or does it promote promiscuity?" Instead, legislators can focus on funding questions. On these issues, compromise comes more easily because the ends of policy have already been established. Many legislators probably would prefer to address the more fundamental questions inherent in the abortion debate—particularly traditionalists, who wish to change the status quo set by the *Roe* decision. They are constrained by the courts, however, and do not have a large enough majority to effect sweeping policy change.

What of homosexuality and school prayer? School prayer probably is the least important issue in the triune. Gay issues receive more legislative attention. Neither issue is tied to the appropriations process to the same extent that abortion is, however, and neither issue has been routinized in the same way reproductive policy has. To the extent that Congress considers these issues, it is forced to confront the fundamental ends of policy. In the gay marriage debate, for example, legislators are directly debating which social relationships are legitimate and which are not. Both issues, however, probably are considered with greater frequency and substance at the state and local levels and in the courts. The truth is that reproductive policy, gay issues, and school prayer are dealt with by all branches of government at all levels of the federal system. This fact speaks to their salience and the need for additional scholarship in this area.

# Appendix A

## Elite Interview Information

I conducted most of my personal interviews of Republican and Democrat representatives and staff, as well as one former Republican House member, in summer 2000. I also conducted a handful in spring 2002. I promised anonymity to all subjects, so their names are not listed. I told interviewees that if they were quoted they would be referred to as "a Republican/ Democrat member/ staffer." I did not select the subjects at random. I sent letters requesting an interview to all Republican and Democratic members of the Judiciary Committee; the Health, Education, and the Workforce Committee; and the Rules and Appropriations Committees. I selected these representatives because gay rights, abortion, and school prayer-related legislation often go through these committees. I made follow-up calls and conducted interviews with whoever responded affirmatively. I conducted thirty-four interviews. Table A.1 provides the partisan and staff/legislator breakdown.

The personal interview is one of several survey research techniques. In deciding which technique to use, researchers face several considerations, such as cost, response rate, and potential bias. Working in a congressional office and knowing the volume of mail received by member offices on a daily basis, I thought self-administered questionnaires (SAQs) would yield a lower than usual response rate. More important, the interviewer has no control over who actually fills out the SAQ; in all

**Table A.1.**  Elite Interview Breakdown

| Interviewee Type | Republicans | Democrats |
|---|---|---|
| Staff | 7 | 8 |
| Representatives | 13 | 7 |
| Total | 20 | 15 |

*Note:* One former representative is included in Republican totals.

likelihood, a staff member would have filled it out. Thus, I proceeded with personal interviews.

The survey instrument comprises a series of open-ended questions. I asked all respondents the same questions. My approach to the interviews was more collaborative than standardized, however. I designed the instrument to mimic the social interaction of a conversation rather than the contrived interaction of a traditional interview. For example, when a respondent asked me to clarify the meaning of a question, I did. Some scholars would argue that this technique compromises both the validity and the reliability of the instrument, but I suggest that "what we are looking for is not the standardization of the interaction but stability of meaning across situations and respondents" (Suchman and Jordan 1992, 262). In this case, the benefits of a collaborative interview outweigh the costs. This is a tradeoff, and I placed more importance on "stability of meaning."

# Appendix B
## Variable Specification, Coding, and Description

### DEPENDENT VARIABLES

My analysis measures the impact of various phenomena on individual legislator support for progressive gay rights policy, progressive reproductive policy, and traditionalistic prayer policy. Logit or ordered logit models are run for each issue in Congress from 103rd to the 107th (1993–2002). The dependent variables are additive indices derived from roll call votes and sponsorship/cosponsorship decisions. I selected relevant legislation after consultation with the *Congressional Record*.

To calculate the roll call indices for the gay rights and reproductive policy models, I gave each legislator a score of +1 for each vote in support of progressive sexuality (supporting gay issues and permissive reproductive policy), –1 for each vote supporting religious traditionalism, and a zero for each missed vote or "present" vote. To calculate the sponsorship/cosponsorship indices, I gave legislators a score of +1 for each bill they sponsored or cosponsored that advocated gay rights or permissive reproductive policy and 0 for every time they did not. High scores indicate high levels of support for progressive sexuality. I include sponsorship and cosponsorship items in the analyses if the legislation in question advanced gay rights or progressive reproductive policy and had at least forty-nine cosponsors.

To calculate the school prayer voting indices, I gave each legislator a score of +1 for each vote in support of school prayer,

–1 for each vote opposing school prayer, and a zero for each missed vote and "present" vote. To calculate the sponsorship/co-sponsorship indices, I gave legislators a score of +1 for each piece of legislation they sponsored or cosponsored that advocated school prayer and a zero for every time they did not. In this case, high scores indicate high levels of support for religious tradition-alism. Again, I include sponsorship and cosponsorship items in the analyses if the legislation in question advanced school prayer and had at least forty-nine cosponsors.

Score range varies by Congress. To facilitate the logit and or-dered logit analysis, I collapsed the range of scores. The loss of fine-grained variation was regrettable but inevitable. When the categories were not collapsed an analytical problem emerged be-cause some of the categories were too small for meaningful analy-sis. The following is a list of index components.

## GAY ISSUES

### 103rd Congress (1993–1994)

#### Votes

| | |
|---|---|
| H.Amdt. 188, H.R. 2492, roll no. 313 | Y = –1, N = +1, P/NV = 0 |
| H.Amdt. 316, H.R. 2401, roll no. 460 | Y = +1, N = –1, P/NV = 0 |
| H.Amdt. 317, H.R. 2401, roll no. 461 | Y = –1, N = +1, P/NV = 0 |
| H.Amdt. 318, H.R. 2401, roll no. 462 | Y = –1, N = +1, P/NV = 0 |
| H.Amdt. 751, H.R. 4649, roll no. 321 | Y = –1, N = +1, P/NV = 0 |
| H.Amdt. 490, H.R. 6, roll no. 92 | Y = +1, N = –1, P/NV = 0 |

#### Sponsorship/Cosponsorship

| | |
|---|---|
| H.R. 431, Civil Rights Act of 1993 | S/C = +1, not S/C = 0 |
| H.R. 4636, Employment Non-Discrimination Act of 1994 | S/C = +1, not S/C = 0 |

### 104th Congress (1995–1996)

#### Votes

| | |
|---|---|
| H.Amdt. 890, H.R. 2546, roll no. 759 | Y = –1, N = +1, P/NV = 0 |
| H.Amdt. 1286, H.R. 3396, roll no. 314 | Y = +1, N = –1, P/NV = 0 |
| H.R. 3396, Defense of Marriage Act, on passage, roll no. 316 | Y = –1, N = +1, P/NV = 0 |

## Sponsorship/Cosponsorship

| | |
|---|---|
| H.R. 1863, Employment Non-Discrimination Act of 1995 | S/C = +1, not S/C = 0 |

## 105th Congress (1997–1998)

### Votes

| | |
|---|---|
| H.Amdt. 789, H.R. 4194, roll no. 349 | Y = –1, N = +1, P/NV = 0 |
| H.Amdt. 855, H.R. 4276, roll no. 398 | Y = –1, N = +1, P/NV = 0 |
| H.Amdt. 871, H.R. 4380, roll no. 414 | Y = –1, N = +1, P/NV = 0 |

### Sponsor/Cosponsorship

| | |
|---|---|
| H.R. 1858, Employment Non-Discrimination Act of 1997 | S/C = +1, not S/C = 0 |
| H.R. 3081, Hate Crimes Prevention Act of 1997 | S/C = +1, not S/C = 0 |

## 106th Congress (1999–2000)

### Votes

| | |
|---|---|
| H.Amdt. 201, H.R. 1501, roll no. 223 | Y = –1, N = +1, P/NV = 0 |
| H.Amdt. 284, H.R. 1691, roll no. 298 | Y = +1, N = –1, P/NV = 0 |
| H.Amdt. 356, H.R. 2587, roll no. 346 | Y = –1, N = +1, P/NV = 0 |
| Graham motion to instruct, H.R. 4205, roll no. 470 | Y = –1, N = +1, P/NV = 0 |
| Conyers motion to instruct, H.R. 4205, roll no. 471 | Y = +1, N = –1, P/NV = 0 |
| H.R. 4892, Scouting for All Act, motion to suspend the rules and pass the bill, roll no. 468 | Y = +1, N = –1, P/NV = 0 |

### Sponsorship/Cosponsorship

| | |
|---|---|
| H.Con.Res. 259, Expressing the concern of Congress regarding human rights violations against lesbians, gay men, bisexuals, and transgendered individuals around the world | S/C = +1, not S/C = 0 |
| H.R. 1082, Hate Crimes Prevention Act of 1999 | S/C = +1, not S/C = 0 |

H.R. 2355, Employment Non-Discrimination    S/C = +1, not S/C = 0
    Act of 1999
H.R. 3650, Permanent Partners Immigration    S/C = +1, not S/C = 0
    Act of 2000

## 107th Congress (2001–2002)

### Votes

H.Amdt. 310, H.R. 2944, roll no. 352    Y = –1, N = +1, P/NV = 0
H.Amdt. 311, H.R. 2944, roll no. 354    Y = –1, N = +1, P/NV = 0
H.Amdt. 312, H.R. 2944, roll no. 353    Y = +1, N = –1, P/NV = 0
H.R. 7, Charitable Choice Act of 2001,    Y = +1, N = –1, P/NV = 0
    motion to recommit, roll no. 253

### Sponsorship/Cosponsorship

H.Con.Res. 173, International Human    S/C = +1, not S/C = 0
    Rights Equality Resolution
H.R. 638, Domestic Partnership Benefits    S/C = +1, not S/C = 0
    and Obligations Act of 2001
H.R. 690, Permanent Partners Immigration    S/C = +1, not S/C = 0
    Act of 2001
H.R. 1343, Local Law Enforcement Hate    S/C = +1, not S/C = 0
    Crimes Prevention Act of 2001
H.R. 2692, Employment Non-Discrimination    S/C = +1, not S/C = 0
    Act of 2001

## REPRODUCTIVE POLICY

### 103rd Congress (1993–1994)

### Votes

H.Amdt. 11, H.R. 4, roll no. 64    Y = –1, N = +1, P/NV = 0
H.Amdt. 12, H.R. 4, roll no. 60    Y = +1, N = –1, P/NV = 0
H.Amdt. 106, H.R. 2333, roll no. 232    Y = –1, N = +1, P/NV = 0
H.Amdt. 185, H.R. 2518, roll no. 309    Y = –1, N = +1, P/NV = 0
H.R. 670, Family Planning Amendments    Y = +1, N = –1, P/NV = 0
    Act, on passage, roll no. 107
H.R. 796, Freedom of Access to Clinic    Y = –1, N = +1, P/NV = 0
    Entrances Act, on motion to recommit,
    roll no. 582

## Sponsorship/Cosponsorship

| | |
|---|---|
| H.R. 25, Freedom of Choice Act | S/C = +1, not S/C = 0 |
| H.R. 26, Reproductive Health Equity Act | S/C = +1, not S/C = 0 |

## 104th Congress (1995–1996)

### Votes

| | |
|---|---|
| H.Amdt. 403, H.R. 1561, roll no. 350 | Y = –1, N = +1, P/NV = 0 |
| H.Amdt. 404, H.R. 1561, roll no. 349 | Y = +1, N = –1, P/NV = 0 |
| H.Amdt. 436, H.R. 1530, roll no. 382 | Y = +1, N = –1, P/NV = 0 |
| H.Amdt. 477, H.R. 1868, roll no. 433 | Y = –1, N = +1, P/NV = 0 |
| H.Amdt. 478, H.R. 1868, roll no. 432 | Y = +1, N = –1, P/NV = 0 |
| H.Amdt. 566, H.R. 2020, roll no. 526 | Y = +1, N = –1, P/NV = 0 |
| H.Amdt. 651, H.R. 2076, roll no. 574 | Y = +1, N = –1, P/NV = 0 |
| H.Amdt. 728, H.R. 2127, roll no. 620 | Y = +1, N = –1, P/NV = 0 |
| H.Amdt. 753, H.R. 2126, roll no. 641 | Y = +1, N = –1, P/NV = 0 |
| H.Amdt. 946, H.R. 3019, roll no. 51 | Y = +1, N = –1, P/NV = 0 |
| H.Amdt. 1054, H.R. 3230, roll no. 167 | Y = +1, N = –1, P/NV = 0 |
| H.Amdt. 1276, H.R.3755, roll no. 307 | Y = +1, N = –1, P/NV = 0 |
| H.Amdt. 1280, H.R.3755, roll no. 310 | Y = +1, N = –1, P/NV = 0 |
| H.Amdt. 1295, H.R. 3756, roll no. 320 | Y = +1, N = –1, P/NV = 0 |
| H.Amdt. 1309, H.R. 3845, roll no. 332 | Y = +1, N = –1, P/NV = 0 |
| H.R. 1833, Partial-Birth Abortion Ban Act, on passage, roll no. 756 | Y = –1, N = +1, P/NV = 0 |

## Sponsorship/Cosponsorship

| | |
|---|---|
| H.Res. 118, Expressing the sense of the House of Representatives with respect to restricting medical professionals from providing to women full and accurate medical information on reproductive health options | S/C = +1, not S/C = 0 |
| H.R. 1952, Women's Choice and Reproductive Health Protection Act | S/C = +1, not S/C = 0 |
| H.R. 3057, Comstock Cleanup Act | S/C = +1, not S/C = 0 |

## 105th Congress (1997–1998)

### Votes

| | |
|---|---|
| H.Amdt. 156, H.R. 1757, roll no. 194 | Y = –1, N = +1, P/NV = 0 |
| H.Amdt. 157, H.R. 1757, roll no. 167 | Y = +1, N = –1, P/NV = 0 |

H.Amdt. 187, H.R. 1119, roll no. 217 — Y = +1, N = –1, P/NV = 0
H.Amdt. 312, H.R. 2159, roll no. 358 — Y = –1, N = +1, P/NV = 0
H.Amdt. 318, H.R. 2159, roll no. 363 — Y = –1, N = +1, P/NV = 0
H.Amdt. 319, H.R. 2159, roll no. 362 — Y = +1, N = –1, P/NV = 0
H.Amdt. 334, H.R. 2264, roll no. 379 — Y = +1, N = –1, P/NV = 0
H.Amdt. 335, H.R. 2264, roll no. 378 — Y = +1, N = –1, P/NV = 0
H.Amdt. 348, H.R. 2264, roll no. 388 — Y = –1, N = +1, P/NV = 0
H.Amdt. 385, H.R. 2267, roll no. 447 — Y = +1, N = –1, P/NV = 0
H.Amdt. 643, H.R. 3616, roll no. 171 — Y = +1, N = –1, P/NV = 0
H.Amdt. 705, H.R. 4104, roll no. 260 — Y = –1, N = +1, P/NV = 0
H.Amdt. 725, H.R. 4104, roll no. 288 — Y = +1, N = –1, P/NV = 0
H.Amdt. 728, H.R. 4104, roll no. 290 — Y = +1, N = –1, P/NV = 0
H.Amdt. 735, H.R. 4104, roll no. 292 — Y = –1, N = +1, P/NV = 0
H.Amdt. 835, H.R. 4276, roll no. 387 — Y = +1, N = –1, P/NV = 0
H.Amdt. 865, H.R. 4380, roll no. 408 — Y = +1, N = –1, P/NV = 0
H.Amdt. 923, H.R. 4274, roll no. 504 — Y = –1, N = +1, P/NV = 0
H.J.Res. 36, Population Planning resolution, on passage, roll no. 22 — Y = +1, N = –1, P/NV = 0
H.R. 581, Population Planning bill, on passage, roll no. 23 — Y = –1, N = +1, P/NV = 0
H.R. 1122, Partial Birth Abortion bill, on passage, roll no. 65 — Y = –1, N = +1, P/NV = 0
H.R. 3682, Child Custody Protection bill, on passage, roll no. 280 — Y = –1, N = +1, P/NV = 0

### Sponsorship/Cosponsorship

H.Res. 358, Expressing the sense of the House of Representatives with respect to the protection of reproductive health services clinics — S/C = +1, not S/C = 0
H.R. 2525, Family Planning and Choice Protection Act of 1997 — S/C = +1, not S/C = 0

## 106th Congress (1999–2000)

### Votes

H.Amdt. 142, H.R. 1906, roll no. 173 — Y = 0, N = 1, P/NV = 0
H.Amdt. 156, H.R. 1401, roll no. 184 — Y = 1, N = 0, P/NV = 0
H.Amdt. 286, H.R. 2490, roll no. 301 — Y = 1, N = 0, P/NV = 0
H.Amdt. 304, H.R. 2415, roll no. 312 — Y = 1, N = 0, P/NV = 0
H.Amdt. 359, H.R. 2606, roll no. 349 — Y = 0, N = 1, P/NV = 0
H.Amdt. 360, H.R. 2606, roll no. 350 — Y = 1, N = 0, P/NV = 0
H.Amdt. 380, H.R. 2606, roll no. 360 — Y = 0, N = 1, P/NV = 0

| | |
|---|---|
| H.Amdt. 399, H.R. 2670, roll no. 373 | Y = 1, N = 0, P/NV = 0 |
| H.Amdt. 508, H.R. 2436, roll no. 463 | Y = 0, N = 1, P/NV = 0 |
| H.Amdt. 722, H.R. 4205, roll no. 203 | Y = 1, N = 0, P/NV = 0 |
| H.Amdt. 882, H.R. 4690, roll no. 318 | Y = 1, N = 0, P/NV = 0 |
| H.Amdt. 956, H.R. 1304, roll no. 371 | Y = 0, N = 1, P/NV = 0 |
| H.Amdt. 962, H.R. 4461, roll no. 373 | Y = 0, N = 1, P/NV = 0 |
| H.Amdt. 997, H.R. 4811, roll no. 396 | Y = 1, N = 0, P/NV = 0 |
| H.Amdt. 1017, H.R. 4871, roll no. 422 | Y = 1, N = 0, P/NV = 0 |
| H.R. 1218, Child Custody Protection Act, on passage, roll no. 26 | Y = 0, N = 1, P/NV = 0 |
| H.R. 2436, Unborn Victims of Violence Act of 1999, on passage, roll no. 465 | Y = 0, N = 1, P/NV = 0 |
| H.R. 3660, Partial-Birth Abortion bill, on passage, roll no. 104 | Y = 0, N = 1, P/NV = 0 |
| H.R. 4292, To protect infants who are born alive, motion to suspend the rules and pass the bill, roll no. 495 | Y = 0, N = 1, P/NV = 0 |

## Sponsorship/Cosponsorship

None

## 107th Congress (2001–2002)

### Votes

| | |
|---|---|
| H.Amdt. 27, H.R. 503, roll no. 88 | Y = 1, N = 0, P/NV = 0 |
| H.Amdt. 34, H.R. 1646, roll no. 115 | Y = 0, N = 1, P/NV = 0 |
| H.Amdt. 171, H.R. 2500, roll no. 235 | Y = 1, N = 0, P/NV = 0 |
| H.Amdt. 317, H.R. 2586, roll no. 357 | Y = 1, N = 0, P/NV = 0 |
| H.Amdt. 377, H.R. 3061, roll no. 379 | Y = 0, N = 1, P/NV = 0 |
| H.Amdt. 478, H.R. 4546, roll no. 153 | Y = 1, N = 0, P/NV = 0 |
| H.R. 476, Child Custody Protection Act, on passage, roll no. 97 | Y = 0, N = 1, P/NV = 0 |
| H.R. 503, Fetal Protection bill, on passage, roll no. 89 | Y = 0, N = 1, P/NV = 0 |
| H.R. 4691, Abortion Non-Discrimination Act, on passage, roll no. 412 | Y = 0, N = 1, P/NV = 0 |
| H.R. 4965, Partial-Birth Abortion bill, on passage, roll no. 343 | Y = 0, N = 1, P/NV = 0 |

## Sponsorship/Cosponsorship

| | |
|---|---|
| H.R. 185, Women's Right to Know Act of 2001 | S/C = +1, not S/C = 0 |

H.R. 755, Mexico City Policy bill            S/C = +1, not S/C = 0
H.R. 3877, Emergency Contraception          S/C = +1, not S/C = 0
   Education Act
H.R. 4113, Compassionate Care for Female    S/C = +1, not S/C = 0
   Sexual Assault Survivors Act

## SCHOOL PRAYER

## 103rd Congress (1993–1994)

### Votes

H.Amdt. 482, H.R. 6, roll no. 75    Y = –1, N = +1, P/NV = 0
H.Amdt. 483, H.R. 6, roll no. 74    Y = +1, N = –1, P/NV = 0

### Sponsorship/Cosponsorship

H.J.Res. 22, Proposing an amendment to       S/C = +1, not S/C = 0
   the Constitution of the United States
   relating to voluntary prayer in public
   schools

## 104th Congress (1995–1996)

### Votes

None

### Sponsorship/Cosponsorship

H.J.Res. 127, Proposing a religious liberties    S/C = +1, not S/C = 0
   amendment to the Constitution of the
   United States to secure the people's right
   to acknowledge God according to the
   dictates of conscience

## 105th Congress (1997–1998)

### Vote

H.J.Res. 78, Proposing an amendment        Y = +1, N = –1, P/NV = 0
   to the Constitution of the United States
   restoring religious freedom, roll no. 201

## Sponsorship/Cosponsorship

None

## 106th Congress (1999–2000)

### Votes

| | |
|---|---|
| H.Amdt. 198, H.R. 1501, roll no. 219 | Y = +1, N = –1, P/NV = 0 |
| H.Amdt. 199, H.R. 1501, roll no. 220 | Y = +1, N = –1, P/NV = 0 |
| H.Amdt. 200, H.R. 1501, roll no. 221 | Y = +1, N = –1, P/NV = 0 |
| H.Amdt. 1044, H.R. 4678, roll no. 455 | Y = –1, N = +1, P/NV = 0 |

### Sponsorship/Cosponsorship

| | |
|---|---|
| H.J.Res. 66, Proposing an amendment to the Constitution of the United States restoring religious freedom | S/C = +1, not S/C = 0 |

## 107th Congress (2001–2002)

### Votes

None

### Sponsorship/Cosponsorship

| | |
|---|---|
| H.J.Res. 81, Proposing an amendment to the Constitution of the United States restoring religious freedom | S/C = +1, not S/C = 0 |

## INDEPENDENT VARIABLES

*% College Educated*: Percentage of the district with a college degree, taken from various editions of *CQ's Politics in America* and based on 1990 Census Bureau data.

*% African American*: Percentage of the district that identifies as African American, data provided by John Green and based on the 1990 Census. This is used as a proxy for the proportion of Black Protestants in each district.

*% Latino*: Percentage of the district that identifies as Latino, taken from various editions of *CQ's Politics in America* and based on 1990 Census Bureau data.

*% Urban*: Percentage of the district classified as urban, based on Census Bureau data and taken from Adler (no date).

*District Partisanship*: Percentage of the district's vote going to the Democratic candidate in the most recent presidential election. For the 103rd and 104th Congresses, this variable is the percentage of the vote that went to Gov. Bill Clinton in the 1992 election. For the 105th and 106th Congresses, it is the percentage of the vote that went to President Clinton in the 1996 election. For the 107th Congress, it is the percentage of the vote that went to Vice President Al Gore in the 2000 election. These data are taken from various editions of *CQ's Politics in America*.

*District Religion*: Percentages of the district classified as religiously conservative and Roman Catholic. These variables are derived from the 1992 Glenmary Research Center enumeration of denominations (Bradley et al. 1992); the data were graciously provided by John Green. See table 4.1 for a list of which denominations are classified as religiously conservative.

*Out Gay or Lesbian*: Legislator variable, measured as a dummy variable (out gay or lesbian = 1, straight = 0). Only gays and lesbians who were out during their service or subsequently came out are coded as 1.

*Gender*: legislator variable measured as a dummy variable (male = 1, female = 0).

*Contributions from HRC, NARAL, and Eagle Forum*: Amount in dollars contributed to the primary and general election campaigns of each legislator by each political action committee during the 103rd, 104th, 105th, 106th, and 107th Congress election cycles. The source of these data is the Center for Responsive Politics.

*Party I.D.*: Legislator variable, measured as a dummy variable (Democrat = 1, Republican = 0).

*Ideology*: Legislator variable operationalized with DW-NOMINATE (Poole and Rosenthal 1991) scores, which are available at http://voteview.com. Scores range from –1 to +1, with –1 being the most liberal and +1 the most conservative. Initial analysis revealed high levels of collinearity between elite partisanship and ideology. The collinearity reduced the significance of the elite partisanship variable and reversed the direction of its effect. Borrowing a technique from Haider-Markel (2001) and Wattier and Tatalovich (1995), I reduced the collinearity by regressing elite partisanship on ideology and using the residuals from that equation in place of the DW-NOMINATE scores. This technique eliminates the ability to make substantive interpretations of the ideology coefficients in the models, but it should reasonably approximate the correct direction of the ideology effect without interfering with the effect of elite partisanship. I took several steps to ensure that the new ideology measure acts as a reasonable proxy for ideology. I ran full models with the DW-NOMINATE scores and reran them with the residual substitution. In both rounds, the significance and direction of the ideology effect are constant. The difference between the two rounds is in the performance of the elite party measure. Substituting the residual measure, elite partisanship emerges as significant, and the direction of the effect is as predicted. The new ideology measure also was correlated with district-level Democratic partisanship. The direction association between these two variables should be negative, assuming that the new ideology measure approximates ideology; in all but one instance, it is.

*Legislator Religion*: A series of dummy variables used to capture legislator religion: white Catholic = 1, white religious conservative = 1, African American Protestant = 1.

# Notes

## NOTES TO INTRODUCTION

1. The line is taken from Winthrop's 1630 sermon "A Model of Christian Charity."
2. Available at http://www.reaganfoundation.org/reagan/speeches/farewell.asp.
3. This is not meant to discount the likelihood that self-interest and a concern for safety affect gun control attitudes. See Wolpert and Gimpel (1998).
4. The Supreme Court struck down a portion of the Brady Act, however, in *Printz v. United States,* 521 U.S. 898 (1997).
5. Shweta Govindarajan, "Dems in tight races oppose gun ban," *The Hill* (June 23, 2004), 20; Rachel L. Swarns, "Clock ticks on extension of gun ban," *New York Times* (July 23, 2004), A9; Aparna H. Kumar, "GOP: Congress won't vote on weapons ban," *Associated Press* (September 9, 2004)
6. See also Sanders (1997) on the effect of urbanization on civil rights voting.
7. See http://www.whitehouse.gov/news/releases/2003/01/20030115-7.html.
8. Unless otherwise specified, I use the term "gay" throughout this volume in an inclusive manner, referring to gay men, lesbians, bisexuals, and transgendered persons. I hope the reader will be forgiving of this shorthand, for the sake of prose.
9. Scholars may use the terms "morality policy" or "social regulatory policy" to refer to the kinds of conflicts I address here.

10. In another example, it is interesting to note that at public universities in Texas, undergraduates are required to take and pass six hours of introductory American Government. The political science department at the University of North Texas surveys these students each semester and regularly finds that although they are overwhelmingly concerned about "moral decay," many approve of drug use and casual sex. Of course, it is unclear whether these survey results suggest a lack of constraint or that students simply define moral decay in unconventional terms. (Questions about these data may be directed to Dr. Steven Forde, professor of political science, University of North Texas.)

## NOTES TO CHAPTER 1

1. See Dodd (2001) for a useful discussion of the goal orientation literature.
2. Even at Baylor University—the world's largest Baptist university and a place where homosexuality is prohibited in the student handbook—there is some division among the student body on this issue. In February 2004 the student newspaper, *The Lariat*, published an editorial in support of gay rights—although the editorial board was rebuked by Baylor president Robert Sloan, as well as by alumni and students. See Todd Ackerman, "Gay marriage stance sparks Baylor furor; officials assail student paper editorial," *Houston Chronicle* (March 2, 2004), A13.
3. I use the terms "moral" and "cultural" interchangeably here.
4. Interview with the author, July 19, 2000.
5. Interview with the author, July 11, 2000.
6. Interview with the author, July 13, 2000.
7. Interview with the author, July 11, 2000.
8. Interview with the author, August 9, 2000.
9. Interview with the author, June 6, 2002.
10. Interview with the author, July 18, 2000.
11. Interview with the author, July 19, 2000.
12. Interview with the author, August 2, 2000.
13. Legislative director's interview with the author, August 1, 2000.
14. Administrative assistant's interview with the author, August 8, 2000.
15. Interview with the author, July 18, 2000.
16. Interview with the author, August 8, 2000.
17. Interview with the author, July 18, 2000.
18. Democratic staffer's interview with the author, May 30, 2002.
19. Democratic staffer's interview with the author, June 14, 2002.
20. Democratic staffer's interview with the author, May 30, 2002.
21. Interview with the author, June 14, 2002.

22. Interview with the author, August 9, 2000.
23. Democratic chief of staff's interview with the author, June 14, 2002.
24. Former Republican representative's interview with the author, June 29, 2000.
25. Interview with the author, August 2, 2000.
26. Interview with the author, June 18, 2002.
27. Interview with the author, June 29, 2000.
28. Interview with the author, July 19, 2000.
29. Interview with the author, June 29, 2000.
30. Interview with the author, June 5, 2002.
31. Interview with the author, June 29, 2000.
32. Republican representative's interview with the author, July 18, 2000.
33. Democratic representative's interview with the author, July 11, 2000.
34. Interview with the author, July 18, 2000.
35. Interview with the author, June 28, 2000.
36. Interview with the author, August 15, 2000.
37. Interview with the author, August 2, 2000.
38. Interview with the author, July 19, 2000.
39. Interview with the author, July 31, 2000.
40. Republican legislative director's interview with the author, August 8, 2000.
41. Republican staffer's interview with the author, August 9, 2000.
42. Democratic legislative director's interview with the author, August 7, 2000.
43. Interview with the author, June 28, 2000.
44. Republican representative's interview with the author, June 29, 2000.
45. Democratic legislative director's interview with the author, August 1, 2000.
46. Interview with the author, August 8, 2000.
47. Democratic legislative director's interview with the author, August 8, 2000.
48. Republican representative's interview with the author, June 29, 2000.
49. Interview with the author, June 29, 2000.
50. Rep. Robert Bauman (R-MD) served in the U.S. House of Representatives from 1973 to 1981.

## NOTES TO CHAPTER 2

1. I do not use the term *progressive* to denote anything other than "changing." Whether changing social relations are for the better is best left to the reader.
2. Nevertheless, abortion has been practiced in some form for many

years. It was even practiced in ancient Greece and the Roman
Empire (McFarlane and Meier 2001, 20–23; O'Connor 1996, 19).
3. The term *quickening* refers to movement of the fetus. A prequickening abortion would take place before initial fetal movement, and a postquickening abortion would take place after initial fetal movement.
4. As McFarlane and Meier (2001, 36) note, "the rationale for therapeutic abortions expanded over time." During the Depression, poverty was considered a therapeutic rationale.
5. 1977 Pregnancy Disability Amendment to Title VII of the 1964 Civil Rights Act (P.L. 95-555).
6. 1979 Amendments to the Public Health Service Act (P.L. 96-76).
7. The law did not take effect immediately because of legal challenges to it.
8. *Stenberg v. Carhart*, 530 U.S. 914 (2000).
9. Cheryl Wetzstein, "High court will review repeal of abortion law," *Washington Times* (May 24, 2005), A01.
10. This story was reported on *Frontline* in "The Clinton Years," which aired on PBS on January 16, 2001.
11. *Congressional Record*, July 12, 1996, pages H74808–87.
12. According to election 2000 exit poll data, 4 percent of voters surveyed (or slightly more than 4 million nationwide) identified themselves as gay or lesbian; 70 percent of these gays and lesbians indicated that they voted for Al Gore. That figure represents about 2.8 million votes for Gore from the gay community. About 25 percent of gays and lesbians (or slightly more than 1 million nationwide) indicated that they voted for George W. Bush.
13. Quoted in Raphael Lewis, "SJC affirms gay marriage," *Boston Globe* (February 5, 2004); available at http://www.boston.com/news/local/massachusetts/articles/2004/02/05/sjc_affirms_gay_marriage/.
14. Christie MacDonald and Bill Dedman, "About 2,500 gay couples sought licenses in 1st week," *Boston Globe* (June 17, 2004); available at http://www.boston.com/news/specials/gay_marriage/articles/2004/06/17/about_2500_gay_couples_sought_licenses_in_1st_week/.
15. Theo Emery, ""State reaches one-year mark of legal same sex marriage," *Associated Press State & Local Wire* (May 17, 2005).
16. Ibid.
17. Tom Benner, "Lull in gay marriage battle, but some planning new fight," *The Patriot Ledger* (Quincy, Mass.) (May 16, 2005) 1.
18. Pam Belluck, "Eight diverse gay couples join to fight Massachusetts," *New York Times* (June 18, 2004); available at http://www.nytimes.com/2004/06/18/national/18gay.html.

19. Shaun Sutner, "Gay marriage foes continue litigation on residencies; SJC may have to decide on license availability for out-of-state couples," Worcester, Mass., *Telegram & Gazette* (November 19, 2004).
20. Jay Lindsay, "High court to hear challenge to marriage law," *Associated Press State and Local Wire* (February 24, 2005).
21. Michael Levenson, "Judge in Fla. won't accept gay couple's Mass. wedding," *Boston Globe* (January 20, 2005).
22. It does not appear to be a slam-dunk for either side. See Lea Brilmayer, "A marriage license only goes so far," *Washington Post* (February 15, 2004), final, B1.
23. Available at http://www.whitehouse.gov/news/releases/2004/01/20040120-7.html.
24. Carl Hulse, "Senators block initiative to ban same-sex unions," *New York Times* (July 15, 2004); available at http://www.nytimes.com/2004/07/15/politics/15gay.html.
25. Ibid.
26. Jonathan Kaplan, "New GOP gay-ban tactics," *The Hill* (July 15, 2004), 1.
27. H.J. Res. 39 by Rep. Daniel E. Lungren (R-CA) on March 17, 2005; S.J. Res. 1 by Sen. Wayne Allard (R-CO) on January 24, 2005; S.J. Res. 13 by Sen. Sam Brownback (R-KS) on April 14, 2005; H.R. 72 by Rep. Jo Ann Davis (R-VA) on January 4, 2005.
28. Robert Tanner, "New England a regional holdout in march to ban gay marriages," *Associated Press State and Local Wire* (April 7, 2005).
29. Kevin O'Hanlon, "Judge strikes down Nebraska's same-sex marriage ban," *Associated Press State and Local Wire* (May 12, 2005); Charles Yoo, "Same-sex marriage gets a boost," *Cox News Service* (May 22, 2005).
30. James Dao, "Renewed state efforts made against same-sex marriage," *New York Times* (July 16, 2004); available at www.nytimes.com/2004/07/16/national/16amend.html.
31. Tanner, "New England a regional holdout."
32. The text of Justice Scalia's opinion is available at http://caselaw.lp.findlaw.com/scripts/getcase.pl?court=US&friend=oyez&vol=000&invol=02-102.

## NOTES TO CHAPTER 3

1. It is less clear that Buchanan's culture war rhetoric appealed to uncommitted voters and independents. Indeed, third-party candidate Ross Perot received more than 18 percent of the popular vote, and Bill Clinton won the election with a plurality of a little more than 43 percent. The incumbent, President George H. W. Bush, received just 37.45 percent of the popular vote.

2. The term "fundamentalist" generally refers to a belief in the inerrancy of the Bible, the importance of personal salvation, and the need for disengagement from the secular world. The term "evangelical" also refers to beliefs in the inerrancy of the Bible and personal salvation through acceptance of Jesus Christ as one's personal savior. In addition, evangelicals emphasize the need to spread the Gospel to nonbelievers. Evangelicals tend not to emphasize the need for separation from the secular world. There also is some disagreement between fundamentalists and evangelicals over exactly how inerrant the Bible actually is. Fundamentalists tend to take a harder line on this question. Although the terms refer to two different religious movements within Christianity, they are not necessarily mutually exclusive.

3. For example, see http://www.law.umkc.edu/faculty/projects/ftrials/scopes/menk.htm.

4. John Hanna, "Kansas debate over evolution also about defining science," *Associated Press State and Local Wire* (May 14, 2005).

5. See Wald (2003), chapter 1, for a good discussion of modernism.

6. Notably, if one defines status as a demographic characteristic like race or class, the status politics model probably will yield different results (Wood and Hughes 1984).

7. Available from http://www.cnn.com/2001/US/09/14/Falwell.apology/.

8. Ralph Z. Hallow, "Christian, but no longer a powerful coalition; Finances retard a once-major force," *The Washington Times* (March 14, 2001), A1; Ralph Z. Hallow, "Religious right loses its political potency," *Washington Times* (May 20, 2001), A1; Joyce Howard Price, "Robertson resigns from Christian Coalition," *Washington Times* (December 6, 2001), A3.

9. Hanna Rosin and Dana Milbank, "A political 'heretic' is cast out; Supporting McCain costs Bauer his place on the religious right," *Washington Post* (March 26, 2000), A6.

10. Alan Cooperman, "Gay marriage as 'the New Abortion'; Debate becomes polarizing as both sides become better organized, spend millions," *Washington Post* (July 26, 2004), A3.

11. Alan Cooperman, "Same-sex bans fuel conservative agenda," *Washington Post* (November 4, 2004), A39.

12. Jim VandeHei and Michael A. Fletcher, "Bush upsets some supporters; President is urged to press ban on same-sex marriage," *Washington Post* (January 19, 2005), A11

13. Ralph Z. Hallow, "Bush backpedal on marriage irks right," *Washington Times* (January 26, 2005), A4.

14. C. L. Loudonville, "Ashcroft's Views on Abortion Rights a Problem," Albany, N.Y., *Times Union*, (January 24, 2001), sec. A.

15. Sean Scully, "House GOP tries to avert criticism of its gun policy; Issue is sensitive as Columbine anniversary nears," *Washington Times* (April 12, 2000), A3.

16. See *Rosenberger v. University of Virginia*, 515 U.S. 819 (1995); *Agostini v. Felton*, 521 U.S. 203 (1997); *Good News Club v. Milford Central School*, 533 U.S. 98 (2001); and *Zelman v. Simmons-Harris*, 536 U.S. 639 (2002).

17. David Hoffman, "On social issues, gains 'far short' of right's hopes," *Washington Post* (January 31, 1984), A7.

18. R. T. Reid, "Helms to offer alternatives; Prayer backers plan new drive," *Washington Post* (March 23, 1984), A2.

19. Larry Witham, "Top women's group gives Istook award; Lauds his support for school prayer," *Washington Times* (September 21, 1996), A4.

20. Adrien Seybert, "Debate draws extremes from local lawmakers," *States News Service* (January 3, 1995); Major Garrett, "Path to school prayer seen as constitutional; Speaker: No need for amendment," *Washington Times* (April 10, 1995), A1.

21. Ralph Z. Hallow, "GOP vows to push religious-right issues; Conservative activists remain skeptical," *Washington Times* (April 10, 1998), A1; Thomas B. Edsall and Ceci Connolly, "A gaping GOP rift; Christian right increasingly resentful," *Washington Post* (March 27, 1998), A1.

22. Available from http://www.diocesecs.org/bishopsOffice/pastoralLetter1.htm.

23. Julia Duin, "Catholic bishops face vexing issues; Maverick politicians on agenda," *Washington Times* (June 14, 2004), A10.

24. Laurie Goodstein, "Politicians face censure from bishops on abortion rights," *New York Times* (June 19, 2004); available from http://www.nytimes.com/2004/06/19/national/19BISH.final.html.

25. Available from http://www.usccb.org/bishops/catholicsinpoliticallife. htm.

26. Dan Balz and Alan Cooperman, "Bush, Pope to meet today at Vatican," *Washington Post* (June 4, 2004), A8.

27. Alan Cooperman, "Bush tells Catholic group he will tackle its issues," *Washington Post* (August 4, 2004), A4; David A. Kirkpatrick and Jason Horowitz, "Bush sought Vatican official's help on issues, report says," *New York Times* (June 13, 2004), sec. 1, p. 38.

28. Available from http://www.vatican.va/holy_father/paul_vi/encyclicals/documents/hf_p-vi_enc_25071968_humanae-vitae_en.html.

29. Notably, however, in March 2005 the Catholic bishops in the United States launched "a more prominent effort to bar the death penalty." Neela Bannerjee, "Bishops fight death penalty in new drive," *New York Times* (March 21, 2005), A19.

30. Raphael Lewis and Michael Paulson, "Church gives pre-election scorecard; Gay marriage votes identified in mailings," *Boston Globe* (June 15, 2004), A1.
31. Available from http://www.vatican.va/roman_curia/congregations/ cfaith/documents/rc_con_cfaith_doc_19751229_persona-humana_ en.html.

## NOTES TO CHAPTER 4

1. Republican legislative director's interview with the author, August 8, 2000.
2. The legislative items used to calculate the indices for each Congress are listed in Appendix B.
3. This is not meant to suggest that the effect of religion on social life is necessarily conservative. Indeed, Smith (1996, 6) is quick to elaborate on the argument that the very sacred transcendence that gives religion a conservative "thrust" can also spark "radical social criticism" and change.
4. John Green graciously provided district-level data.
5. Representatives Baldwin, Frank, Gunderson, Huffington, Kolbe, and Studds.
6. Carolyn Curiel, "How Hispanics Voted Republican," *New York Times* (November 8, 2004), A22.
7. The vast array of Christian Right organizations may function as a proximate hierarchy for the purposes of communication and mobilization. This empirical question, put forth by Brian Calfano in a conversation with the author, deserves scholarly attention.

## NOTES TO CHAPTER 5

1. Anne Swardson and Tom Kenworthy, "Wright ekes out tax bill's passage; Speaker literally turns back clock to overcome party rebellion," *Washington Post* (October 30, 1987), A16.
2. "O'Neill assails a Republican and is rebuked by the chair," *New York Times* (May 16, 1984), A16.
3. Russell Baker, "Blades and pants," *New York Times* (May 31, 1989), A23.
4. Tom Kenworthy, "House committee charges Wright with 69 ethics-rules violations; Improper gifts, 'scheme' to evade income limit by book sales cited," *Washington Post* (April 18, 1989), A1; Tom Kenworthy, "Wright to resign speaker's post, House seat; Texan again rebuts charges, decries conflict over ethics," *Washington Post* (June 1, 1989), A1.

5. Susan B. Glasser, "High Court hears term limits case Tuesday at 10 a.m," *Roll Call* (November 28, 1994).
6. David E. Rosenbaum, "Big hurdle for the tax bill: the 'Rule,'" *New York Times* (April 1, 1995),] sec. 1, p. 20.
7. Joel Connelley, "Foley calls for a more genteel era," *Seattle Post-Intelligencer* (April 4, 1996), A1.
8. "The Contract with America: Scorecard," *Washington Post* (April 3, 1995), A17.
9. Interview with the author, August 15, 2000.
10. Quoted in Richard E. Cohen, "The Rise and Fall of Newt," *National Journal* (March 5, 1999), 603.
11. Cohen, "The Rise and Fall of Newt," 598–606.
12. Ibid.
13. Richard E. Cohen, "It's Campaign 2000, Stupid!" *National Journal* (September 25, 1999), 2714–16.
14. Charlie Cook, "Crisis Dims Democrats' Recruitment Prospects," *National Journal* (September 29, 2001), 3022–23.
15. E. J. Dionne, "Democratic catastrophe," *Washington Post* (November 7, 2002), A25.
16. David Broder, "'Accidental' no more," *Washington Post* (November 7, 2002), A25.
17. John Cochran, "Disorder in the House—and no end in sight," *CQ Weekly* (April 3, 2004), 790.
18. Alan K. Ota, "No pat on the back for GOP as intraparty issues dominate," *CQ Weekly* (January 10, 2005), 66.
19. "The main GOP factions," *CQ Weekly* (September 4, 2004), 2027.
20. Keith Perine, "House conservatives seek voters' attention with action on gay marriage amendment," *CQ Weekly* (October 2, 2004); David Nather and Adriel Bettelheimm, "Social Security FYI: Bush's top priority vs. queasy GOP," *CQ Weekly* (January 24, 2005), 170.
21. Ota, "No pat on the back for GOP," 66.
22. William Safire, "The dangers of lopsidedness," *New York Times* (November 4, 2004).
23. Audrey Hudson, "President's domestic agenda to include marriage amendment," *Washington Times* (November 8, 2004), A1.
24. John Cochran, "Religious right lays claim to big role in GOP agenda," *CQ Weekly* (November 13, 2004), 2684.
25. Ken Herman, "How to get straight to the people: Control the message and stage the event," *Cox News Service* (February 11, 2005); Jim VandeHei and Michael A. Fletcher, "Bush upsets some supporters; President is urged to press ban on same-sex marriage," *Washington Post* (January 19, 2005), A11.

26. Democratic chief of staff's interview with the author, June 14, 2004.
27. Republican legislative director's interview with the author, August 9, 2000.
28. Republican representative's interview with the author, June 29, 2000.
29. Interview with the author, August 7, 2000.
30. Interview with the author, August 8, 2000.
31. Ibid.
32. Republican legislative director's interview with the author, July 31, 2000.
33. Interview with the author, August 2, 2000.
34. Interview with the author, August 8, 2000.
35. Ibid.
36. Republican legislative director's interview with the author, August 2, 2000.
37. Republican legislative director's interview with the author, August 8, 2000.
38. Democratic administrative assistant's interview with the author, August 8, 2000.
39. Republican legislative director's interview with the author, August 15, 2000.
40. Interview with the author, August 8, 2000.
41. Interview with the author, August 9, 2000.
42. Interview with the author, June 14, 2002.
43. Interview with the author, June 6, 2002.
44. I note that the Republican leadership also made this tool available to Democrats.
45. Interview with the author, August 15, 2000.
46. Interview with the author, July 18, 2000.
47. Interview with the author, August 9, 2000.
48. Interview with the author, June 28, 2000.
49. Republican representative's interview with the author, July 11, 2000.
50. Interview with the author, July 19, 2000.
51. Ibid.
52. Democratic representative's interview with the author, July 19, 2000.
53. Republican legislative director's interview with the author, August 8, 2000.
54. Interview with the author, July 31, 2000.
55. Interview with the author, July 19, 2000.
56. Interview with the author, August 8, 2000.
57. Interview with the author, August 2, 2000.
58. Democratic legislative director's interview with the author, August 1, 2000.

59. Republican legislative director's interview with the author, July 31, 2000.
60. Republican staffer's interview with the author, August 9, 2000.
61. In addition to the author, the interviewee, and one of the interviewee's staffers, the car included Reps. Diane DeGette (D-CO), Ralph Hall (R-TX, though at the time he was a Democrat), Gerald Nadler (D-N.Y.), and Lincoln Diaz-Balart (R-FL).
62. Republican staffer's interview with the author, August 9, 2000.
63. Republican legislator's interview with the author, July 13, 2000.
64. Republican legislator's interview with the author, June 29, 2000.
65. Interview with the author, August 15, 2000.
66. Republican representative's interview with the author, July 19, 2000; Democratic representative's interview with the author, July 19, 2000.
67. Republican representative's interview with the author, July 18, 2000.
68. Democratic legislative director's interview with the author, August 8, 2000.
69. Democratic legislative director's interview with the author, August 1, 2000.
70. Interview with the author, August 9, 2000.
71. Republican legislative director's interview with the author, July 31, 2000.
72. The interviewee refers to Rep. James Greenwood (D-PA), a prochoice Republican who often offers prochoice amendments to legislation.
73. Republican legislator's interview with the author, July 13, 2000; Republican legislator's interview with the author, July 19, 2000; Republican legislative director's interview with the author, July 31, 2000.
74. Republican legislator's interview with the author, June 18, 2002.
75. Interview with the author, July 11, 2000.
76. Interview with the author, August 8, 2000. This point was echoed in several other interviews, e.g., Democratic staffer's interview with the author June 14, 2002; Democratic chief of staff's interview with the author, June 14, 2002.
77. Interview with the author, June 5, 2002.
78. Interview with the author, August 8, 2000.
79. Interview with the author, July 31, 2000.
80. Interview with the author, August 7, 2000.
81. For example, moderate Republican Ralph Regula (Ohio) was passed over as chair of the House Appropriations Committee in the 109th Congress. See Ota, "No pat on the back for GOP," 66.
82. Although the Defense of Marriage Act passed during the period of strong party governance during the Gingrich years, it also had the support of Democratic President Clinton.

83. Susan Milligan, "Back-room dealing a Capitol trend," *Boston Globe* (October 3, 2004).

## NOTES TO CHAPTER 6

The chapter epigraph is from an interview with the author, July 19, 2001, and is attributed to Rep. Price with his permission.

1. Tony Perkins, president of the Family Research Council, characterized opposition to Bush's nominees (by some but not all Democrats) as a "campaign against orthodox religious views"; see Tony Perkins, "It's about religious belief," *Washington Post* (May 14, 2005), A21. A spokesperson for the Family Research Council suggested that "The seven so-called [Republican] centrists who made this deal showed an incredible disconnect with the voters who put their party in power last year"; see Josh Kurtz, "Deal not sparking primaries—yet," *Roll Call* (May 25, 2005).
2. This is not to suggest that only two sociocultural groups have developed. Surely many have blossomed in the modern era.
3. Marginals available from www.cnn.com/ELECTION/2004/pages/results/states/US/P/00/epolls.0.html.
4. Interview with the author, July 19, 2000.
5. See Madison's *Federalist 10*.
6. The Democrats of the 89th Congress, during the Johnson Administration, offer stiff competition.
7. *Fox News Sunday*, November 7, 2004.

# Bibliography

Abramowitz, Alan I. 1995. "It's Abortion, Stupid: Policy Voting in the 1992 Presidential Election." *Journal of Politics* 57: 176–86.

Adams, G. D. 1997. "Abortion: Evidence of an Issue Evolution." *American Journal of Political Science* 41: 718–37.

Adler, E. Scott. No date. "Congressional District Data File, 103rd–107th Congresses." Data set. University of Colorado, Boulder.

Adorno,Theodor. 1950. *The Authoritarian Personality.* New York: Harper.

Aldrich, John H., and David W. Rohde. 2000. "The Republican Revolution and the House Appropriations Committee." *Journal of Politics* 62: 1–33.

———. 2001. "The Logic of Conditional Party Government." In *Congress Reconsidered,* ed. Lawrence C. Dodd and Bruce I. Oppenheimer. Washington, D.C.: CQ Press.

———. 2004. "Congressional Committees in the Partisan Era." In *Congress Reconsidered,* ed. Lawrence C. Dodd and Bruce I. Oppenheimer. Washington, D.C.: CQ Press.

Arnold, R. Douglas. 1990. *The Logic of Congressional Action.* New Haven, Conn.: Yale University Press.

Barber, James David. 1992. *Presidential Character: Predicting Performance in the White House.* New York: Pearson Education.

Benson, Peter L., and Dorothy L. Williams. 1982. *Religion on Capitol Hill: Myths and Realities.* San Francisco: Harper & Row.

Benzel, R. F. 1984. *Sectionalism and American Political Development: 1880–1980.* Madison: University of Wisconsin Press.

Bradley, Martin B., Norman M. Green, Dale E. Johnson, Mac Lynn, and Lou McNeil. 1992. *Churches and Church Membership in the United Sates, 1990.* Atlanta: Glenmary Research Center.

Brady, David, and Barbara Sinclair. 1984. "Building Majorities for Policy Change in the House of Representatives." *Journal of Politics* 46: 1033–60.

Bratton, Kathleen A., and Kerry L. Haynie. 1999. "Agenda Setting and Legislative Success in State Legislatures: The Effects of Race and Gender." *Journal of Politics* 61: 658–79.

Brewer, P. R. 2003. "The Shifting Foundations of Public Opinion about Gay Rights." *Journal of Politics* 65: 1208–20.

Bryner, Gary C. 1998. "Affirmative Action: Minority Rights or Reverse Discrimination?" In *Moral Controversies in American Politics: Cases in Social Regulatory Policy*, ed. Raymond Tatalovich and Byron W. Daynes. Armonk, N.Y.: M. E. Sharpe, Inc.

Burris, Val. 1983. "Who Opposed ERA? An Analysis of the Social Bases of Antifeminism." *Social Science Quarterly* 64: 305–17.

Button, James W., Barbara A. Rienzo, and Kenneth D. Wald. 1997. *Private Lives, Public Controversies: Battles over Gay Rights in American Communities*. Washington, D.C.: CQ Press.

Byrnes, Timothy. 1991. *The Catholic Bishops in American Politics*. Princeton, N.J.: Princeton University Press.

———. 1993. "The Politics of American Catholic Hierarchy." *Political Science Quarterly* 108: 497–515.

Calfano, Brian Robert, and Elizabeth Anne Oldmixon. 2005. "Catholic Clergy Activism in the 2004 Election: Tipping the Scales with Gay Marriage." Presented at the annual meeting of the American Political Science Association, Washington, D.C., September 1–4.

Calfano, Brian Robert, Elizabeth Anne Oldmixon, and Peter VonDoepp. 2005. "Religious Advocacy in the Texas Legislature." In *Representing God at the Statehouse: Religion and Politics in the American States*, ed. Edward L. Cleary and Allen Hertzke. Lanham, Md.: Rowman & Littlefield.

Campbell, Ballard. 1980. *Representative Democracy: Public Policy and Midwestern Legislatures in the Late 19th Century*. Cambridge, Mass.: Harvard University Press.

Campbell, Colton C., and Roger H. Davidson. 2000. "Gay and Lesbian Issues in the Congressional Arena." In *The Politics of Gay Rights*, ed. Craig A. Rimmerman, Kenneth Donald, and Clyde Wilcox. Chicago: University of Chicago Press.

Carmines, Edward G., and James A. Stimson. 1980. "The Two Faces of Issue Voting." *American Political Science Review* 74: 78–91.

———. 1986. "On the Structure and Sequence of Issue Evolution." *American Political Science Review* 80: 901–20.

Clausen, Aage R. 1973. *How Congressmen Decide: A Policy Focus*. New York: St. Martin's Press.

Combs, M. W., and S. Welch. 1982. "Blacks, Whites, and Attitudes Toward Abortion." *Public Opinion Quarterly* 46: 510–20.

Connelly, William F., Jr., and John J. Pitney Jr. 1994. *Congress' Permanent Minority?* Lanham, Md.: Rowman & Littlefield.

Conway, M. Margaret. 2000. *Political Participation in the United States*, 3rd ed. Washington, D.C.: CQ Press.

Conway, M. Margaret, Gertrude A. Steuernagel, and David W. Ahern. 1997. *Women and Political Participation: Cultural Change in the Political Arena*. Washington, D.C.: CQ Press.

Cook, Elizabeth Adell. 1997. "Public Opinion and Abortion law in the Post-Webster Era." In *Understanding Public Opinion*, ed. Barbara Norrander and Clyde Wilcox. Washington, D.C.: CQ Press.

Cook, Elizabeth Adell, Ted G. Jelen, and Clyde Wilcox. 1992. *Between Two Absolutes: Public Opinion and the Politics of Abortion*. Boulder, Colo.: Westview Press.

———. 1993. "Catholicism and Abortion Attitudes in the American States: A Contextual Analysis." *Journal for the Scientific Study of Religion* 32: 223–30.

Cooper, Joseph, and David W. Brady. 1981. "Institutional Context and Leadership Style: The House from Cannon to Rayburn." *American Political Science Review* 75: 411–25.

Costain, Anne N. 1992. *Inviting Women's Rebellion: A Political Process Interpretation of the Women's Movement*. Baltimore: Johns Hopkins University Press.

Cox, Gary W., and Mathew D. McCubbins. 1993. *Legislative Leviathan: Party Government in the House*. Berkeley: University of California Press.

Crawford, Alan. 1980. *Thunder on the Right*. New York: Pantheon.

Cruikshank, Margaret. 1992. *The Gay and Lesbian Liberation Movement*. London: Routledge, Chapman and Hall Inc.

Currinder, Marian. 2003. "Leadership PAC Contribution Strategies and House Member Ambitions." *Legislative Studies Quarterly* 28: 551–77.

Davidson, Roger H., and Walter J. Oleszek. 2000. *Congress and Its Members*. Washington, D.C.: CQ Press.

Deering, Christopher J., and Steven S. Smith. 1997. *Committees in Congress*. Washington, D.C.: CQ Press.

D'Emilio, John. 2000. "Cycles of Change, Questions of Strategy: The Gay and Lesbian Movement after Fifty Years." In *The Politics of Gay Rights*, ed. Craig A. Rimmerman, Kenneth D. Wald, and Clyde Wilcox. Chicago: University of Chicago Press.

Dienes, C. T. 1972. *Law, Politics, and Birth Control*. Urbana: University of Illinois Press.

Dierenfield, Bruce J. 1997. "'Somebody Is Tampering with America's Soul': Congress and the School Prayer Debate." *Congress & the Presidency* 24: 167–205.

Dodd, Lawrence C. 1977. "Congress and the Quest for Power." In *Congress Reconsidered*, ed. Lawrence C. Dodd and Bruce I. Oppenheimer. New York: Praeger Publishers.

———. 1981. "Congress, the Constitution, and the Crisis of Legitimation." In *Congress Reconsidered*, 2nd. ed., ed. Lawrence C. Dodd and Bruce I. Oppenheimer. Washington, D.C.: CQ Press.

———. 1983. "Coalition-Building by Party Leaders: A Case Study of House Democrats." *Congress and the Presidency* 10: 147–68.

———. 1986a. "The Cycles of Legislative Change: Building a Dynamic Theory." In *Political Science: The Science of Politics*, ed. Herbert F. Weisberg. New York: Agathon Press.

———. 1986b. "A Theory of Congressional Cycles: Solving the Puzzle of Change." In *Congress and Policy Change*, ed. Gerald C. Wright Jr., Leroy N. Rieselbach, and Lawrence C. Dodd. New York: Agathon Press.

———. 1993. "Congress and the Politics of Renewal: Redressing the Crisis of Legitimation." In *Congress Reconsidered*, 5th ed., ed. Lawrence C. Dodd and Bruce I. Oppenheimer. Washington, D.C.: CQ Press.

———. 2001. "Re-Envisioning Congress: Theoretical Perspectives on Congressional Change." In *Congress Reconsidered*, 7th ed., ed. Lawrence C. Dodd and Bruce I. Oppenheimer. Washington, D.C.: CQ Press.

Dodd, Lawrence C., and Bruce I. Oppenheimer. 1997. "Congress and the Emerging Order: Conditional Party Government or Constructive Party Government?" In *Congress Reconsidered*, 6th ed., ed. Lawrence C. Dodd and Bruce I. Oppenheimer. Washington, D.C.: CQ Press.

———. 2001a. "A House Divided: The Struggle for Partisan Control, 1994–2000." In *Congress Reconsidered*, 7th ed., ed. Lawrence C. Dodd and Bruce I. Oppenheimer. Washington, D.C.: CQ Press.

———. 2001b. "Congress and the Emerging Order: Assessing the 2000 Elections." In *Congress Reconsidered*, 7th ed., ed. Lawrence C. Dodd and Bruce I. Oppenheimer. Washington, D.C.: CQ Press.

———. 2005. "A Decade of Republican Control: The House of Representatives, 1995–2005." In *Congress Reconsidered*, 8th ed., ed. Lawrence C. Dodd and Bruce I. Oppenheimer. Washington, D.C.: CQ Press.

Dodson, Debra L., and Susan J. Carroll. 1991. *Reshaping the Agenda: Women in State Legislatures*. New Brunswick, N.J.: Center for American Women and Politics, Eagleton Institute of Politics, Rutgers–The State University of New Jersey.

Duke, James T., and Barry L. Johnson. 1992. "Religious Affiliation and Congressional Representation." *Journal for the Scientific Study of Religion* 31: 324–29.

Edelman, Murray. 1964. *The Symbolic Uses of Politics*. Urbana: University of Illinois Press.

————. 1971. *Politics as Symbolic Action*. Chicago: Markham Publishing Co.

Elifson, Kirk W., and C. Kirk Hadaway. 1985. "Prayer in Public Schools: When Church and State Collide." *Public Opinion Quarterly* 49: 317–29.

Ellis, Margaret. 1998. "Gay Rights: Lifestyle or Immorality?" In *Moral Controversies in American Politics: Cases in Social Regulatory Policy*, ed. Raymond Tatalovich and Byron Daynes. Armonk, N.Y.: M. E. Sharpe.

Erikson, Robert S., and Kent L. Tedin. 1995. *American Public Opinion*, 5th ed. New York: Addison Welsey Longman, Inc.

Evans, C. Lawrence. 2001. "Committees, Leaders, and Message Politics." In *Congress Reconsidered*, 7th ed., ed. Lawrence C. Dodd and Bruce I. Oppenheimer. Washington, D.C.: CQ Press.

Evans, C. Lawrence, and Walter J. Oleszek. 1997. "Congressional Tsunami? The Politics of Committee Reform." In *Congress Reconsidered*, 6th ed., ed. Lawrence C. Dodd and Bruce I. Oppenheimer. Washington, D.C.: CQ Press.

Fabrizio, Paul J. 2001. "Evolving into Morality Politics: U.S. Catholic Bishops' Statements on U.S. Politics from 1972 to the Present." In *The Public Clash of Private Values: The Politics of Morality Policy*, ed. Christopher Z. Mooney. Chatham, England: Chatham House Press.

Faderman, Lillian. 1991. *Odd Girls and Twilight Lovers: A History of Lesbian Life in Twentieth-Century America*. New York: Penguin.

Fairbanks, David. 1977. "Religious Forces and 'Morality' Policies in the American States." *Western Political Quarterly* 30: 411–17.

Fastnow, Chris, J. Tobin Grant, and Thomas J. Rudolf. 1999. "Holy Roll Calls: Religious Tradition and Voting Behavior in the U.S. House." *Social Science Quarterly* 80: 687–701.

Fenno, Richard F. 1962. "The House Appropriation Committee as a Political System: The Problem of Integration." *American Political Science Review* 56: 310–24.

————. 1966. *The Power of the Purse*. Boston: Little, Brown and Co.

————. 1973. *Congressmen in Committees*. Boston: Little, Brown and Co.

Findlay, James F. 1990. "Religion and Politics in the Sixties: The Church and the Civil Rights Act of 1964." *Journal of American History* 77: 66–92.

Fiorina, Morris P., Samuel J. Abrams, and Jeremy C. Pope. 2004. *Culture War? The Myth of a Polarized America*. New York: Longman.

Fowler, Robert Booth, Allen D. Hertzke, and Laura R. Olson. 1999. *Religion and Politics in the United States: Faith, Culture, and Strategic Choices*. Boulder, Colo.: Westview Press.

Froman, Lewis A., Jr., and Randall B. Ripley. 1965. "Conditions for Party Leadership." *American Political Science Review* 59: 52–63.

Glynn, Carroll J., Susan Herbst, Garrett J. O'Keefe, and Robert Y. Shapiro. 1999. *Public Opinion*. Boulder, Colo.: Westview Press.

Gordon, Joshua. 2004. "The (Dis)Integration of the House Appropriations Committee: Revisiting *The Power of the Purse* in a Partisan Era." In *Congress Reconsidered*, 8th ed., ed. Lawrence Dodd and Bruce Oppenheimer. Washington, D.C.: CQ Press.

Gray, John. 1996. *Isaiah Berlin*. Princeton, N.J.: Princeton University Press.

Green, John C. 2000. "Antigay: Varieties and Opposition to Gay Rights." In *The Politics of Gay Rights*, ed. Craig A. Rimmerman, Kenneth D. Wald, and Clyde Wilcox. Chicago: University of Chicago Press.

Green, John C., and James L. Guth. 1989. "The Missing Link: Political Activists and Support for School Prayer." *Public Opinion Quarterly* 53: 41–57.

———. 1991. "Religion, Representatives, and Roll Calls." *Legislative Studies Quarterly* 16: 571–84.

Gusfield, Joseph. 1963. *Symbolic Crusade: Status Politics and the American Temperance Movement*. Urbana: University of Illinois Press.

Guth, James L., and Lyman A. Kellstedt. 2001. "Religion and Congress." In *In God We Trust: Religion and American Political Life*, ed. Corwin E. Smidt. Grand Rapids, Mich.: Baker Academic.

Guth, James L., Corwin E. Smidt, Lyman A. Kellstedt, and John C. Green. 1993. "The Sources of Antiabortion Attitudes: The Case of Religious Political Activists." *American Politics Quarterly* 27: 65–80.

Habermas, Jurgen. 1973. *Legitimation Crisis*. Boston: Beacon Press.

Haeberle, Steven H. 1996. "Gay Men and Lesbians in City Hall." *Social Science Quarterly* 77: 190–97.

Haider-Markel, Donald P. 1998. "The Politics of Social Regulation Policy: State and Federal Hate Crimes Policy and Implementation Effort." *Political Research Quarterly* 51: 69–88.

———. 1999a. "Redistributive Values in Congress: Interest Group Influence Under Sub-Optimal Conditions." *Political Research Quarterly* 52: 113–44.

———. 1999b. "Morality Policy and Individual-Level Political Behavior: The Case of Legislative Voting on Lesbian and Gay Issues." *Policy Studies Journal* 27: 735–49.

———. 2001. "Morality in Congress? Legislative Voting on Gay Issues." In *The Public Clash of Private Values: The Politics of Morality Policy*, ed. Christopher Z. Mooney. Chatham, England: Chatham House Press.

Haider-Markel, Donald P., and Kenneth J. Meier. 1996. "The Politics of Gay and Lesbian Rights: Expanding the Scope of the Conflict." *Journal of Politics* 58: 332–49.

Haider-Markel, Donald P., Mark R. Joslyn, and Chad J. Kniss. 2000. "Minority Group Interests and Political Representation: Gay Elected Officials in the Policy Process." *Journal of Politics* 62: 568–77.

Hall, Elaine J., and Myra Marx Ferree. 1986. "Race Differences in Abortion Attitudes." *Public Opinion Quarterly* 50: 193–207.

Hammond, Susan W. 1991. "Congressional Caucuses and Party Leaders in the House of Representatives." *Political Science Quarterly* 106: 277–94.

———. 1997. "Congressional Caucuses in the 104th Congress." In *Congress Reconsidered*, ed. Lawrence C. Dodd and Bruce I. Oppenheimer. Washington, D.C.: CQ Press.

———. 1998. *Congressional Caucuses in National Policy Making.* Baltimore: Johns Hopkins University Press.

Harvey, Anna L. 1998. *Votes without Leverage: Women in American Electoral Politics, 1920–1970.* New York: Cambridge University Press.

Henshaw, Stanley K., and Jennifer Van Vort. 1994. "Abortion Services in the United States, 1991 and 1992." *Family Planning Perspectives* 26: 100–106, 112.

Herman, Didi. 2000. "The Gay Agenda Is the Devil's Agenda." In *The Politics of Gay Rights*, ed. Craig A. Rimmerman, Kenneth D. Wald, and Clyde Wilcox. Chicago: University of Chicago Press.

Hertzke, Allen D. 1988. *Representing God in Washington: The Role of Religious Lobbies in the American Polity.* Knoxville: University of Tennessee Press.

Hibbing, John R., and James T. Smith. 2001. "What Americans Want Congress to Be." In *Congress Reconsidered*, 7th ed., ed. Lawrence C. Dodd and Bruce I. Oppenheimer. Washington, D.C.: CQ Press.

Huntington, Samuel. 1974. "Postindustrial Politics: How Benign Will It Be?" *Comparative Politics* 6: 163–91.

Inglehart, Ronald. 1990. *Cultural Shift in Advanced Industrial Society.* Princeton, N.J.: Princeton University Press.

Jelen, Ted G. 1997. "Religion and Public Opinion in the 1990s: An Empirical Overview." In *Understanding Public Opinion*, ed. Barbara Norrander and Clyde Wilcox. Washington, D.C.: CQ Press.

———. 1998. "God or Country: Debating Religion in Public Life." In *Moral Controversies in American Politics: Cases in Social Regulatory Policy*, ed. Raymond Tatalovich and Byron W. Daynes. Armonk, N.Y.: M. E. Sharpe.

Jost, Kenneth. 1997. "Gun Control Standoff." *CQ Researcher* 7: 1105–28.

Kaczorowski, Robert J. 1987. "To Begin the Nation Anew: Congress, Citizenship, and Civil Rights after the Civil War." *American Historical Review* 92: 45–68.

Katz, Jonathan Ned. 1976. *Gay American History: Lesbians and Gay Men in the U.S.A.* New York: Meridian.

Kellstedt, Lyman A., and John C. Green. 1993. "Knowing God's Many People: Denominational Preference and Political Behavior." In *Rediscovering the Religious Factor in American Politics*, ed. David C. Leege and Lyman A. Kellstedt. Armonk, N.Y.: M. E. Sharpe.

226    *Bibliography*

Kinsey, Alfred, Warell B. Pomeroy, and Clyde E. Martin. 1948. *Sexual Behavior in the Human Male*. Philadelphia: W. B. Saunders.
Kleck, Gary. 1996. "Crime, Culture Conflict and Sources of Support for Gun Control." *American Behavioral Scientist* 3: 387–404.
Koopman, Douglas L. 1996. *Hostile Takeover: The House Republican Party, 1980–1995*. Lanham, Md.: Rowman & Littlefield.
Kroger, Gregory. 2003. "Position Taking and Cosponsorship in the U.S. House." *Legislative Studies Quarterly* 28: 225–46.
Langbein, Laura I., and Mark A. Lotwis. 1990. "The Political Efficacy of Lobbying and Money: Gun Control in the U.S. House, 1986." *Legislative Studies Quarterly* 15: 413–40.
Leege, David C., Kenneth D. Wald, Brian S. Krueger, and Paul D. Mueller. 2002. *The Politics of Cultural Differences: Social Change and Voter Mobilization in the Post–New Deal Period*. Princeton, N.J.: Princeton University Press.
Lewis, Gregory B., and Jonathan L. Edelson. 2000. "DOMA and ENDA." In *The Politics of Gay Rights*, ed. Craig A. Rimmerman, Kenneth D. Wald, and Clyde Wilcox. Chicago: University of Chicago Press.
Liebman, Robert C. 1983. "Mobilizing the Moral Majority." In *The New Christian Right*, ed. Robert C. Wuthnow. New York: Aldine.
Lowi, Theodore. 1998. "Forward: New Dimensions in Policy and Politics." In *Moral Controversies in American Politics: Cases in Social Regulatory Policy*, ed. Raymond Tatalovich and Byron W. Daynes. Armonk, N.Y.: M. E. Sharpe.
Lytle, Clifford M. 1966. "The History of the Civil Rights Bill of 1964." *Journal of Negro History* 51: 275–96.
March, James G., and Herbert A. Simon. 1958. *Organizations*. New York: John Wiley and Sons.
Marshall, Patrick. 2001. "Religion in Schools." *CQ Researcher* 11: 1–24.
Mayhew, David R. 1974. *Congress: The Electoral Connection*. New Haven, Conn.: Yale University Press.
McFarlane, Deborah R., and Kenneth J. Meier. 2001. *The Politics of Fertility Control*. Chatham, England: Chatham House Publishers.
Meier, Kenneth J. 1994. *The Politics of Sin*. Armonk, N.Y.: M. E. Sharpe.
———. 1999. "Sex, Drugs, Rock, and Roll: A Theory of Morality Politics." *Policy Studies Journal* 27: 681–95.
———. 2001. "Sex, Drugs, and Rock and Roll: A Theory of Morality Politics." In *The Public Clash of Private Values: The Politics of Morality Policy*, ed. Christopher Z. Mooney. Chatham, England: Chatham House Publishers.
Meier, Kenneth J., and Cathy M. Johnson. 1990. "The Politics of Demon Rum: Regulating Alcohol and Its Deleterious Consequences." *American Politics Quarterly* 18: 404–29.

Meier, Kenneth J. and Deborah R. McFarlane. 1993. "The Politics of Funding Abortion." *American Politics Quarterly* 21: 81–101.

Melich, Tanya. 1996. *The Republican War against Women: An Insider's Report from behind the Lines.* New York: Bantam Books.

Mill, John Stuart. 1863. *On Liberty.* Boston: Ticknor and Fields.

Moen, Matthew C. 1984. "School Prayer and the Politics of Life-Style Concern." *Social Science Quarterly* 65: 1065–71.

———. 1989. *The Christian Right and Congress.* Tuscaloosa: University of Alabama Press.

———. 1992. *The Transformation of the Christian Right.* Tuscaloosa: University of Alabama Press.

———. 1995. "From Revolution to Evolution: The Changing Nature of the Christian Right." In *The Rapture of Politics*, ed. Steve Bruce, Peter Kivisto, and William Swatos. New Brunswick, N.J.: Transaction.

Mooney, Christopher Z. 2001. "The Public Clash of Private Values: The Politics of Morality Policy." In *The Public Clash of Private Values: The Politics of Morality Policy*, ed. Christopher Z. Mooney. Chatham, England: Chatham House Publishers.

Mooney, Christopher Z., and Mei-Hsien Lee. 1995. "Legislating Morality in the American States: The Case of Pre-Roe Abortion Regulation Reform." *American Journal of Political Science* 39: 599–627.

———. 1999. "The Temporal Diffusion of Morality Policy: The Case of Death Penalty Legislation in the American States." *Policy Studies Journal* 27: 766–81.

———. 2000. "The influence of Values on Consensus and Contentious Morality Policy: U.S. Death Penalty Reform, 1956–1982." *Journal of Politics* 62: 223–39.

Morgan, David R., and Kenneth J. Meier. 1980. "Politics and Morality: The Effect of Religion on Referenda Voting." *Social Science Quarterly* 61: 144–48.

Norrander, Barbara, and Clyde Wilcox. 2001. "Public Opinion and Policymaking in the States: The Case of Post-*Roe* Abortion Policy." In *The Public Clash of Private Values: The Politics of Morality Policy*, ed. Christopher Z. Mooney. Chatham, England: Chatham House Publishers.

O'Connor, Karen. 1996. *No Neutral Ground? Abortion Politics in an Age of Absolutes.* Boulder, Colo.: Westview Press.

Oldmixon, Elizabeth A. 2002. "Culture Wars in the Congressional Theater: How the U.S. House of Representatives Legislates Morality, 1993–1998." *Social Science Quarterly* 83: 775–88.

Oldmixon, Elizabeth A., Beth Rosenson, and Kenneth D. Wald. 2005. "Conflict over Israel: The Role of Religion, Race, Party and Ideology in the U.S. House of Representatives, 1997–2002." *Terrorism and Political Violence* 17: 407–26.

228

Bibliography

Page, Ann L., and Donald A. Clelland. 1978. "The Kanawha County Textbook Controversy: A Study of the Politics of Life Style Concern." *Social Forces* 57: 265–81.

Peltzman, Sam. 1984. "Constituent Interest and Congressional Voting." *Journal of Law and Economics* 27: 181–210.

Peterson, Bill E., Richard M. Doty, and David G. Winter. 1993. "Authoritarianism and Attitudes toward Contemporary Social Issues." *Personality and Social Psychology Bulletin* 19: 174–84.

Polsby, Nelson W. 1968. "The Institutionalization of the U.S. House of Representatives." *American Political Science Review* 62: 144–68.

———. 2003. *How Congress Evolves: Social Bases of Institutional Change.* Oxford: Oxford University Press.

Poole, Keith T., and Howard Rosenthal. 1991. "Patterns of Congressional Voting." *American Journal of Political Science* 35: 228–78.

Putnam, Robert D., Robert Leonardi, and Raffaella Y. Nanetti. 1994. *Making Democracy Work.* Princeton, N.J.: Princeton University Press.

Reingold, Beth. 2000. *Representing Women: Sex, Gender, and Legislative Behavior in Arizona and California.* Chapel Hill: University of North Carolina Press.

Rimmerman, Craig A. 2002. *From Identity to Politics: The Lesbian and Gay Movements in the United States.* Philadelphia: Temple University Press.

Rohde, David W. 1991. *Parties and Leaders in the Postreform House.* Chicago: University of Chicago Press.

Roof, Wade Clark, and William McKinney. 1987. *American Mainline Religion.* New Brunswick, N.J.: Rutgers University Press.

Rosenblatt, R. 1992. *Life Itself: Abortion in the American Mind.* New York: Random House.

Rozell, Mark J., and Clyde Wilcox. 1995. "The Past as Prologue: The Christian Right in the 1996 Elections." In *God at the Grassroots: The Christian Right in the 1994 Elections,* ed. Mark J. Rozell and Clyde Wilcox. Lanham, Md.: Rowman & Littlefield.

Sanders, Francine. 1997. "Civil Rights Roll-Call Voting in the House of Representatives, 1957–1991: A Systematic Analysis." *Political Research Quarterly* 50: 483–502.

Schecter, David. 2002. "What Drives the Voting on Abortion Policy? Investigating Partisanship and Religion in the State Legislative Arena." *Women & Politics* 23: 61–84.

Schickler, Eric. 2001. *Disjointed Pluralism: Institutional Innovation and the Development of the U.S. Congress.* Princeton, N.J.: Princeton University Press.

Schroedel, Jean Reith, and Oamela Fiber. 2000. "Lesbian and Gay Policy Priorities." In *The Politics of Gay Rights,* ed. Craig A. Rimmerman, Kenneth D. Wald, and Clyde Wilcox. Chicago: University of Chicago Press.

Sharpe, Elaine B., ed. 1999. *Culture Wars and Local Politics.* Lawrence: University of Kansas Press.

Sheeran, P. J. 1987. *Women, Society, the State, and Abortion: A Structuralist Analysis.* New York: Praeger.

Simon, Herbert A. 1957. *Administrative Behavior.* New York: Macmillan.

Sinclair, Barbara. 1983. *Majority Leadership in the U.S. House.* Baltimore: Johns Hopkins University Press.

———. 1989. "House Majority Party Leadership in the Late 1980s." In *Congress Reconsidered*, 4th ed., ed. Lawrence C. Dodd and Bruce I. Oppenheimer. Washington, D.C.: CQ Press.

———. 1990. *The Transformation of the U.S. Senate.* Baltimore: Johns Hopkins University Press.

———. 1997. "Party Leaders and the New Legislative Process." In *Congress Reconsidered*, 6th ed., ed. Lawrence C. Dodd and Bruce I. Oppenheimer. Washington, D.C.: CQ Press.

Skocpol, Theda. 1992. *Protecting Soldiers and Mothers: The Political Origins of Social Policy in the United States.* Cambridge, Mass.: Belknap Press of Harvard University Press.

———. 1994a. "Early U.S. Social Policies: A Challenge to Theories of the Welfare State." In *New Perspectives on American Politics*, ed. Lawrence C. Dodd and Calvin Jillson. Washington, D.C.: CQ Press.

———. 1994b. "The Origins of Social Policy in the United States: A Policy Centered Analysis." In *The Dynamics of American Politics: Approaches and Interpretations*, ed. Lawrence C. Dodd and Calvin Jillson. Boulder, Colo.: Westview Press.

Skocpol, Theda, Marjorie Abend-Wein, Christopher Howard, and Susan Goodrich Lehmann. 1993. "Women's Associations and the Enactment of Mothers' Pensions in the United States." *American Political Science Review* 87: 686–701.

Smidt, Corwin E. 2001. "Religion and American Public Opinion." In *In God We Trust: Religion and American Political Life*, ed. Corwin E. Smidt. Grand Rapids, Mich.: Baker Academic.

Smith, Christian. 1996. "Correcting a Curious Neglect, or Bringing Religion Back In." In *Disruptive Religion: The Force of Faith in Social Movement Activism*, ed. Christian Smith. New York: Routledge.

Smith, Kevin B. 2001. "Clean Thoughts and Dirty Minds: The Politics of Porn." In *The Public Clash of Private Values: The Politics of Morality Policy*, ed. Christopher Z. Mooney. Chatham, England: Chatham House Publishers.

Smith, Steven S., and Eric D. Lawrence. 1997. "Party Control of Committees in the Republican Congress." In *Congress Reconsidered*, 6th ed., ed. Lawrence C. Dodd and Bruce I. Oppenheimer. Washington, D.C.: CQ Press.

Spitzer, Robert J. 1998a. *The Politics of Gun Control*, 2nd ed. New York: Chatham House Publishers.

———. 1998b. "Gun Control: Constitutional Mandate or Myth?" In *Moral Controversies in American Politics: Cases in Social Regulatory Policy*, ed. Raymond Tatalovich and Byron W. Daynes. Armonk, N.Y.: M. E. Sharpe.

Steiner, Gilbert Y., ed. 1983. *The Abortion Dispute in the American System*. Washington, D.C.: Brookings Institution Press.

Stetson, Dorothy McBride. 1997. *Women's Rights in the USA: Policy Debates and Gender Roles*, 2nd ed. New York: Garland Publishing, Inc.

Strickland, Ruth Ann. 1998. "Abortion: Prochoice versus Prolife." In *Moral Controversies in American Politics: Cases in Social Regulatory Policy*, ed. Raymond Tatalovich and Byron W. Daynes. Armonk, N.Y.: M. E. Sharpe.

Studlar, Donley T. 2001. "What Constitutes Morality Policy? A Cross-National Analysis." In *The Public Clash of Private Values: The Politics of Morality Policy*, ed. Christopher Z. Mooney. Chatham, England: Chatham House Publishers.

Suchman, Lucy, and Brigitte Jordan. 1992. "Validity and the Collaborative Construction of Meaning in Face-to-Face Surveys." In *Questions about Questions: Inquiries into the Cognitive Bases of Surveys*, ed. Judith Tanur. New York: Russell Sage Foundation.

Swers, Michele L. 1998. "Are Women More Likely to Vote for Women's Issues Bills Than Their Male Colleagues?" *Legislative Studies Quarterly* 23: 435–48.

Swidler, Ann. 1986. "Culture in Action: Symbols and Strategies." *American Sociological Review* 51: 273–86.

Tatalovich, Raymond. 1997. *The Politics of Abortion in the United States and Canada*. Armonk, N.Y.: M. E. Sharpe.

Tatalovich, Raymond, and Byron W. Daynes. 1998. "Introduction: Social Regulations and Moral Conflict." In *Moral Controversies in American Politics: Cases in Social Regulatory Policy*, ed. Raymond Tatalovich and Byron W. Daynes. Armonk, N.Y.: M. E. Sharpe.

Tatalovich, Raymond, and David Schier. 1993. "The Persistence of Ideological Cleavage in Voting on Abortion Legislation in the House of Representatives, 1973–1988." *American Politics Quarterly* 21: 125–39.

Tatalovich, Raymond, and T. Alexander Smith. 2001. "Status Claims and Cultural Conflict: The Genesis of Morality Policy." *Policy Currents* 10: 2–8.

Thomas, Sue. 1994. *How Women Legislate*. New York: Oxford University Press.

Thomas, Sue, and Susan Welch. 1991. "The Impact of Gender on Activities and Priorities of State Legislators." *Western Political Quarterly* 44: 445–56.

Vega, Arturo, and Juanita M. Firestone. 1995. "The Effects of Gender on Congressional Behavior and the Substantive Representation of Women." *Legislative Studies Quarterly* 20: 213–22.

Vinovskis, Maris A. 1980. "The Politics of Abortion in the U.S. House of Representatives in 1976." In *The Law and Politics of Abortion*, ed. Carl E. Schneider and Maris A. Vinovskis. Lexington, Mass.: Lexington Books.

Wald, Kenneth D. 1987. *Religion and Politics in the United States*. New York: St. Martin's Press.

———. 1997. *Religion and Politics in the United States*, 3rd ed. Washington, D.C.: CQ Press.

———. 2000. "The Context of Gay Politics." In *The Politics of Gay Rights*, ed. Craig A. Rimmerman, Kenneth D. Wald, and Clyde Wilcox. Chicago: University of Chicago Press.

———. 2003. *Religion and Politics in the United States*, 4th ed. Lanham, Md.: Rowman & Littlefield.

Wald, Kenneth D., James W. Button, and Barbara A. Rienzo. 1996. "The Politics of Gay Rights in American Communities: Explaining Anti-discrimination Ordinances and Policies." *American Journal of Political Science* 40: 1152–78.

———. 2001. "Morality Politics v. Political Economy: The Case of School-Based Health Centers." *Social Science Quarterly* 82: 221–33.

Wald, Kenneth D., Dennis E. Owen, and Samuel S. Hill. 1989. "Evangelical Politics and Status Issues." *Journal for the Scientific Study of Religion* 28: 1–16.

Wattier, Mark J., and Raymond Tatalovich. 1995. "Senate Voting on Abortion Legislation over Two Decades: Testing a Reconstructed Partisanship Variable." *American Review of Politics* 16: 167–83.

Welch, Susan. 1985. "Are Women More Liberal Than Men in the U.S. Congress?" *Legislative Studies Quarterly* 10:125–34.

Westfield, Louis P. 1974. "Majority Party Leadership and the Committee System in the House of Representatives." *American Political Science Review* 68: 1593–1604.

White, Mel. 1995. *Stranger at the Gate: To Be Gay and Christian in America*. New York: Plume.

Wilcox, Clyde. 1988. "The Christian Right in Twentieth Century America: Continuity and Change." *Review of Politics* 50: 659–81.

———. 1990. "Race Differences in Abortion Attitudes: Some Additional Evidence." *Public Opinion Quarterly* 54: 248–55.

———. 1996. *Onward Christian Soldiers? The Religious Right in American Politics*. Boulder, Colo.: Westview Press.

———. 2000. *Onward Christian Soldiers? The Religious Right in American Politics*, 2nd ed. Boulder, Colo.: Westview Press.

Wilcox, Clyde, and Barbara Norrander. 2002. "Of Moods and Morals: The Dynamics of Opinion on Abortion and Gay Rights." In *Under-*

*standing Public Opinion*, 2nd ed., ed. Barbara Norrander and Clyde Wilcox. Washington, D.C.: CQ Press.

Wilcox, Clyde, and Robert Wolpert. 2000. "Gay Rights in the Public Sphere: Public Opinion on Gay and Lesbian Equality." In *The Politics of Gay Rights*, ed. Craig A. Rimmerman, Kenneth D. Wald, and Clyde Wilcox. Chicago: University of Chicago Press.

Wilcox, Clyde, Ted G. Jelen, and David C. Leege. 1993. "Religious Group Identifications: Toward a Cognitive Theory of Religious Mobilization." In *Rediscovering the Religious Factor in American Politics*, ed. David C. Leege and Lyman A. Kellstedt. Armonk, N.Y.: M. E. Sharpe.

Wildavsky, Aaron. 1987. "Choosing Preferences by Constructing Institutions: A Cultural Theory of Preference Formation." *American Political Science Review* 81: 3–44

Wolpert, Robin M., and James G. Gimpel. 1998. "Self-Interest, Symbolic Politics, and Public Attitudes toward Gun Control." *Political Behavior* 20: 241–62.

Wood, Michael, and Michael Hughes. 1984. "The Moral Basis of Moral Reform: Status Discontent vs. Culture and Socialization as Explanations of Anti-Pornography Social Movement Adherence." *American Sociological Review* 49: 86–99.

Wright, Fiona. 2000. "The Caucus Reelection Requirement and the Transformation of House Committee Chairs, 1959–94." *Legislative Studies Quarterly*, 25: 469–80.

Wuthnow, Robert. 1983. "The Political Rebirth of American Evangelicals." In *The New Christian Right*, ed. Robert C. Liebman and Robert Wuthnow. New York: Aldine.

———. 1987. *Meaning and Moral Order: Explorations in Cultural Analysis*. Berkeley: University of California Press.

Yamane, David, and Elizabeth A. Oldmixon. In press. "Affiliation, Salience, Advocacy: Three Religious Factors in Public Policy-Making."

Young, James Sterling. 1986. *The Washington Community*. New York: Columbia University Press.

Zhou, Xueguang. 1993. "The Dynamics of Organizational Rules." *American Journal of Sociology* 98: 1134–66.

# Index

238 *Index*